MW01256142

Information Technology Protection and Homeland Security

FRANK R. SPELLMAN

Homeland Security Series

Lanham • Boulder • New York • London

Published by Bernan Press
An imprint of The Rowman & Littlefield Publishing Group, Inc.
4501 Forbes Boulevard, Suite 200, Lanham, Maryland 20706
www.rowman.com
800-865-3457; info@bernan.com

6 Tinworth Street, London SE11 5AL, United Kingdom

Copyright © 2019 by The Rowman & Littlefield Publishing Group, Inc.

All rights reserved. No part of this book may be reproduced in any form or by any electronic
or mechanical means, including information storage and retrieval systems, without written
permission from the publisher, except by a reviewer who may quote passages in a review. Bernan
Press does not claim copyright in U.S. government information.

British Library Cataloguing in Publication Information Available

Library of Congress Cataloging-in-Publication Data

Names: Spellman, Frank R., author.
Title: Information technology protection and homeland security / Frank R.
  Spellman.
Description: Lanham : Bernan Press, [2019] | Series: Homeland security series
  | Includes bibliographical references and index.
Identifiers: LCCN 2019004274| ISBN 9781641433242 (pbk. : alk. paper) | ISBN
  9781641433259 (ebook)
Subjects: LCSH: Cyberterrorism—United States—Prevention. | Computer
  security—United States. | National security—United States.
Classification: LCC HV6773.15.C97 S64 2019 | DDC 363.325—dc23 LC record available at https://
lccn.loc.gov/2019004274

∞™ The paper used in this publication meets the minimum requirements of
American National Standard for Information Sciences—Permanence of Paper
for Printed Library Materials, ANSI/NISO Z39.48-1992.

Printed in the United States of America

For Joan Price-Bayer

Contents

Acronyms and Abbreviations

ACH	Automated Clearing House
APEC	Asia-Pacific Economic Cooperation
APM	Asset Prioritization Model
ATM	Automated Teller Machine
ATM	Asynchronous Transfer Mode
BCPEI	Business Continuity Plan Exercise
BCPI	Business Continuity Plan Index
CMI	Consequences Measurement Index
BIS	Bureau of Industry and Security
BSS	Broadcast Satellite Service
CATV	Cable Television
CERT	Computer Emergency Readiness Team
CFR	Code of Federal Regulations
CFTC	Commodity Futures Trading Commission
CHIPS	The Clearing House Interbank Payments System
CII	Critical Infrastructure Information
CIKR	Critical Infrastructure and Key Resources
CINS	FS-ISAC's Critical Infrastructure Notification System
CIP	Critical Infrastructure Protection
CLEC	Competitive Local Exchange Carrier
CME	Chicago Mercantile Exchange
CS	Commercial Services
CSBS	Conference of State Bank Supervisors
CS/IA	Cybersecurity/Information Assurance
DCIP	Defense Critical Infrastructure Program
DHS	Department of Homeland Security
DIB	Defense Industrial Base
DOC	Department of Commerce
DOD	Department of Defense
Dodd	Department of Defense Directive

Dodin	Department of Defense Instruction
DOJ	Department of Justice
DOS	Department of State
DPAS	Defense Priorities and Allocations System
ECIP	Enhanced Critical Infrastructure Protection (program)
E.O.	Executive Order
FAA	Federal Aviation Administration
FBIIC	Financial and Banking Information Infrastructure Committee
FCA	Farm Credit Administration
FDIC	Federal Deposit Insurance Corporation
FEMA	Federal Emergency Management Agency
FOIA	Federal of Information Act
GDP	Gross Domestic Product
GPS	Global Positioning System
HSPD	Homeland Security Presidential Directive
IA	Information Assurance
IMCC	Incident Management & Command Center
IP	Office of Infrastructure Protection
IST	Infrastructure Survey Tool
IT	Information Technology
IXC	Interexchange Carrier
LEC	Local Exchange Carrier
MAUT	Multi-attribute Utility Theory
MOA	Memoranda of Agreement
MOU	Memoranda of Understanding
NCIP	National Critical Infrastructure Protection
NCS	National Communications System
NG	National Guard
NIAC	National Infrastructure Council
PMI	Protective Measures Index
PPD	Presidential Policy Directive
PrI	Preparedness Index
PSA	Protective Security Advisor
PSPrep	Private Sector Preparedness Program
PSTN	Public Switched Telephone Network
QA	Quality Assurance
RI	Resilience Index
RMI	Resilience Measurement Index
SAA	Significant Assets/Areas
SME	Subject Matter Expert
SSA	Sector Specific Agency
SSP	Sector Specific Plan
TSA	Transportation Security Administration
UAS	Unmanned Aircraft Systems

Preface

The eleventh volume of a new, well-received, and highly acclaimed series on critical infrastructure and homeland security, *Information Technology Protection and Homeland Security* is an eye-opening account and an important resource of a diverse and complex sector. This book was designed and written to serve and advise Information Technology (IT) personnel, public and private computer operators, financial planners, project designers, engineers, communications technicians, law enforcement and security specialists, managers, small business owners and superintendents and/or supervisors, and responsible-managers-in-charge of protecting the multifaceted nature of critical infrastructure in the United States. Whenever I mentioned to a particular colleague that I was in the process of writing another volume for this series and I described the topic to be covered, she was surprised as always that I would again embark on such a mind-numbing and difficult task. I remember that bewildered look on her face and her exact words when she asked: "How can you . . . or anyone . . . write about and describe the U.S. Information Technology Infrastructure sector when it is so deep, tall, 'cloudy' and wider-than-wide and all encompassing and almost indefinable in terms of total reach, scope, extent etc., etc., etc.?" I had heard this question many times in the past, but my reaction remained the same when I remember scratching my head and trying to answer her again in an impressive way (not easy) and finally coming up with what, for me, was the ultimate answer. I replied, "If it exists, it can be written about and described." Then she scratched her head and smiled while nodding her head side to side (meaning no way, Jose) and then she just changed the subject.

Anyway, currently, the IT critical infrastructure sector includes a diverse range of sites that draw large number of users (a terrorist's dream situation) for public and private communication, shopping on-line, business, entertainment, or lodging. Facilities within the sector operate on the principle of open public access (a key factor for terrorists), meaning that the general public can communicate within or search the web freely without the deterrent of highly visible or obstructive security barriers (or so it would seem). The majority of these facilities are privately owned and operated, with minimal interaction with the federal government and other regulatory agencies.

This book is organized to simplify and present in a logical and sequential manner a discussion of not only the elements comprising the IT sector in the United States but also many of the security measures employed to protect the various entities and equipment involved.

Let's face today's reality, those who want quick answers to complicated questions—to help employers and employees handle security threats—must be prepared to meet and deal with the threat of terrorism on a 24/7 basis. It is important to point out that this book does not discuss and focus on security concerns related to natural disasters; on the contrary, the focus here is on the security aspects in the design of systems that need to be able to deal robustly with possible sources of disruption, specifically from malicious acts; moreover, the focus includes the added dimension of preventing mis-use and malicious behavior. In the post-September 11, 2001, world, the possibility of IT sector infrastructure terrorism—the malicious use of substances, weapons, and cy-ber intrusion to cause devastating damage to IT sector infrastructure and its associated subsectors along with—literally—its cascading effects—is very real. Thus, the need is clear and real and so is the format and guidelines presented in this text to improve protection and resilience of IT sector infrastructure.

This book describes the sector- subsector-wide process required to identify and prioritize assets, assess risk in the sector, implement protective programs and resil-ience strategies, and measure their effectives. This book and the complete sixteen volumes (upgraded from the original fourteen volumes) of the critical infrastructure sector series were written as a result of 9/11 to address these concerns. It is important to point that our IT sector infrastructure (as is the case with the other fifteen critical infrastructures) cannot be made absolutely immune to all possible intrusions/hacks/attacks; thus, it takes a concerted, well-thought-out effort to incorporate security up-grades in the retrofitting of existing systems and careful security planning for all new facility infrastructure components. These upgrades or design features need to address issues of monitoring, response, critical infrastructure redundancy, and recovery to minimize risk to the facility infrastructure. However, based on personal experience none of these approaches is or can be effective unless IT sector staff members at all levels of the chain of command are cognizant of the threats.

Information Technology Protection and Homeland Security presents commonsense methodologies in a straightforward, almost blunt manner. Why so blunt? At this particular time, when dealing with security of workers, family members, citizens, and society in general—actually, with our very way of life—politically correct presenta-tions on security might be the norm, might be expected, and might be demanded, but my view is that there is nothing normal or subtle about killing thousands of innocent people; mass murders certainly should not be expected; the right and need to communicate and the right to live in a free and safe environment is a reasonable demand.

This text is accessible to those who have no experience with or knowledge of the IT sector. If you work through the text systematically, you will gain an understanding of the challenge of domestic preparedness—that is, an immediate need for a heightened state of awareness of the present threat facing the IT sector members as potential terrorist targets. Moreover, you will gain knowledge of security principles and measures that can be implemented—adding a critical component not only to your professional knowledge but also give you the tools needed to combat terrorism in the homeland—our homeland, both by outsiders and insiders (homegrown terrorists).

One final word to readers: this book is written in the conversational, engaging, and reader-friendly style that is the author's trademark. Why? Well, when demonstrating how one . . . or anyone . . . can write about the U.S. IT sector when it is so deep, tall, wide, and all encompassing and almost indefinable in terms of total reach, scope, extent etc., etc., etc., I never apologize for attempting to communicate face-to-face or via cyberspace.

Frank R. Spellman
Norfolk, Virginia

Prologue
The Duct Tape Caper

Note: The following fictitious account is included here in order to set the stage for what follows in the text and to continue the sordid saga of the Williams family. The Williams' are homegrown radicalized terrorists (smart, brutal, and not Muslim; you might say they are clones of Timothy McVeigh types) who have done whatever they could do to bring about the death and destruction of innocents in the United States; with particular attention being paid to attacking, impacting, and/or destroying sectors of critical infrastructure.

* * * * *

Have you ever heard the phrase: "Terrorism is like duct tape, it fixes everything." Well, if you haven't heard it, keep in mind that terrorism is something that is needed on occasion to get the attention of the vested interests and that of all the other wackos, weirdoes, snowflakes, and degenerates occupying or running (and ruining) our country.

Well, at least that is my take on the abysmal mess . . . we need to do some serious house cleaning, so to speak. You know when you are incarcerated in Seattle's finest lockup (the liberals that run the place make sure the bad girls like me have all the comforts of home . . . funny, but true), time and quiet lends itself to some serious thinking . . . thinking can be dangerous but it also can lift the veil that enshrouds the mysteries of life and all its encumbrances; it makes ones' thoughts as clear as a pristine mountain stream.

Okay, guess I ought to begin my story at the beginning. First, I am B. M. Williams IX. Yes, if you guessed or ascertained that I am part and parcel of the infamous Williams' family known for terrorist acts here, there, and anywhere, you are one smart Tootsie Roll. Unfortunately, most of my blood (i.e., my family members, relatives, and relations) are incarcerated for life in places like supermax. People and mostly the bleeding-heart left-wing media (aka fake news—those who parrot out vacuous drivel from their warped technophobic minds) have branded me and my blood as terrorists of the worst sort: cold blooded killers with zero empathy for anyone. This is true, of course. But I am somewhat different . . . in my family circle I am known as the wimp . . . the jellyfish (no backbone) of the family . . . also as the tall, attractive red-headed beauty with the too-soft heart. Why? Well, I do not mind death and lots of destruction . . . so long as it is not mine or precipitated by me. Blood and guts spattered here, there, and everywhere is not my thing . . . can't stand the sight of such nasty stuff. Instead, I think about destroying critical infrastructure differently. I believe in the old saying about there is more than one way to skin a liberal . . . and there is, of course. And the plan I came up with was perfect . . . no bloodshed or explosions . . . just chaos. I just love chaos, don't you?

Anyway, you want to know how I became incarcerated and ended up receiving a four-year sentence in Walla Walla's famous women's federal prison. . . .

It all begins when I was born. I am a terrorist and will always be a card-carrying terrorist until death. However, again, I take a different slant on homegrown terrorism than most of my blood. I do not necessarily need to kill people, blow up buildings, burn ISIS flags, or spit on alt-left wingers to accomplish my goal(s). No, Maria and Jose; I have my own view and modus operandi. You see, if you kill humans or blow things up or burn the crazies' flag(s), you will either die in the performance of such applaudable actions or you will end up in super duper max for life. Of course, that is better than the rope, electric chair, firing squad, being tree-shredded, or gassed to death in one of them Nazi-like gas chambers. You see, comrades, even though I know that if you commit capital crimes in bleeding-heart liberal wacko places like Washington State, Oregon, California, and a few East Coast states, the death penalty is never exercised . . . the bleeders protect killers and ignore victims—that is a given . . . but a lengthy prison sentence is no fun either . . . not for me . . . I have too many future catastrophic events to initiate and to see fulfilled.

Back to the plan . . . my ultimate plan was to accomplish some house-cleaning operations. Specifically, I came up with a plan to hack into all local male and a few female politicians' computers and to plant very incriminating information. You see, besides being filthy rich and nineteen years old and an incomparable genius, I am also a computer whiz kid. I can do things with a computer that you can only dream about . . . it is nothing to get into anyone's computer and plant the kind of incriminating information that will destroy them. You see, I am sure you have noticed all the recent allegations about infidelity, about beating women, abusing women, groping women or kissing them and then dumping them for another woman or a man . . . that's all in the current news. Allegations are powerful and the good news is that a mere allegation can shatter lives. I just love to shatter lives . . . so satisfying, don't you agree?

You see, being the genius that I am, a former child prodigy in all things mathematical and computer-based, I was an expert in technical things by age twelve, I knew more about most things than any of my teachers, professors, or others and could outdo them all anytime in their fields or specialties. So, being the genius that I am and being filthy rich, like all my blood, I came up with the perfect terrorist scenario, plain and simple, or so I thought at the time . . . sigh, the best laid plans of mice and women . . . etc., etc., etc.

Anyway, the plan was simple to put into motion. I simply made a list of all the male bleeding-heart liberal politicians in the Northwest (and a few women too) and I inserted child and adult pornography into their computers, into both their work and personal computers . . . I also installed videos showing brutality toward women.

You understand there is nothing, with the exception of murder, of course, that will undermine any politician's career than a computer full of sordid trash . . . demonstrations of brutality, lewdness, vulgarity, vileness toward women and children . . . they are devastating. I call them the ultimate term limits! Don't you just love it? I sure did . . . you see my opinion is that voters are fools and keep putting worthless bleeding-heart liberals, commies, snowflakes, and other jackasses into office, over and over again. Where is their sense of smarts? Well, they have none; they are brain-dead.

So, now you are asking yourself if my plan was so brilliant and so sure to succeed what happened. Why am I now in Seattle lockup awaiting transfer to federal prison? Well, I have to admit that I got greedy. Success makes one continue on . . . like robbing banks . . . rob a few banks and get away with it . . . well, then you do it again and again because you will never get caught, right? Well, I got caught.

Here is what happened. I hacked a couple of the worst bleeding-heart liberal pols here and filled their computers with nasty trash and then ratted them out to local newspapers. Wow! You should have been here to witness the uproar (well, maybe you were here) . . . even the liberal newspapers (aren't they all) went crazy and destroyed the politicians without any kind of due process (only happens in America, right?).

It turned out that the deeper the newspapers and other media investigated, the more they found even more devastating information that sealed the politicians fate forever. Funny thing is I did not plant that additional incriminating information. You gotta love it. I know I sure did.

So where does the greed come into this bawdy tale? Hold on, grasshoppers, I am getting to it. What I did was wallow in the glory of my success in destroying those horrible male politicians. I am not one of those American women who you must listen to me roar . . . no way, Maria. I do not roar; instead, I bite . . . I bite hard . . . and harder.

Anyway, while enjoying my overblown feelings of glee and glory I decided to expand my operation and branch out to those other two horrible states, California and

Oregon. Nowhere, except New York and a couple of those other commie eastern states are they more liberal and messed up than the United States West Coast region.

What I did was make a huge error in judgment (rare for the likes of me). I needed help to expand so I enlisted one of my cousins, sweet Joan Williams and trained her to fill local politician's computers in California and Oregon with terrible and discriminating pornography. Well, all that worked for awhile. Again, even in those two bastions of brain-dead voters, the voters demanded that politicians resign. Again, term limits in progress, for sure.

Well, all good things, sooner or later, come to an end. And my computer hacking scheme sure did. What happened is sweet cousin Joan (another beautiful redhead) loved hacking so much that she started hacking banks and ripping them off. Hmmm-mmmmmmm, well, what can I say? She got caught and quickly negotiated via a plea-bargain deal for testimony against my dumb self; into jail I went while she got away clean. So, today instead of calling here "sweet Joan" it is now "sour Joan." I thought I had totally corrupted her but she turned out to be a Goody Two-shoes . . . nothing worse than that except that it is unforgivable when your own blood turns against you to save her own skin. Kind of fits the mold at the present time, don't you agree?

So here I sit in this lockup waiting to be transferred to serve out my time while Joan is as free as a bird . . . probably out chasing horrible men. You know what really torques my jaws is that she ratted me out. They say that terrorism is like duct tape and it fixes everything . . . well, I could use some of that duct tape right now. However, the only consolation I have is that warm and fuzzy feeling I get when I think about all those sleazebag pols that are no longer in power. Also, knowing that I will be locked up for only a short time and will have the chance for further escapades and daring do . . . WOW, what a turn on . . . but only on my own . . . never with a partner . . . only as a lone wolf, one that bites, of course.

1

Introduction

WHAT IS TERRORISM?

Since 9/11, we have heard it said by many of our teachers, neighbors, security specialists, and students (and many others) that there is controversy about the definition of
the politically-charged word *terrorism*. Terrorism, like pollution, is a judgment call.
For example, with regard to defining pollution, if two neighbors live next door to an
air polluting facility, one neighbor who has no personal connection with the polluting
plant is likely to label the plant's output as pollution. The other neighbor who is an
employee of the plant may see the plant's pollution as dollar bills—dollars that are his
or her livelihood. I have heard workers who dive into ponds full of raw sewage to find
a leak in an effluent pipe say that the sewage in the pond and its associated odor is
money in the bank . . . and long-term employment because toilets and their function
are not likely to vanish anytime soon. Why a money-making enterprise? Because there
are few people around who would join them in diving into trenches filled with raw
sewage and in doing their work. On the terrorism front, when someone deliberately
spikes a tree to prevent loggers from cutting it down, the tree-spiker might feel he or
she is a patriot, just a knight in shining green armor and definitely not a terrorist. On
the other hand, the logger who has to take the tree down and puts his or her life and
limbs at risk in taking down the spiked tree has little doubt in his or her mind on what
to call the tree-spiker, and what the tree-spiker is called certainly has nothing to do
with patriotism. Thus, what we are saying here in the example presented, pollution
versus terrorism, is that along with attempting to define pollution, trying to define
terrorism may be a judgment call, especially in the view of the terrorists.

SETTING THE STAGE

When I taught college-level courses in environmental health and science, I never
stopped being amazed by the morphing looks on graduate and undergraduate student
faces when I handed out the course syllabus and reviewed its contents with them. I

1

watched with amusement as I began to discuss each requirement, one item at a time. Whenever I got to the last entry on the syllabus, the one requiring a 1,250 word (minimum) research paper, that is when I could not only see the changes, the morphing, sweep over their faces, like a cloud bank covering bright sunlight, but also basically the change from curiosity to disgust, including many moans and groans because of the realization that they would have to complete a hated research paper.

There was a time in the beginning of my teaching career when I was totally motivated but very unknowingly unaware of real-world thinking generated in younger folks brain cells (we did not call them snowflakes in my era), so I would wait until they squashed their disgust about having to write a term paper and explained my view to them. For example, routinely I would explain that there was a time, not too far in the distant past, when I would have a question pop into my mind about anything, the type of question that I wanted an answer to but I quickly became frustrated because the answer was not easily accessible. Unless I had the right reference book close at hand, or could find the reference book I needed at the local library, it was almost impossible for me to find the correct answer to my question. Oh, then there were the term papers that I had to write. Trying to find credible source material for my papers was not easy. In fact it was hard and frustrating work. I remember going to the library on several occasions to find source material and not finding much of what I needed because they did not have the book or journal or it was checked out or it was simply missing; a real headache-maker for sure.

During my rambling presentation the students were checking their e-mails, or surfing the web, or just falling asleep at their desks; surprise, there were even a few paying attention. I went on to explain how lucky they were that they had laptop computers and Internet to search for the answers, sources, research data, or whatever else they needed to write any paper. Oh, how things have changed I would say. And as many of the students finally focused on what I was saying, they would look at me with wonder when I finished by saying, "How did we ever live, survive, maintain, and/or even exist without personal computers and the Internet?"

Today, in my advanced age, I realize that we existed without the personal computer and the Internet in the past just as we existed before electricity, the light bulb, telephone, airplane, automobile, and television set because we simply morphed from one era to the next. The funny thing is during the transition from one innovative period to the next the transition never really got our attention; that is, not until someone inadvertently turned off the lights.

INFORMATION TECHNOLOGY INFRASTRUCTURE

It is clear that the Information Technology (IT) sector provides an extremely diverse range of products and services that support the efficient operation of today's global information-based society. These products and services are integral to the operations and services provided by other critical infrastructures Sectors. Although IT sector operations, products, services, and functions enhance efficiency and effectiveness and increase the resilience of the sector, they face numerous multifaceted global threats from natural and manmade events on a daily basis. Many of these events occur frequently but do not have significant consequences because of individual entities' existing security and response capabilities. Simply, given the national and international visibility and potential human and economic consequences associated with IT entities, it is important for the federal government and the IT sector to work together to ensure the protection of our Nation's prominent business centers and gathering places.

Working together and assigning responsibility is the key requirement in providing protection for the IT sector. The primary tandem entities responsible for protecting IT sector infrastructure and assets is U.S. Department of Homeland Security and the private sector. In conjunction with the federal government, the private sector is able to predict, anticipate, and respond to sector hackers, predators, system interruptions, site outages, and understand how they might affect the ability to continue whatever service they are designed or configured to provide. This is especially the case during times of crisis, and when impact affects the operations of other sectors, and affects response and recovery efforts.

The IT sector functions encompass the full set of processes involved in creating IT products and services, including research and development, manufacturing , distribution, upgrades, and maintenance. They also support the sector's ability to produce and provide high-assurance products, services, and practices that are resilient to threats and can be rapidly recovered. A fundamental aspect of all critical IT functions is assurance. The functions referred to here are not limited by geographic or political boundaries, further defining its virtual and distributed nature. This distribution underlines the increasing need for international cooperation and synchronization for risk assessment activities, effective security practices, and protective program design and implementation. Moreover, the crucial functions may be developed and maintained by small, medium, or large companies with varied resources and capabilities highlighting the need for risk management strategies and protective programs that map and scale to a wide range of needs.

IT Sector Critical Functions and Interdepencies
As shown in figure 1.1 there are six critical functions that support the IT sector's ability to provide high assurance IT products and services for various sectors. These functions are required to maintain or reconstitutes networks (e.g., the Internet, local networks, and wide area networks) and their associated services. The functions reflect industry consensus (also within interdependencies; see figure 1.2) on critical functions

DID YOU KNOW?

Owners and operators and their respective associations provide IT hardware, software, systems, and services. IT services include development, integration, operations, communications, testing, and security

that are vital to the nation's economic security and public health, safety, and confidence. These functions are distributed across a broad network of infrastructure, managed proactively, and therefore, can withstand and rapidly recover from most threats.

IT Sector Risks

After some time, experience (lessons-learned), and considerable thought, the IT sector has identified its five greatest risks of concern facing the six critical functions of the sector shown in figure 1.1. On a regular basis these risks of concern are validated and

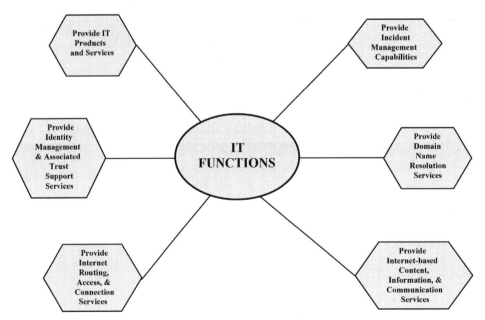

FIGURE 1.1
IT sector functions.

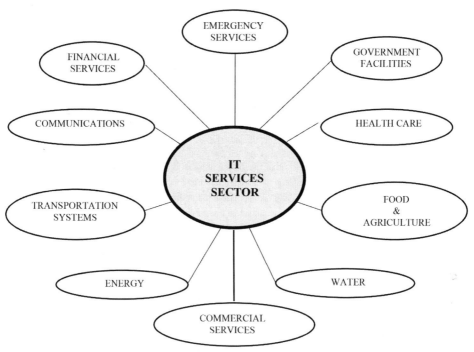

FIGURE 1.2
Critical sector interdependencies.

updated during subsequent risk assessments conducted by the sector. The IT sector
has focused its risk management activities on these areas. These risks of concern are
(DHS, 2016):

- Production or distraction of untrustworthy critical product/service through a successful manmade deliberate attack on a supply chain vulnerability.
- Breakdown of a signal interoperable Internet through a human-made attack and
  resulting failure of governance policy. A large-scale human-made Denial-of-Service
  attack on the Domain Name System infrastructure.
- Human-made unintentional incident caused in Internet content services result in a
  significant loss of e-commerce capabilities.
- Partial or complete loss of routing capabilities through a deliberate human-made
  attack on the Internet routing infrastructure.
- Impact to detection capabilities due to lack of data availability resulting from a
  natural threat.

THE BOTTOM LINE

In addition to the critical interdependencies for the IT sector mentioned to this point, it is important to note that physical security of sector facilities (covered in detail later) is important but, actually, the focus of security of this sector is a different kind and relatively new to most. Much of the IT sector infrastructure is vulnerable to cyber-attack from either inside or outside of the network. Cybersecurity is addressed later.

The bottom line is that from this discussion, it is clear that any number of inside and outside interdependencies could threaten one of the key components of our critical national infrastructure and the IT sector. These factors are the "realities" of the IT sector and go beyond just the core precepts of good system development and design. Cleary, there is a great deal of interdependence on other outside factors that could threaten information services and other key resources. Without the active participation of each of these sectors, the key and essential facilities of the IT sector could be very vulnerable—a fact that is not acceptable for the protection of our national interests.

REFERENCES AND RECOMMENDED READING

DHS (2016). *Information Technology Sector—An Annex to the National Infrastructure Protection Plan.* Washington, DC: Department of Homeland Security.

Haimes, Y. Y. (2004). *Risk Modeling, Assessment, and Management,* 2nd Edition. New York: John Wiley & Sons, p. 699.

Henry, K. (2002). New face of security. *Gov. Security,* Apr., pp. 30–37.

NSHS (2006). *National Strategy for Homeland Security.* Accessed 5/13/06 @ www.whitehouse/homeland.

Sauter, M. A. and Carafano, J. J. (2005). *Homeland Security: A Complete Guide to Understanding, Preventing, and Surviving Terrorism.* NY: McGraw-Hill.

Spellman, F. R. (1997). *A Guide to Compliance for Process Safety Management/Risk Management Planning (PSM/RMP).* Lancaster, PA: Technomic Publishing Company.

Digital Network Security

We depend on critical infrastructure every day. Our ability to travel, to communicate with friends and family, to conduct business, to handle our finances, and even our ability to access clean, safe food and water are all reliant upon our Nation's critical infrastructure networks and systems. These essential services that underlie daily life in American society are increasingly being run on digital networks. Every day, people connect to the national grid without even realizing it from their smart phones, computers, and tablets. As a result, these critical systems are prime targets for cyber attacks from those seeking to cause out country harm.

—DHS (2016)

Note: In this book we use the terms information technology (IT), cyberspace, and digital network interchangeably.

On April 23, 2000, police in Queensland, Australia, stopped a car on the road and found a stolen computer and radio inside. Using commercially available technology, a disgruntled former employee had turned his vehicle into a pirate command center of sewage treatment along Australia's Sunshine Coast. The former employee's arrest solved a mystery that had troubled the Maroochy Shire wastewater system for two months. Somehow the system was leaking hundreds of thousands of gallons of putrid sewage into parks, rivers, and the manicured grounds of a Hyatt Regency hotel—marine life died, the creek water turned black, and the stench was unbearable for residents. Until the former employee's capture—during his 46th successful intrusion—the utility's managers did not know why.

Specialists study this case of cyber-terrorism because, at the time, it was the only one known in which someone used a digital control system deliberately to cause harm. The former employee's intrusion shows how easy it is to break in—and how restrained he was with his power.

To sabotage the system, the former employee set the software on his laptop to identify itself as a pumping station, and then suppressed all alarms. The former employee was the "central control station" during his intrusions, with unlimited command of 300 SCADA nodes governing sewage and drinking water alike.

The bottom line: as serious as the former employee's intrusions were they pale in comparison with what he could have done to the fresh water system—he could have done anything he liked.

—Barton Gellman, 2002

Other reports of digital network exploits illustrate the debilitating effects such attacks can have on the nation's security, economy, and on public health and safety.

- In May 2015, media sources reported that data belonging to 1.1 million health insurance customers in the Washington, D.C., area were stolen in a cyberattack on a private insurance company. Attackers accessed a database containing names, birth dates, e-mail addresses, and subscriber ID numbers of customers.
- In December 2014, the industrial Control Systems Cyber Emergency Response Team (ICS-CERT; works to reduce risks within and across all critical infrastructure sectors by partnering with law enforce agencies) issued an updated alert on a sophisticated malware camping compromising numerous industrial control system environments. Their analysis indicated that this campaign had been ongoing since at least 2011.
- In the January 2014 to April 2014 release of its Monitor report, ICS-CERT reported that a public utility had been compromised when a sophisticated threat actor gained unauthorized access to its control system network through a vulnerable remote access capability configured on the system. The incident highlighted the need to evaluate security controls employed at the perimeter and ensure that potential intrusion vectors are configured with appropriate security controls, monitoring, and detection capabilities.
- In December 2016, a Wisconsin couple was charged after the duo allegedly defrauded Enterprise Credit Union in Brookfield out of more than $300,000 after one of the defendants, who managed the bank's accounts had her co-conspirator cash bank checks worth $980 several times each week beginning in May 2015. The charges allege that the couple used the money to buy drugs. (Source: http://www. wauwatrosanow.com/story/news/cirme/2016/12/09/two-charged-allegedly-scamming-credit-unions-over-300k/95207718/.)

In 2000, the FBI identified and listed threats to critical infrastructure. These threats are listed and described in table 2.1. In 2015, the GAO described the sources of digital network-based threats. These threats are listed and described in detail in table 2.2.

DID YOU KNOW?

Presidential Policy Directive 21 defined "All hazards" as a threat to an incident natural or manmade that warrants action to protect life, property, the environment, and public health or safety, and to minimize disruptions of government, social, or economic activities.

Table 2.1.   Threats to Critical Infrastructure Observed by the FBI

Threat	Description
Criminal groups	There is an increased use of cyber intrusions by criminal group who attack systems for purposes of monetary gain.
Foreign intelligence services	Foreign intelligence services use cyber tools as part of their information gathering and espionage activities.
Hackers	Hackers sometimes crack into networks for the thrill of the challenge or for bragging rights in the hacker community. While remote cracking once required a fair amount of skill or computer knowledge, hackers can now download attack scripts and protocols from the Internet and launch them against victim sites. Thus, while attack tools have become more sophisticated, they have also become easier to use.
Hacktivists	Hacktivism refers to politically motivated attacks on publicly accessible web pages or e-mail servers. These groups and individuals overload e-mail servers and hack into websites to send a political message.
Information warfare	Several nations are aggressively working to develop information warfare doctrine, programs, and capabilities. Such capabilities enable a single entity to have a significant and serious impact by disrupting the supply, communications, and economic infrastructures that support military power—impacts that, according to the director of Central Intelligence, can affect the daily lives of Americans across the country.
Inside threat	The disgruntled organization insider is a principal source of computer crimes. Insiders may not need a great deal of knowledge about computer intrusions because their knowledge of a victim system often allows them to gain unrestricted access to cause damage to the system or to steal system data. The insider threat also includes outsourcing vendors.
Virus writers	Virus writers are posing an increasingly serious threat. Several destructive computer viruses and "worms" have harmed files and hard drives, including the Melissa Macro Virus, the Explore.Zip worm, the CIH (Chernobyl) Virus, Nimda, and Code Red.

Source: FBI, 2000; 2014.

Table 2.2. Common Digital Network Threat Sources

Source	Description
Non-adversarial-malicious	
Failure in information technology equipment	Failures in displays, sensors, controllers, and information Information technology hardware responsible for data storage, processing, and communications
Failure in environmental controls	Failures in temperature/humidity controllers or power supplies
Software coding errors	Failures in operating systems, networking, and general-purpose and mission-specific applications
Natural or man-made disaster	Events beyond an entity's control such as fires, floods/tsunamis, tornadoes, hurricanes, and earthquakes
Unusual or natural event	Natural events beyond the entity's control that are not considered to be disasters (e.g., sunspots)
Infrastructure failure or outage	Failure or outage of telecommunications or electrical power
Unintentional user errors	Failures resulting from erroneous, accidental actions taken by individuals (both system users and administrators) in the course of executing their everyday responsibilities
Adversarial	
Hackers or hacktivists	Hackers break networks for the challenge, revenge, stalking, or monetary gain, among other reasons. Hactivists are ideologically motivated actors who use cyber exploits to further political goals.
Malicious insiders	Insiders (e.g., disgruntled organization employees, including contractors) may not need a great deal of knowledge about computer intrusions because their position with the organization often allows them to gain unrestricted access and cause damage to the target system or to steal system data. These individuals engage in purely malicious activities and should not be confused with non-malicious insider accidents.
Nations	Nations, including nation-state, state-sponsored, and state-sanctioned programs use cyber tools as part of their information-gathering and espionage activities. In addition, several nations are aggressively working to develop information warfare doctrine, programs, and capabilities.
Criminal groups and organize crime	Criminal groups seek to attack systems for monetary gain. Specifically, organized criminal groups use cyber exploits to commit identity theft, online fraud, and computer extortion.
Terrorist	Terrorists seek to destroy, incapacitate, or exploit critical infrastructures in order to threaten national security, cause mass casualties, weaken the economy, and damage public morale and confidence.
Unknown malicious outsiders	Unknown malicious outsiders are threat sources or agents that, due to a lack of information, agencies are unable to classify as being one of the five types of threat sources or agents listed above.

Source: GAO analysis of unclassified government and nongovernmental data. GAO 16-79.

Threats to systems supporting critical infrastructure are evolving and growing. As shown in Table 2.2, cyber threats can be unintentional or intentional. Unintentional or non-adversarial threats include equipment failures, software coding errors, and the actions of poorly trained employees. They also include natural disasters and failures of critical infrastructure on which the organization depends but are outside of its control. Intentional threats include both targeted and untargeted attacks from a variety of sources, including criminal groups, hackers, disgruntled employees, foreign nations engaged in espionage and information warfare, and terrorists. These threat adversaries vary in terms of the capabilities of the actors, their willingness to act, and their motives, which can include seeking monetary gain or seeking an economic, political, or military advantage (GAO, 2015).

THE DIGITAL NETWORK

Today's developing "information age" technology has intensified the importance of critical infrastructure protection in which digital network or cybersecurity has become as critical as physical security to protecting virtually all critical infrastructure sectors. The Department of Defense (DoD) determined that cyber threats to contractors' unclassified information systems represented an unacceptable risk of compromise to DoD information and posed a significant risk to U.S. national security and economic security interests.

In the past few years, especially since 9/11, it has been somewhat routine for us to pick up a newspaper, magazine, or view a television news program where a major topic of discussion is cybersecurity or the lack there of. For example, recently there has been discussion about Russian hackers trying to influence the U.S. 2016 elections. Many of the cyber intrusion incidents we read or hear about have added new terms or new uses for old terms to our vocabulary. For example, old terms such as Botnets (short for robot networks, also balled bots, zombies, botnet fleets, and many others) are groups of computers that have been compromised with malware such as Trojan horses, worms, backdoors, remote control software, and viruses have taken on new connotations in regards to cybersecurity issues. Relatively new terms such as scanners, Windows NT hacking tools, ICQ hacking tools, mail bombs, sniffer, logic bomb, nukers, dots, backdoor Trojan, key loggers, hackers' Swiss knife, password crackers, blended threats, Warhol worms, flash threats, targeted attacks, and BIOS crackers are now commonly read or heard. New terms have evolved along with various control mechanisms. For example, because many control systems are vulnerable to attacks of varying degrees, these attack attempts range from telephone line sweeps (war dialing), to wireless network sniffing (war driving), to physical network port scanning, and to physical monitoring and intrusion. When wireless network sniffing is performed at (or near) the target point by a pedestrian (war walking), meaning that instead of a person being in an automotive vehicle, the potential intruder may be sniffing the network for weaknesses or vulnerabilities on foot, posing as a person walking, but they may have a handheld PDA device or laptop computer (Warwalking 2003). Further, adversaries can leverage common computer software programs, such as Adobe Acrobat and Microsoft Office, to deliver a threat by embedding exploits within software files that can be activated when a user opens a file within its corresponding program. Finally, the communications infrastructure and the utilities are extremely dependent on the IT sector. This dependency is due to the reliance of the communications systems on the software that runs the control mechanism of the operations systems, the management software, the billing software, and any number of other software packages is used by industry. Table 2.3 provides descriptions of common exploits or techniques, tactics, and practices used by digital/cyber adversaries.

Table 2.3. Common Methods of Digital/Cyber Exploits

Exploit	Description
Watering hole	A method by which threat actors exploit the vulnerabilities of carefully selected websites frequented by users of the targeted system. Malware is then injected to the targeted system via the compromised websites.
Phishing and spear phishing	A digital form of social engineering that uses authentic-looking e-mails, websites, or instant messages to get users to download malware, open malicious attachments, or open links that direct then to a website that requires information or executes malicious code.
Credentials based	An exploit that takes advantage of a system's insufficient user authentication and/or any elements of cybersecurity supporting it, to include not limiting the number of failed login attempts, the use of hard-coded credentials, and the use of a broken or risky cryptographic algorithm.
Trusted third parties	An exploit that takes advantage of the security vulnerabilities of trusted third parties to gain access to an otherwise secure system.
Classic buffer overflow	An exploit that involves the intentional transmission of more data than a program's input buffer can hold, leading to the deletion of critical data and subsequent execution of malicious code.
Cryptographic weakness	An exploit that takes advantage of a network employing insufficient encryption when either storing or transmitting data, enabling adversaries to read and/or modify the data stream.
Structured Query Language (SQL) Injection	An exploit that involves the alteration of a database search in a web-based application, which can be used to obtain unauthorized across to sensitive information in a database, resulting in data loss at corruption, denial or service, or complete host takeover.
Operating system command injection	An exploit that takes advantage of a system's inability to properly neutralize special elements used in operating system commands, allowing the adversaries to execute unexpected commands on the system by either modifying already evoked commands or evoking their own.

Exploit	Description
Cross-site scripting	An exploit that uses third-party web resources to run lines of programming code (referred to as scripts) within the victim's web browser or scriptable application. This occurs when a user, using a browser, visits a malicious website or clicks a malicious link. The most dangerous consequences can occur when this method is used to exploit additional vulnerabilities that may permit an adversary to steal cookies (data exchanged between a web server and a browser), log key stokes, capture screen shots, discover and collect network information, or remotely access and control the victim's machine.
Cross-site request forgery	An exploit takes advantage of an application that cannot, or does not, sufficiently verify whether a well-formed, valid, consistent request was intentionally provided by the user who submitted the request, tricking the victim into executing a falsified requires that results in the system or data being compromised.
Path traversal	An exploit that seeks to gain access to files outside of a restricted directory by modifying the directory pathname in an application that does not properly neutralize special elements (e.g., '...', '/', '.../', etc.)
Integer overflow	An exploit where malicious code is inserted that leads to unexpected integer overflow, or wraparound, which can be used by adversaries to control looping or make security decisions in order to cause program crashes, memory corruption, or the execution of arbitrary code via buffer overflow.
Uncontrolled format string	Adversaries manipulate externally-controlled format strings in print-style functions to gain access to information and/or execute unauthorized code or commands.
Open redirect	An exploit where the victim is tricked into selecting a URL (website location) that has been modified to direct them to an external, malicious site that may contain malware that can compromises the victim's machine.
Heap-based buffer overflow	Similar to classic buffer overflow, but the buffer that is overwritten is allocated in the heap portion of memory, generally meaning that the buffer was allocated using a memory allocation routine, such as "malloc ( )."
Unrestricted upload of files	An exploit that takes advantage of insufficient upload restrictions, enabling adversaries to upload malware (e.g., .php) in place of the intended file type (e.g., .jpg).
Inclusion of functionality from untrusted sphere	An exploit that uses trusted, third-party (e.g., web widget or library) as a means of executing malicious code in software whose protection mechanism are unable to determent whether functionality a from a trusted sources, modified in transit, or being spoofed.
Certificate and certificate authority compromise	Exploits facilitated via the issuance of fraudulent digital certificates (e.g., transport layer security and Secure Socket Layer). Adversaries use these certificates to establish secure connections with the target organization or individual by mimicking a trusted third-party.
Hybrid of others	An exploit that combines elements of two or more of the aforementioned techniques.

Source: GAO, (2015).

Not all relatively new and universally recognizable information technology, digital, or cyber terms have sinister connotation or meaning, of course. Consider, for example, the following digital terms: backup, binary, bit byte, CD-ROM, CPU, database, e-mail, HTML, icon, memory, cyberspace, modem, monitor, network, RAM, Wi-Fi (wireless fidelity), record, software, World Wide Web—none of these terms normally generate thoughts of terrorism in most of us.

THE BOTTOM LINE

The United States Department of Homeland Security, in collaboration with many of the information technology sector stakeholders, identified cyber risk as significant to all critical infrastructure sectors. In the next chapter, as an example, we detail SCADA and its importance, significances, and vulnerabilities, all of which point to the need for planning, preparation, and mitigation procedures to ensure the resilience of digital network systems and applications.

REFERENCES AND RECOMMENDED READING

Associated Press (AP) (2009). *Goal: Disrupt.* From the 04/04/09 The Virginian-Pilot, Norfolk, Va.

DHS (2009). *National Infrastructure Protection Plan.* Accessed 05/11/17 @http://www.dhs. gov/ xlibrary/assets/NIPP.Plan.pdf.

DHS (2003). The National Strategy for the Physical Protection of Critical Infrastructures and Key Assets. Accessed @ https://www.dhs.gov/xlibrary/assets/physical_Strat.

DHS (2013). Homeland Security Directive 7: Critical Infrastructure Identification, Prioritization, and Protection. Accessed @ https://www.dihs.gov/xabout/laws/ gc_1214597989952.shtm.

DOE (2001). *21 Steps to improve cyber security of SCADA networks.* Washington, DC: Department of Energy.

FEMA (2008). *FEMA452: Risk Assessment A How to Guide.* Accessed 05/01/08 @fema.gov/ library/file?type=published/filetofile.

FEMA (2015). *Protecting Critical Infrastructure Against Insider Threats.* Accessed 17 April 2015 @ http://emilms.fema.gov/IS0915/IABsummary.htm.

FBI (2000). *Threat to Critical Infrastructure.* Washington, DC: Federal Bureau of Investigation.

FBI (2007). *Ninth Annual Computer Crime and Security Survey.* FBI: Computer Crime Institute and Federal Bureau of Investigations.

FBI (2014). *Protecting Critical Infrastructure and the Importance of Partnerships.* Accessed @ https://www.fib.gov/news/speeches/protecitng-critical-infrastruce-andt-the-importantce-o.

GAO (2003). *Critical Infrastructure Protection: Challenges in Securing Control System.* Washington, DC: United States General Accounting Office.

GAO (2015). *Critical Infrastructure Protection: Sector-Specific Agencies Need to Better Measure Cybersecurity Progress.* Washington, DC: United States Government Accountability Office.

Gellman, B. (2002). Cyber-Attacks by Al Qaeda Feared: Terrorists at Threshold of Using Internet as Tool of Bloodshed, Experts Say. *Washington Post,* June 27; p. A01.

Minter, J. G. (1996). Prevention Chemical Accidents Still A Challenge. *Occupational Hazards,* September.

National Infrastructure Advisory Council (2008). *First Report and Recommendations on the Insider Threat to Critical Infrastructure.* Washington, DC.

NIPC (2002). *National Infrastructure Protection Center Report.* Washington, DC: National Infrastructure Protection Center.

Spellman, F. R. (1997). *A Guide to Compliance for PSM/RMP.* Lancaster, PA: Technomic Publishing Company.

Stamp, J. et al. (2003). *Common Vulnerabilities in Critical Infrastructure Control Systems,* 2nd ed. Sandia National Laboratories.

US DOE (2002). *Vulnerability Assessment Methodology: Electric Power Infrastructure.* Washington, DC.

USEPA (2005). EPA Needs to Determine What Barriers Prevent Water Systems from Securing Known SCADA Vulnerabilities. In: Harris, J. Final Briefing Report. Washington, DC: USEPA.

Warwalking (2003). Accessed 05/09/08 @ http://warwalking.tribe.net.

3

SCADA

Nobody has ever been killed by a cyberterrorist.
Unless people are injured, there is less drama and emotional appeal.

—Dorothy Denning

WHAT IS SCADA?

The critical infrastructure of many countries is increasingly dependent on SCADA systems.

If we were to ask the specialist to define SCADA, the technical response could be outlined as follows:

- A multitier system or interfaces with multitier systems
- It is used for physical measurement and control endpoints via an Remote Terminal Unit (RTU) and Program Logic Controller (PLC) to measure voltage, adjust a value, or flip a switch
- It is an intermediate processor normally based on commercial third-party OSes—VMS, Unix, Windows, Linux
- It human interfaces, for example, with graphical user interface (Windows GUIs)
- Its communication infrastructure consists of a variety of transport mediums such as analog, serial, Internet, radio, Wi-Fi

How about the non-specialist response—for the rest of us who are non-specialists? Well, for those of us in this category we could simply say that SCADA is a computer-based control system that remotely controls and monitors processes previously controlled and monitored manually. The philosophy behind SCADA control systems can be summed up by the phrase "If you can measure it, you can control it." SCADA allows an operator using a central computer to supervise (control and monitor) multiple networked computers at remote locations. Each remote computer can control mechanical processes (mixers, pumps, valves, etc.) and collect data from sensors at its remote location. Thus, the phrase: **S**upervisory **C**ontrol **a**nd **D**ata **A**cquisition, or **SCADA**.

The central computer is called the Master Terminal Unit, or MTU. The MTU has two main functions: periodically obtain data from RTUs/PLCs; and control remote devices through the operator station. The operator interfaces with the MTU using software called Human Machine Interface, or HMI. The remote computer is called Program Logic Controller (PLC) or Remote Terminal Unit (RTU). The RTU activates a relay (or switch) that turns mechanical equipment "on" and "off." The RTU also collects data from sensors. Sensors perform measurement and actuators perform control.

In the initial stages, utilities ran wires, also known as hardwire or landlines, from the central computer (MTU) to the remote computers (RTUs). Because remote locations can be located hundreds of miles from the central location, utilities began to use public phone lines and modems, leased telephone company lines, and radio and microwave communication. More recently, they have also begun to use satellite links, Internet, and newly developed wireless technologies.

DID YOU KNOW?

Modern RTUs typically use a ladder-logic approach to programming due to its similarity to standard electrical circuits. An RTU that employees this ladder logic programming is called a Programmable Logic Controller (PLC).

Because SCADA systems' sensors provided valuable information, many critical infrastructure entities, utilities and other industries established "connections" between their SCADA systems and their business system. This allowed utility/industrial management and other staff access to valuable statistics, such as chemical usage. When utilities/industries later connected their systems to the Internet, they were able to provide stakeholders/stockholders with usage statistics on the IT segment and utility/in-

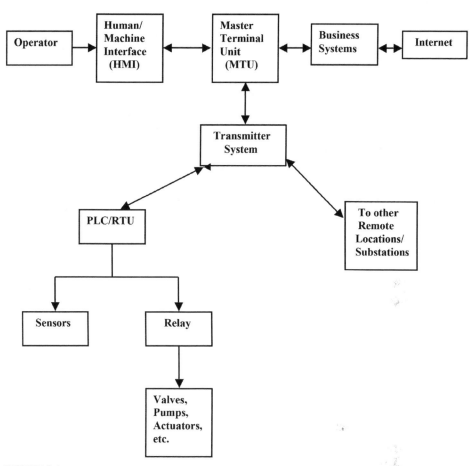

FIGURE 3.1
Representative SCADA network.

dustrial web pages. Figure 3.1 provides a basic illustration of a representative SCADA network. Note that firewall protection would normally be placed between Internet and business system and between business system and the MTU.

SCADA APPLICATIONS

As stated above, SCADA systems can be designed to measure a variety of equipment operating conditions, and parameters or volumes and flow rates or electricity, natural gas and oil or oil and petrochemical mixture quality parameters, and to respond to change in those parameters either by alerting operators or by modifying system op- eration through a feedback loop system without having to physically visit each valve, process, or piece of other equipment on a daily basis to check it and/or ensure that it is functioning properly. Automation and integration of large-scale diverse assets required SCADA systems to provide the utmost in flexibility, scalability, openness, and reliability. SCADA systems are used to automate certain energy production functions; these can be performed without initiation by an operator. In addition to process equipment, SCADA systems can also integrate specific security alarms and equipment, such as cameras, motion sensors, lights, data from card reading systems, etc. thereby providing a clear picture of what is happening at areas throughout a facility. Finally, SCADA systems also provide constant, real-time data on processes, equipment, location access, etc. the necessary response to be made quickly. This can be extremely useful during emergency conditions, such as when energy distribution lines or piping breaks or when potentially disruptive chemical reaction spikes appear in chemical processing operations. Currently, it can be said that SCADA has evolved from a simple indicating light and pushbutton control system into a comprehensive operation and handling system for very complex process control and safety shutdown systems. In a nutshell, SCADA results in an oversight system that requires fewer operators.

Today, many common digital system applications for SCADA systems include, but are not limited to those shown below.

- Boiler controls
- Bearing temperature monitors (electric generators and motors)
- Gas processing
- Plant monitoring
- Plant energy management
- Power distribution monitoring
- Electric power monitoring
- Fuel oil handling system
- Hydroelectric load management
- Petroleum pilot plants
- Plant monitoring
- Process controls
- Process stimulators
- Tank controls
- Utility monitoring
- Safety parameter display systems and shutdown systems
- Tank level control and monitoring
- Turbine controls
- Turbine monitoring
- Virtual annunciator panels

- Alarm systems
- Security equipment
- Event logging

Because these systems can monitor multiple processes, equipment, and infrastructure and then provide quick notification of, or response to, problems or upsets, SCADA systems typically provide the first line of detection for atypical or abnormal conditions. For example, a SCADA system connected to sensors that measure specific machining quality parameters are measured outside of a specific range. A real-time customized operator interface screen could display and control critical systems monitoring parameters.

The system could transmit warning signals back to the operators, such as by initiating a call to a personal pager. This might allow the operators to initiate actions to prevent power outages or contamination and disruption of the energy supply. Further automation of the system could ensure that the system initiated measures to rectify the problem. Preprogrammed control functions (e.g., shutting a valve, controlling flow, throwing a switch, or adding chemicals) can be triggered and operated based on SCADA utility.

SCADA VULNERABILITIES

U.S. Electric Grid Gets Hacked Into
    The Associated Press (AP) reported April 9, 2009 that spies hacked into the U.S. energy grid and left behind computer programs (Trojan Horses) that would enable them to disrupt service, exposing potentially catastrophic vulnerabilities in key pieces of national infrastructure.

Even though terrorists, domestic and/or foreign, tend to aim their main focus around the critical devices that control actual critical infrastructure production and delivery activities, according to USEPA (2005), SCADA networks were developed with little attention paid to security, making the security of these systems often weak. Studies have found that, while technological advancements introduced vulnerabilities, many critical infrastructure sector plans/sites and utilities have spent little time securing their SCADA networks. As a result, many SCADA networks may be susceptible to attacks and misuse. SCADA systems languished in obscurity and this was the essence of their security; that is, until technological developments transformed SCADA from a backroom operation to a front-and-center visible control system.

Remote monitoring and supervisory control of processes began to develop in the early 1960s and adopted many technological advancements. The advent of minicomputers made it possible to automate a vast number of once manually-operated switches.

Advancements in radio technology reduced the communication costs associated with installing and maintaining buried cable in remote areas. SCADA systems continued to adopt new communication methods including satellite and cellular. As the price of computers and communications dropped, it became economically feasible to distribute operations and to expand SCADA networks to include even smaller facilities.

Advances in information technology and the necessity of improved efficiency have resulted in increasingly automated and interlinked infrastructures, and created new vulnerabilities due to equipment failure, human error, weather, and other natural causes, and physical and cyberattacks. Some areas and examples of possible SCADA vulnerabilities include (Wiles et al., 2007):

- Human—People can be tricked or corrupted, and may commit errors.
- Communications—Messages can be fabricated, intercepted, changed, deleted, or blocked.
- Hardware—Security features are not easily adapted to small self-contained units with limited power supplies.
- Physical—Intruders can break into a facility to steal or damage SCADA equipment.
- Natural—Tornadoes, floods, earthquakes, and other natural disasters can damage equipment and connections.
- Software—Programs can be poorly written.

Specific SCADA weaknesses and potential attack vectors include:

- Does not require any authorization
- Does not use encryption
- Does not properly recognize and properly handle errors and exceptions
- Not authentication is required
- Data could be intercepted
- Manipulation of data
- Service denial
- IP address spoofing—Internet protocol packets with a false source IP address
- Session hijacking
- Unsolicited responses
- Packet fuzzing—involves imputing false information, etc.
- Unauthorized control
- Log data medication

SCADA system computers and their connections are susceptible to different types of information system attacks and misuse such as those mentioned above. The

Computer Security Institute and Federal Bureau of Investigation conduct an annual Computer Crime and Security Survey (FBI, 2007). The survey reported on ten types of attacks or misuse, and reported that virus and denial of service had the greatest negative economic impact. The same study also found that 15 percent of the respondents reported abuse of wireless networks, which can be a SCADA component. On average, respondents from all sectors did not believe that their organization invested enough in security awareness. For example, utilities as a group reported a lower average computer security expenditure/investment per employee than many other sectors such as transportation, telecommunications, and finance.

Sandia National Laboratories' *Common Vulnerabilities in Critical Infrastructure Control Systems* described some of the common problems it has identified in the following five categories (Stamp et al., 2003):

1. **System Data**—Important data attributes for security include availability, authenticity, integrity, and confidentiality. Data should be categorized according to its sensitivity, and ownership and responsibility must be assigned. However, SCADA data is often not classified at all, making it difficult to identify where security precautions are appropriate (e.g., which communication links to secure, databases requiring protection, etc.).
2. **Security Administration**—Vulnerabilities emerge because many systems lack a properly structured security policy (security administration is notoriously lax in the case of control systems), equipment and system implementation guides, configuration management, training, and enforcement and compliance auditing.
3. **Architecture**—Many common practices negatively affect SCADA security. For example, while it is convenient to use SCADA capabilities for other purposes such as fire and security systems, these practices create single points of failure. Also, the connection of SCADA networks to other automation systems and business networks introduces multiple entry points for potential adversaries.
4. **Network** (including communication links)—Legacy systems' hardware and software have very limited security capabilities, and the vulnerabilities of contemporary systems (based on modern information technology) are publicized. Wireless and shared links are susceptible to eavesdropping and data manipulation.
5. **Platforms**—Many platform vulnerabilities exist, including default configurations retained, poor password practices, shared accounts, inadequate protection for hardware, and nonexistent security monitoring controls. In most cases, important security patches are not installed, often due to concern about negatively impacting system operation; in some cases technicians are contractually forbidden from updating systems by their vendor agreements.

The following incident helps to illustrate some of the risks associated with SCADA vulnerabilities.

During the course of a conduction vulnerability assessment, a contractor stated that personnel from his company penetrated the information system of a utility within minutes. Contractor personnel drove to a remote substation and noticed a wireless network antenna. Without leaving their vehicle, they plugged in their wireless radios and connected to the network within five minutes. Within twenty minutes they had mapped the network, including SCADA equipment, and accessed the business network and data. This illustrates what a cybersecurity advisor from Sandia National Laboratories specializing in SCADA stated, that utilities are moving to wireless communication without understanding the added risks.

THE INCREASING RISK

According to GAO (2015), historically, security concerns about control systems (SCADA included) were related primarily to protecting against physical attack and misuse of refining and processing sites or distribution and holding facilities. However, more recently there has been a growing recognition that control systems are now vulnerable to cyberattacks from numerous sources, including governments, terrorist groups, disgruntled employees, and other malicious intruders.

In addition to control system vulnerabilities mentioned earlier, several factors have contributed to the escalation of risk to control systems, including (1) the adoption of standardized technologies with known vulnerabilities, (2) the connectivity of control systems to other networks, (3) constraints on the implementation of existing security technologies and practices, (4) insecure remote connections, and (5) the widespread availability of technical information about control systems.

Adoption of Technologies with Known Vulnerabilities

When a technology is not well-known, not widely used, not understood or publicized, it is difficult to penetrate it and thus disable it. Historically, proprietary hardware, software, and network protocols made it difficult to understand how control systems operated—and therefore how to hack into them. Today, however, to reduce costs and improve performance, organizations have been transitioning from proprietary systems to less expensive, standardized technologies such as Microsoft Windows and Unix-like operating systems and the common networking protocols used by the Internet. These widely used standardized technologies have commonly known vulnerabilities, and sophisticated and effective exploitation tools are widely available and relatively easy to use. As a consequence, both the number of people with the knowledge to wage attacks and the number of systems subject to attack have increased. Also, common communication protocols and the emerging use of Extensible Markup

Language (commonly referred to as XML) can make it easier for a hacker to interpret the content of communications among the components of a control system.

Control systems are often connected to other networks—enterprises often integrate their control system with their enterprise networks. This increased connectivity has significant advantages, including providing decision makers with access to real-time information and allowing engineers to monitor and control the process control system from different points on the enterprise network. In addition, the enterprise networks are often connected to the networks of strategic partners and to the Internet. Further, control systems are increasingly using wide area networks and the Internet to trans-mit data to their remote or local stations and individual devices. This convergence of control networks with public and enterprise networks potentially exposes the control systems to additional security vulnerabilities. Unless appropriate security controls are deployed in the enterprise network and the control system network, breaches in enterprise security can affect the operation of controls system.

According to industry experts, the use of existing security technologies, as well as strong user authentication and patch management practices, are generally not imple-mented in control systems because they operate in real-time, typically are not designed with cybersecurity in mind, and usually have limited processing capabilities.

Existing security technologies such as authorization, authentication, encryption, intrusion detection, and filtering of network traffic and communications require more bandwidth, processing power, and memory than control system components typically have. Because controller stations are generally designed to do specific tasks, they use low-cost, resource-constrained microprocessors. In fact, some devices in the electrical industry still use the Intel 8088 processor, introduced in 1978. Consequently, it is difficult to install existing security technologies without seriously degrading the performance of the control system.

Further, complex passwords and other strong password practices are not always used to prevent unauthorized access to control systems, in part because this could hinder a rapid response to safety procedures during an emergency. As a result, accord-ing to experts weak passwords that are easy to guess, share, and infrequently change are reportedly common in control systems, including the use of default passwords or even no password at all.

In addition, although modern control systems are based on standard operating systems, they are typically customized to support control system applications. Con-sequently, vendor-provided software patches are generally either incompatible or cannot be implemented without compromising service shutting down "always-on" systems or affecting interdependent operations.

Potential vulnerabilities in control systems are exacerbated by insecure connections. Organizations often leave access links—such as dial-up modems to equipment and control information—open for remote diagnostics, maintenance, and examination of system status. Such links may not be protected with authentication of encryption, which increases the risk that hackers could us these insecure connections to break into remotely controlled systems. Also, control systems often use wireless communications systems, which are especially vulnerable to attack, or leased lines that pass through commercial telecommunications facilities. Without encryption to protect data as it flows through these insecure connections or authentication mechanisms to limit access, there is limited protection for the integrity of the information being transmitted.

Public information about infrastructures and control systems is available to potential hackers and intruders. The availability of this infrastructure and vulnerability data was demonstrated by a university graduate student, whose dissertation reportedly mapped every business and industrial sector in the U.S. economy to the fiber-optic network that connects them—using material that was available publicly on the Internet, none of which was classified.

Cyber Threats to Control Systems

There is a general consensus—and increasing concern—among government officials and experts on control systems about potential cyber threats to the control systems that govern our critical infrastructures. As components of control systems increasingly make critical decisions that were once made by humans, the potential effect of a cyber threat becomes more devastating. Such cyber threats could come from numerous sources, ranging from hostile governments and terrorist groups to disgruntled employees and other malicious intruders.

In July 2002, National Infrastructure Protection Center (NIPC) reported that the potential for compound cyber and physical attacks, referred to as "swarming attacks," is an emerging threat to the U.S. critical infrastructure. As NIPC reports, the effects of a swarming attack include slowing or complicating the response to a physical attack. For instance, a cyberattack that disabled the water supply or the electrical system in conjunction with a physical attack could deny emergency services the necessary resources to manage the consequences—such as controlling fires, coordinating actions, and generating light.

Control systems, such as SCADA, can be vulnerable to cyberattacks. Entities or individuals with malicious intent might take one or more of the following actions to successfully attack control systems:

- disrupt the operation of control systems by delaying or blocking the flow of information through control networks, thereby denying availability of the networks to control system operations

- make unauthorized changes to programmed instructions in PLCs, RTUs, or DCS controllers, change alarm thresholds, or issue unauthorized commends to control equipment, which could potentially result in damage to equipment (if tolerances are exceeded), premature shutdown of processes (such as prematurely shutting down transmission lines), or even disabling of control equipment
- send false information to control system operators either to disguise unauthorized changes or to initiate inappropriate actions by system operators
- modify the control system software, producing unpredictable results, and
- interfere with the operation of safety systems

In addition, in control systems that cover a wide geographic area, the remote sites are often unstaffed and may not be physically monitored. If such remote systems are physically breached, the attackers could establish a cyber connection to the control network.

Securing Control Systems

Several challenges must be addressed to effectively secure control systems against cyber threats. These challenges include: (1) the limitations of current security technologies in securing control systems; (2) the perception that securing control systems may not be economically justifiable; and (3) the conflicting priorities within organizations regarding the security of control systems.

A significant challenge in effectively securing control systems is the lack of specialized security technologies for these systems. The computing resources in control systems that are needed to perform security functions tend to be quite limited, making it very difficult to use security technologies within control system networks without severely hindering performance.

Securing control systems may not be perceived as economically justifiable. Experts and industry representatives have indicated that organizations may be reluctant to spend more money to secure control systems. Hardening the security of control systems would require industries to expend more resources, including acquiring more personnel, providing training for personnel, and potentially prematurely replacing current systems that typically have a lifespan of about twenty years.

Finally, several experts and industry representatives indicated that the responsibility for securing control systems typically includes two separate groups: IT security personnel and control system engineers and operators. IT security personnel tend to focus on securing enterprise systems, while control system engineers and operators tend to be more concerned with the reliable performance of their control systems. Further, they indicate that, as a result, those two groups do not always fully understand each other's requirements and collaborate to implement secure control systems.

STEPS TO IMPROVE SCADA SECURITY

The President's Critical Infrastructure Protection Board and the Department of Energy (DOE) have developed the steps outlined below to help organizations improve the security of their SCADA networks. DOE (2001) points out that these steps are not meant to be prescriptive or all-inclusive. However, they do address essential actions to be taken to improve the protection of SCADA networks. The steps are divided into two categories: specific actions to improve implementation and actions to establish essential underlying management processes and policies.

21 Steps to Increase SCADA Security (DOE, 2001)

The following steps focus on specific actions to be taken to increase the security of SCADA networks:

1. **Identify all connections to SCADA networks.**

   Conduct a thorough risk analysis to assess the risk and necessity of each connection to the SCADA network. Develop a comprehensive understanding of all connections to the SCADA network, and how well those connections are protected. Identify and evaluate the following types of connections:
   - Internal local area and wide area networks, including business networks
   - The Internet
   - Wireless network devices, including satellite uplinks
   - Modem or dial-up connections
   - Connections to business partners, vendors or regulatory agencies

2. **Disconnect unnecessary connections to the SCADA network.**

   To ensure the highest degree of security of SCADA systems, isolate the SCADA network from other network connections to as great a degree as possible. Any connection to another network introduces security risks, particularly if the connection creates a pathway from or to the Internet. Although direct connections with other networks may allow important information to be passed efficiently and conveniently, insecure connections are simply not worth the risk; isolation of the SCADA network must be a primary goal to provide needed protection. Strategies such as utilization of "demilitarized zones" (DMZs) and data warehousing can facilitate the secure transfer of data from the SCADA network to business networks. However, they must be designed and implemented properly to avoid introduction of additional risk through improper configuration.

3. **Evaluate and strengthen the security of any remaining connections to the SCADA networks.**

   Conduct penetration testing or vulnerability analysis of any remaining connections to the SCADA network to evaluate the protection posture associated with these pathways. Use this information in conjunction with risk management processes to develop a robust protection strategy for any pathways to the SCADA network. Since the SCADA network is only as secure as its weakest connecting point, it is essential to implement firewalls, intrusion detection systems (IDSs), and other appropriate security measures at each point of entry. Configure firewall rules to prohibit access from and to the SCADA network, and be as specific as possible when permitting approved connections. For example, an Independent System Operator (ISO) should not be granted "blanket" network access simply because there is a need for a connection to certain components of the SCADA system. Strategically place IDSs at each entry point to alert security personnel of potential breaches of network security. Organization management must understand and accept responsibility or risks associated with any connection to the SCADA network.

4. **Harden SCADA networks by removing or disabling unnecessary services.**
SCADA control servers built on commercial or open-source operating systems can be exposed to attack default network services. To the greatest degree possible, remove or disable unused services and network demons to reduce the risk of direct attack. This is particularly important when SCADA networks are interconnected with other networks. Do not permit a service or feature on a SCADA network unless a thorough risk assessment of the consequences of allowing the service/feature shows that the benefits of the service/feature far outweigh the potential for vulnerability exploitation. Examples of services to remove from SCADA networks include automated meter reading/remote billing systems, email services, and Internet access. An example of a feature to disable is remote maintenance. Numerous secure configurations such as the National Security Agency's series of security guides. Additionally, work closely with SCADA vendors to identify secure configurations and coordinate any and all changes to operational systems to ensure that removing or disabling services does not cause downtime, interruption of service, or loss of support.

5. **Do not rely on proprietary protocols to protect your system.**
Some SCADA systems are unique, proprietary protocols for communications between field devices and servers. Often the security of SCADA systems is based solely on the secrecy of these protocols. Unfortunately, obscure protocols provide very little "real" security. Do not rely on proprietary protocols or factor default configuration setting to protect your system. Additionally, demand that vendors disclose any backdoors or vendor interfaces to your SCADA systems, and expect them to provide systems that are capable of being secured.

6. **Implement the security features provided by device and system vendors.**
Older SCADA systems (most systems in use) have no security features whatsoever, SCADA system owners must insist that their system vendor implement security

features in the form of product patches or upgrades. Some newer SCADA devices are shipped with basic security features, but these are usually disabled to ensure ease of installation.

Analyze each SCADA device to determine whether security features are present. Additionally, factory default security settings (such as in computer network firewalls) are often set to provide maximum usability, but minimal security. Set all security features to provide the maximum security only after a thorough risk assessment of the consequences of reducing the security level.

7. **Establish strong controls over any medium that is used as a backdoor into the SCADA network.**

Where backdoors or vendor connections do exist in SCADA systems, strong authentication must be implemented to ensure secure communications. Modems, wireless, and wired networks used for communications and maintenance represent a significant vulnerability to the SCADA network and remote sites. Successful "war dialing" or "war driving" attacks could allow an attacker to bypass all of other controls and have direct access to the SCADA network or resources. To minimize the risk of such attacks, disable inbound access and replace it with some type of callback system.

8. **Implement internal and external intrusion detection systems and establish 24-hour-a-day incident monitoring.**

To be able to effectively respond to cyber attacks, establish an intrusion detection strategy that includes alerting network administrators of malicious network activity originating from internal or external sources. Intrusion detection system monitoring is essential 24 hours a day; this capability can be easily set up through a pager. Additionally, incident response procedures must be in place to allow an effective response to any attack. To complement network monitoring, enable logging on all systems and audit system logs daily to detect suspicious activity as soon as possible.

9. **Perform technical audits of SCADA devices and networks, and any other connected networks, to identify security concerns.**

Technical audits of SCADA devices and networks are critical to ongoing security effectiveness. Many commercial and open-sourced security tools are available that allow system administrators to conduct audits of their systems/networks to identify active services, patch level, and common vulnerabilities. The use of these tools will not solve systemic problems, but will eliminate the "paths of least resistance" that an attacker could exploit. Analyze identified vulnerabilities to determine their significance, and take corrective actions as appropriate. Track corrective actions and analyze this information to identify trends. Additionally, retest systems after corrective actions have been taken to ensure that vulnerabilities were actually eliminated. Scan non-production environments actively to identify and address potential problems.

10. **Conduct physical security surveys and assess all remote sites connected to the SCADA network to evaluate their security.**

    Any location that has a connection to the SCADA network is a target, especially unmanned or unguarded remote sites. Conduct a physical security survey and inventory access points at each facility that has a connection to the SCADA system. Identify and assess any source of information including remote telephone/computer network/fiber optic cables that could be tapped; radio and microwave links that are exploitable computer terminals that could be accessed; and wireless local area network access points. Identify and eliminate single points of failure. The security of the site must be adequate to detect or prevent unauthorized access. Do not allow "live" network access points at remote, unguarded sites simply for convenience.

11. **Establish SCADA "Red Teams" to identify and evaluate possible attack scenarios.**

    Establish a "Red Team" to identify potential attack scenarios and evaluate potential system vulnerabilities. Use a variety of people who can provide insight into weaknesses of the overall network, SCADA system, physical systems, and security controls. People who work on the system every day have great insight into the vulnerabilities of your SCADA network and should be consulted when identifying potential attack scenarios and possible consequences. Also, ensure that the risk from a malicious insider is fully evaluated, given that this represents one of the greatest threats to an organization. Feed information resulting from the "Red Team" evaluation into risk management processes to assess the information and establish appropriate protection strategies. The following steps focus on management actions to establish an effective cyber security program.

12. **Clearly define cyber security roles, responsibilities, and authorities for managers, system administrators, and users.**

    Organization personnel need to understand the specific expectations associated with protecting information technology resources through the definition of clear and logical roles and responsibilities. In addition, key personnel need to be given sufficient authority to carry out their assigned responsibilities. Too often, good cyber security left up to the initiative of the individual, which usually leads to inconsistent implementations and ineffective security. Establish a cyber security organizational structure that defines roles and responsibilities and clearly identifies how cyber security issues are escalated and who is notified in an emergency.

13. **Document network architecture and identify systems that serve critical functions or contain sensitive information that require additional levels of protection.**

    Develop and document robust information security architecture as part of a process to establish an effective protection strategy. It is essential that organizations design their network with security in mind and continue to have a strong understanding of their network architecture throughout its lifecycle. Of particular importance, an in-depth understanding of the functions that the systems perform and the sensitivity of the stored information is required. Without this understanding, risk cannot be properly assessed and protection strategies may not be sufficient. Documenting the information security architecture and its components is critical to understanding the overall protection strategy, and identifying single points of failure.

14. **Establish a rigorous, ongoing risk management process.**

A thorough understanding of the risks to network computing resources from denial-of-service attacks and the vulnerability of sensitive information to compromise is essential to an effective cyber security program. Risk assessments from the technical basis of this understanding are critical to formulating effective strategies to mitigate vulnerabilities and preserve the integrity of computing resources. Initially, perform a baseline risk analysis based on current threat assessment to use for developing a network protection strategy. Due to rapidly changing technology and the emergence of new threats on a daily basis, an ongoing risk assessment process is also needed so that routine changes can be made to the protection strategy to ensure it remains effective. Fundamental to risk management is identification of residual risk with a network protection strategy in place and acceptance of that risk by management.

15. **Establish a network protection strategy based on the principle of defense-in-depth.**

A fundamental principle that must be part of any network protection strategy is defense-in-depth. Defense-in-depth must be considered early in the design phase of the development process, and must be an integral consideration in all technical decision-making associated with the network. Utilize technical and administrative controls to mitigate threats from identified risks to as great a degree as possible at all levels of the network. Single points of failure must be avoided, and cyber security defense must be layered to limit and contain the impact of any security incidents. Additionally, each layer must be protected against other systems at the same layer. For example, to protect against the inside threat, restrict users to access only those resources necessary to perform their job functions.

16. **Clearly identity cyber security requirements**.

Organizations and companies need structured security programs with mandated requirements to establish expectations and allow personnel to be held accountable. Formalized policies and procedures are typically used to establish and institutionalize a cyber security program. A formal program is essential of establishing a consistent, standards-based approach to cyber security through an organization and eliminates sole dependence on individual initiative. Policies and procedures also inform employees of their specific cyber security responsibilities and the consequences of failing to meet those responsibilities. They also provide guidance regarding actions to be taken during a cyber security incident and promote efficient and effective actions during a time of crisis. As part of identifying cyber security requirements, include user agreements and notification and warning banners. Establish requirements to minimize the threat from malicious insiders, including the need for conducting background checks and limiting network privileges to those absolutely necessary.

17. **Establish effective configuration management processes.**

   A fundamental management process needed to maintain a secure network is configuration management. Configuration management needs to cover both hardware configurations and software configurations. Changes to hardware or software can easily introduce vulnerabilities that undermine network security. Processes are required to evaluate and control any change to ensure that the network remains secure. Configuration management begins with well-tested and documented security baselines for your various systems.

18. **Conduct routine self-assessments.**

   Robust performance evaluation processes are needed to provide organizations with feedback on the effectiveness of cyber security policy and technical implementation. A sign of a mature organization is one that is able to self-identify issues, conduct root cause analyses, and implement effective corrective actions that address individual and systemic problems. Self-assessment processes that are normally part of an effective cyber security program include routine scanning for vulnerabilities, automated auditing of the network, and self-assessments of organizational and individual performance.

19. **Establish system backups and disaster recovery plans**.

   Establish a disaster recovery plan that allows for rapid recovery from any emergency (including a cyber attack). System backups are an essential part of any plan and allow rapid reconstruction of the network. Routinely exercise disaster recovery plans to ensure that they work and that personnel are familiar with them. Make appropriate changes to disaster recovery plans based on lessons learned from exercises.

20. **Senior organizational leadership should establish expectations for cyber security performance and hold individuals accountable for their performance.**

   Effective cyber security performance requires commitment and leadership from senior managers in the organization. It is essential that senior management establish an expectation for strong cyber security and communicate this to their subordinate managers throughout the organization. It is also essential that senior organizational leadership establish a structure for implementation of a cyber security program. This structure will promote consistent implementation and the ability to sustain a strong cyber security program. It is then important for individuals to be held accountable for their performance as it relates to cyber security. This includes managers, system administrators, technicians, and users/operators.

21. **Establish policies and conduct training to minimize the likelihood that organizational personnel will inadvertently disclose sensitive information regarding SCADA system design, operations, or security controls.**

Release data related to the SCADA network only on a strict, need-to-know basis, and only to persons explicitly authorized to receive such information. "Social engineering," the gathering of information about a computer or computer network via questions to naïve users, is often the first step in a malicious attack on computer networks. The more information revealed about a computer or computer network, the more vulnerable the computer/network is. Never divulge data revealed to a SCADA network, including the names and contact information about the system operators/administrators, computer operating systems, and/or physical and logical locations of computers and network systems over telephones or to personnel unless they are explicitly authorized to receive such information. Any requests for information by unknown persons need to be sent to a central network security location for verification and fulfillment. People can be a weak link in an otherwise secure network. Conduct training and information awareness campaigns to ensure that personnel remain diligent in guarding sensitive network information, particularly their passwords.

REFERENCES AND RECOMMENDED READING

Associated Press (AP) (2009). *Goal: Disrupt.* From the 04/04/09 The Virginian-Pilot, Norfolk, VA.

Brown, A. S. (2008). *SCADA vs. the hackers.* American Society of Mechanical Engineers. Accessed 05/10/08 @ http://www.memagazine.org/backissues/dec02/features/scadavs/.

Denning, Dorothy (2001). *Is Cyber Terror Next?* Brooklyn, NY: Social Science Research Council.

DOE (2001). *21 Steps to improve cyber security of SCADA networks.* Washington, DC: Department of Energy.

Ezell, B. C. (1998). *Risks of Cyber Attack to Supervisory Control and Data Acquisition.* Charlottesville: University of Virginia.

FEMA (2008). *FEMA452: Risk Assessment A How to Guide.* Accessed 05/01/08 @fema.gov/library/file?type=published/filetofile.

FEMA (2015). *Protecting Critical Infrastructure Against Insider Threats.* Accessed 4/17/15 @ http://emilms.fema.gov/IS0915/IABsummary.htm.

FBI (2000). *Threat to Critical Infrastructure.* Washington, DC: Federal Bureau of Investigation.

FBI (2007). *Ninth Annual Computer Crime and Security Survey.* FBI: Computer Crime Institute and Federal Bureau of Investigations.

FBI (2014). *Protecting Critical Infrastructure and the Importance of Partnerships.* Accessed @ https://www.fib.gov/news/speeches/protecitng-critical-infrastruce-andt-the-importantce-o...

GAO (2003). *Critical Infrastructure Protection: Challenges in Securing Control System.* Washington, DC: United States General Accounting Office.

GAO (2015). *Critical Infrastructure Protection: Sector-Specific Agencies Need to Better Measure Cybersecurity Progress.* Washington, DC: United States Government Accountability Office.

Gellman, B. (2002). Cyber-Attacks by Al Qaeda Feared: Terrorists at Threshold of Using Internet as Tool of Bloodshed, Experts Say. *Washington Post,* June 27; p. A01.

Minter, J. G. (1996). Prevention Chemical Accidents Still A Challenge. *Occupational Hazards,* September.

National Infrastructure Advisory Council (2008). *First Report and Recommendations on the Insider Threat to Critical Infrastructure.* Washington, DC.

NIPC (2002). *National Infrastructure Protection Center Report.* Washington, DC: National Infrastructure Protection Center.

Spellman, F. R. (1997). *A Guide to Compliance for PSM/RMP.* Lancaster, PA: Technomic Publishing Company.

Stamp, J. et al. (2003). *Common Vulnerabilities in Critical Infrastructure Control Systems,* 2nd ed. Sandia National Laboratories.

U.S. Department of Energy (2010). *Energy Sector-Specific Plan: An Annex to the National Infrastructure Protection Plan.* Washington, DC: USDOE.

US DOE (2002). *Vulnerability Assessment Methodology: Electric Power Infrastructure.* Washington, DC.

USEPA (2005). EPA Needs to Determine What Barriers Prevent Water Systems from Securing Known SCADA Vulnerabilities. In: Harris, J. Final Briefing Report. Washington, DC: USEPA.

Warwalking (2003). Accessed 05/09/08 @ http://warwalking.tribe.net.

Wiles, J. et al. (2007). *Techno Security's™ Guide to Securing SCADA .* Burlington, MA: Elsevier, Inc.

Young, M. A. (2004). *SCADA Systems Security.* SANS Institute.

4

IT Security Action Plan

Never underestimate the time, expense, blood, sweat, and effort a terrorist will apply to compromise the security of any industrial facility.

IT SECURITY ACTION ITEMS

IT security policies should follow good design and governance practices—not so long that they become unusable, not so vague that they become meaningless, and reviewed on a regular basis to ensure that they stay pertinent as needs change.

All companies should develop and maintain clear and robust polices for safeguarding critical business data and sensitive information, protecting their reputation, and discouraging inappropriate behavior by employees. These robust policies for safeguarding sensitive digital information should include (based on FCC, 2017):

- Policy development and management
- Scams and fraud
- Network security
- Website security
- E-mail
- Mobile devices
- Employees
- Facility security
- Operational security
- Payment cards
- Incident response and reporting

Note: Implementing the following recommended actions to protect your IT sector systems is highly advised. However, if company funds are available to hire reputable professional IT security professionals to tailor security needs to your system this is always the best course of action; moreover, many of the items detailed below should, or would, be included and accomplished in large companies by outside and/or inside computer experts.

Policy Development and Management

Establish Security Roles and Responsibilities

One of the least expensive and most effective means of preventing serious IT security incidents is to establish a policy that clearly defines the separation of roles and responsibilities with regard to systems and the information they contain. Such polices need to clearly state, at a minimum, the company data ownership and employee roles for security oversight and their inherit privileges, including:

- Necessary roles, and the privileges and constraints accorded to those roles
- The types of employees who should be allowed to assume the various roles
- How long an employee may hold a role before access rights must be reviewed
- If employees may hold multiple roles, the circumstances define when to adopt one role over another

Depending on the types of data regularly handled by your business, it may also make sense to create separate policies governing who is responsible for certain types of data.

Establish an Employee Internet Usage Policy

The limits on employee Internet usage in the workplace vary widely from business to business. Your guidelines should allow employees the maximum degree of freedom they require to be productive (short breaks to surf the web or perform personal tasks online have been shown to increase productivity). However, at the same time, employees must keep in mind that rules of behavior are necessary to ensure that they are aware of boundaries, both to keep them safe and to keep the company successful. Consider, for example:

- Personal breaks to surf the web should be limited to a reasonable amount of time and to certain types of activities.
- If a web filtering system is used, employees should have clear knowledge of how and why their web activities will be monitored, and what types of sites are deemed unacceptable.

- Workplace rules of behavior should be clear, concise, and easy to follow. Employees should feel comfortable performing both personal and professional tasks online without making judgment calls as to what may or may not be deemed appropriate. Businesses may want to include a splash warning upon network sign-on that advises the employees of the businesses' Internet usage polices so that all employees are on notice.

Establish a Social Media Policy

Using technical or procedural solutions to address social networking applications introduces a number of risks that are difficult to address. A strong social media policy is crucial for any business that seeks to use social networking to promote its activities and communicate with its customers. At a minimum, a social media policy should clearly include the following:

- Specific guidance on when to disclose company activities using social media, and what kinds of details can be discussed in a public forum
- Additional rules of behavior for employees using personal social networking accounts to make clear what kinds of discussion topics or posts could cause risk for the company
- Guidance on the acceptability of using a company email address to register for, or get notices from, social media sites
- Guidance on selecting long and strong passwords for social networking accounts, since very few social media sites enforce strong authentication policies for users

Last but not least, all users of social media need to be aware of the risks associated with social networking tools and the types of data that can be automatically discovered online when using social media. Taking the time to educate your employees on the potential pitfalls of social media use, especially in tandem with geo-location services (i.e., the latitude and longitude of a particular location), may be the most beneficial social networking security practice of all.

Identify Potential Reputation Risks

Potential risks to a company's reputation are real and therefore a strategy should be developed to mitigate those risks via polices or other measures. Specific types of reputation risks include:

- Being impersonated online by a criminal organization (e.g., an illegitimate website spoofing a business name and copying site design, then attempting to defraud potential customers via phishing scams or other method

- Having sensitive company or customer information leaked to the public via the web
- Having sensitive or inappropriate employee actions made public via the web or social media sites

All businesses should set a policy for managing these types of risks and plans to address such incidents if and when they occur. Such a policy should cover a regular process for identifying potential risks to the company's reputation in cyberspace, practical measures to prevent those risks from materializing, and reference plans to respond and recover from potential incidents as soon as they occur.

Scams and Fraud

New telecommunications technologies may offer countless opportunities for business, but they also offer cybercriminals many new ways to victimize businesses, scam customers, and hurt reputations.

Train Employees to Recognize Social Engineering

Social engineering, also known as "pretexting," is used by many criminals, both online and off, to trick unsuspecting people into giving away their personal information and/ or installing malicious software onto their computers, devices, or networks. Social engineering is successful because the bad guys are doing their best to make their work look and sound legitimate, sometimes even helpful, which makes it easier to deceive users.

Most offline social engineering occurs over the telephone, but it frequently occurs online, as well. Information gathered from social networks or posted on websites can be enough to create a convincing ruse to trick employees. For example, LinkedIn profiles, Facebook posts, and Twitter messages can allow a criminal to assemble detailed dossiers on employees. Teaching people the risks involved in sharing personal or business details on the Internet can help partner with staff to prevent both personal and organizational losses.

Many criminals use social engineering tactics to get individuals to voluntarily install malicious computer software such as fake antivirus, thinking they are doing something that will help make them more secure. Users who are tricked into loading malicious programs on their computers may be providing remote control capabilities to an attacker, unwittingly installing software that can steal financial information or simply try to sell them fake security software.

Protect against Online Fraud

Online fraud takes on many guises that can impact everyone, including businesses and their employees. It is helpful to maintain consistent and predictable online messaging when communicating with customers to prevent others from impersonating the company.

Be sure to never request personal information or account details through e-mail, social networking, or other only messages. Let customers know their personal information will never be requested through such channels and instruct them to contact the person or company directly should they have any concerns.

Protect against Phishing

Phishing is the technique used by online criminals to trick people into thinking they are dealing with a trusted website or other entity. Businesses face this threat from two directions—phishers may be impersonating them to take advantage of unsuspecting customers and phishers may be trying to steal their employees' online credentials.

Businesses should ensure that their online communications never ask their customers to submit sensitive information via e-mail. Businesses should make clear in their communications reinforcing that the business will never ask for personal information via e-mail so that if someone targets customers, they may realize it is a scam.

The best defense again users being tricked into handing over their usernames and passwords to cybercriminals is employee awareness. Employees need to be informed that they should never respond to incoming messages requesting private information. Also, to avoid being led to a fake site, they should know to never click on a link sent by e-mail from an untrustworthy source. Employees should open an Internet browser window and manually type in the site's web address to make sure the e-mailed link is not maliciously redirecting to a dangerous site. Keep in mind that this is especially critical for protection of online banking accounts belonging to your organization. Criminals are targeting business banking accounts.

Don't Fall for Fake Antivirus Offers

"Scareware" (fake antivirus) and other rouge online security scams have been behind some of the most successful online frauds in recent times. Make sure your organization has a policy in place explaining what the procedure is if an employee's computer becomes infected with a virus.

Employees need to be trained to recognize a legitimate warning message and to properly notify the IT team if something bad or questionable has happened. If possible, business computers should be configured to not allow regular users to have administrative access. This will minimize the risk of them installing malicious software and caution users that adding unauthorized software to work computers is against policy.

Protect against Malware

Businesses can experience a compromise through the introduction of malicious software, or malware, that tracks a user's keyboard strokes, also known as *key logging*.

Many businesses are falling victim to key-logging malware being installed on computer systems in their environment. Once installed, the malware can record keystrokes made on a computer, allowing bad guys to see passwords, credit card numbers, and other confidential data. Keep security software up-to-date and patching computers regularly will make it more difficult for this type of malware to infiltrate business networks.

Develop a Layered Approach to Guard against Malicious Software

Despite progress in creating more awareness of security threats on the Internet, malware authors are not giving up. Based on research, it was found that more than 100,000 malicious software samples were seen every day (FCC, 2017).

Effective protection against viruses, Trojans, and other malicious software requires a layered approach to company defenses. The company must install antivirus software but should also deploy a combination of multiple techniques to keep the workplace environment safe. Moreover, the use of thumb drives and other removable media must be guarded against; they may have malicious software preinstalled that can infect the organization's computer(s). Ensure that the source of the removable media device is trustworthy before installing it.

Whenever web filtering, antivirus signature protection, proactive malware protection, firewalls, strong security policies, and employer training are combined and used, the risk of infection is significantly reduced. Keeping protection software up-to-date along with your operating system and applications increases the safety of your systems.

Verify the Identity of Telephone Information Seekers

The telephone is the preferred communication device used by social engineering criminals. Information gathered through social networks and information posted on websites can be enough to create a convincing ruse to trick company employees. Ensure employees are trained to never disclose customer information, usernames, passwords, or other sensitive details to incoming callers. When someone requests information, always contact the person back using a known phone number or e-mail account to verify the identity and validity of the individual and their request.

Network Security

Securing a company's network consists of (1) identifying all devices and connections on the network, (2) setting boundaries between the company's systems and others, and (3) enforcing controls to ensure that unauthorized access, misuse, or denial-of-service events can be thwarted or rapidly contained and recovered from if they do occur.

Secure Internal Network and Cloud Services

A company's network should be separated from the public Internet by strong user authentication mechanisms and policy enforcement systems such as firewalls and web filtering proxies. Additional monitoring and security solutions, such as antivirus software and intrusion detection systems, should also be employed to identify and stop malicious code or unauthorized access attempts.

Internal Network   After identifying the boundary points on the company's network, each boundary should be evaluated to determine what types of security controls are necessary and how they can be best deployed. Border routers should be configured to only route traffic to and from a company's public IP addresses, firewalls would be deployed to restrict traffic only to and from the minimum set of necessary services, and intrusion prevention systems should be confirmed to monitor for suspicious

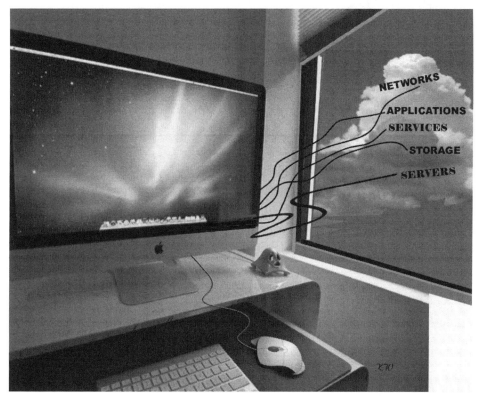

FIGURE 4.1
Cloud computing resources. Illustration by F. R. Spellman and K. Welsh.

activity crossing the network perimeter. In order to prevent bottlenecks, all security systems you deploy to your company's network perimeter should be capable of handling the bandwidth that your carrier provides.

Cloud-based Services   Cloud computing is a model for enabling convenient, on-demand network access to a shared pool of configurable computing resources (see figure 4.1). The terms of service with all cloud service providers should be discussed to ensure that the company's information and activities are protected with the same degree of security that the company would intend to provide on its own. Businesses should request security and auditing from their cloud service providers as applicable to the business' needs and concerns. Review and understand service level agreements of system restoration and reconstitution time. Businesses should also inquire about additional services a cloud service can provide. These services may include backup-and-restore services and encryption services, which may be very attractive to businesses.

Develop Strong Password Policies

Generally speaking, two-factor authentication methods, which require two types of evidence that the employee (or anyone else) is who he or she claims to be, are safer than using static passwords for authentication. One common example is a personal security token that displays changing passcodes to be used in conjunction with an established password. However, two-factor system may not always be possible or practical for your company.

Company password policies should encourage employees to use the strongest passwords possible without creating the need or temptation to reuse passwords or write them down. That means passwords that are random, complex, and long (at least ten characters), that are changed regularly, and that are closely guarded by those who know them.

Security and Encrypt the Company Wi-Fi

Wireless Access Control   A company may operate a wireless local area network (WLAN) for the use of customers, guest, and visitors. If this is the case, it is important that such a WLAN be kept separate from the main company network so that traffic from the public network cannot traverse the company's internal systems at any point.

Internal, non-public WLAN access should be restricted to specific devices and specific users to the greatest extent possible while meeting your company's business needs. Where the internal WLAN has less stringent access controls than your company's wired network, dual connections—where a device is able to connect to both the wireless and wired networks simultaneously—should be prohibited by technical controls on each such capable device (e.g., BIOS-level LAN/WLAN switch settings).

All users should be given unique credentials with preset expiration dates to use when accessing the internal WLAN.

Wireless Encryption   Due to demonstrable security flaws known to exist in older forms of wireless encryption, a company's internal WLAN should only employ Wi-Fi Protected Access 2 (WPA2) encryption.

Encrypt Sensitive Company Data

Encryption should be used to protect any data that a company considers sensitive, in addition to meeting applicable regulatory requirements on information safeguarding. Different encryption schemes are appropriate under different circumstances. However, applications that comply with the OpenPGP standard, such as PGP (**P**retty **G**ood **P**rivacy encryption program) and GnuPG, provide a wide range of options for security data on disk as well as in transit. If you choose to offer security transactions via your company's website, consult with your service provider about available options for an SSL certificate for a business site.

Regularly Update All Applications

All systems and software, including networking equipment, should be updated in a timely fashion as patches and firmware upgrades become available. Use automatic updating services whenever possible, especially for security systems such as antimalware applications, web filtering tools, and intrusion prevention systems.

Set Safe Web Browsing Rules

A company's internal network should only be able to access those services and resources on the Internet that are essential for the business and the needs of employees. Use the safe browsing features included with modern web browsing software and a web proxy to ensure that malicious or unauthorized sites cannot be accessed from your internal network.

If Remote Access is Enabled, Make Sure it is Secure

If a company needs to provide remote access to its internal network over the Internet, one popular and secure option is to use a secure virtual private network (VPN) system accompanied by strong two-factor authentication, using either hardware or software tokens (FCC, 2017).

Website Security

No amount of hyperbole or emphasis is needed when we say that website security is more important than ever. Web servers, which host the data and other content available to customers on the Internet, are often the most targeted and attacked components of a company's network. Cybercriminals are constantly looking for improperly secured websites to attack, while many customers say website security is a top consideration when they choose to shop online. As a result, it is essential to secure severs and the network infrastructure that supports them. The consequences of a security breach are great: loss of revenues, damage to credibility, legal liability, and loss of customer trust. The following are examples of specific security threats to web servers (FCC, 2017):

- Cybercriminals may exploit software bugs in the web server, underlying operating system, or active content to gain unauthorized access to the web server. Examples of unauthorized access include gaining access to files or folders that were not meant to be publicly accessible and being able to execute commands and/or install malicious software on the web server.
- Denial-of-service attacks may be directed at the web server or its supporting network infrastructure to prevent or hinder a company's website users from making use of its services.
- Sensitive information on the web server may be read or modified without authorization.
- Sensitive information on backend databases that are used to support interactive elements of a web application may be compromised through the injection of unauthorized software commands.
- Sensitive unencrypted information transmitted between the web server and the browser may be intercepted.
- Information on the web server may be changed for malicious purposes. Website defacement is a commonly reported example of this threat.
- Cybercriminals may gain unauthorized access to resources elsewhere in the organization's network via a successful attack on the web server.
- Cybercriminals may also attack external entities after compromising a web server. The attacks can be launched directly (e.g., from the compromised server against an external server) or indirectly (e.g., placing malicious content on the compromised web server that attempts to exploit vulnerability in the web browsers of users visiting the site).
- The server may be used as a distribution point for attack tools, pornography, or illegally copied software.

Carefully Plan and Address the Security Aspects of the Deployment of a Public Web Server

Because it is much more difficult to address security once deployment and implementation have occurred, security should be considered from the initial planning stage.

Businesses are more likely to make decisions about configuring computers appropriately and consistently when they develop and use a detailed, well-designed deployment plan. Developing such a plan will support web server administrators in making the inevitable trade-off decisions between usability, performance, and risk.

Businesses also need to consider the human resource requirements for the deployment and continued operation of the web server and supporting infrastructure. The following points list a deployment plan:

- Types of personnel required—for example, system and web server administrators, webmaster, network administrators, and information systems security personnel
- Skills and training required by assigned personnel
- Individual (i.e., the level of effort required of specific personnel types) and collective staffing (i.e., overall level of effort) requirements

Implement Appropriate Security Management Practices and Controls When Maintaining and Operating a Secure Web Server

Appropriate management practices are essential to operating and maintaining a secure web server. Security practices include the identification of the company's information system assets and the development, documentation, and implementation of policies, and guidelines to help ensure the confidentiality, integrity, and availability of information system resources. The following practices and controls are recommended:

- A business-wide information system security policy
- Server configuration and change control and management
- Risk assessment and management
- Standardized software configurations that satisfy the information system security policy
- Security awareness and training
- Contingency, planning, continuity of operations, and disaster recovery planning
- Certification and accreditation

Ensure that Web Server Systems Meet the Organization's Security Requirements

The initial step in securing a web server is securing the underlying operations system. Most commonly available web servers operate on a general-purpose operating system. Many security issues can be avoided if the operating systems underlying web servers are configured appropriately. Default hardware and software configurations are typically set by manufacturers to emphasize features, functions, and ease of use at the expense of security. Because manufacturers are not aware of each organization's security needs, each web server administrator must configure new servers to reflect their

48 CHAPTER 4

business' security requirements and reconfigure them as those requirements change. Using security configuration guides or checklists can assist administrators in security systems consistently and efficiently. Initially securing an operating system initially generally includes the following steps:

- Patch and upgrade the operating system.
- Change all default passwords.
- Remove or disable unnecessary services and applications.
- Configure operating system user authentication.
- Configure resource controls.
- Install and configure additional security controls.
- Perform security testing of the operating system.

Ensure the Web Server Application Meets the Organization's Security Requirements
In many respects, the security installation and configuration of the web server application will mirror the operating system process discussed above. The overarching principle is to install the minimal amount of web server services required and eliminate any known vulnerabilities through patches or upgrades. If the installation program installs any unnecessary applications, services, or scripts, they should be removed immediately after the installation process concludes. Securing the web server application generally includes the following steps:

- Patch and upgrade the web server application.
- Remove or disable unnecessary services, applications, and sample content.
- Configure web server user authentication and access controls.
- Configure web server resource controls.
- Test the security of the web server application and web content.

Ensure That Only Appropriate Content is Published on the Organization's Website
Typically, it is an organization's website that is often one of the first places cybercriminals search for valuable information. In spite of everything, many businesses lack a web publishing process or policy that determines what type of information to publish openly, what information to publish with restricted access, and what information should not be published to any publicly accessible repository. Some general accepted examples of what should not be pulled or at least should be carefully examined and reviewed before being published on a public website include:

- Classified or proprietary business information
- Sensitive information relating to a business' security

- Medical records
- A business' detailed physical and information security safeguards
- Details about a business' network and information system infrastructure—for example, address ranges, naming conventions, and access numbers
- Information that specifies or implies physical security vulnerabilities
- Detailed plans, maps, diagrams, aerial photographs, and architectural drawings of business buildings, properties, or installations
- Any sensitive information about individuals that might be subject to federal, state, or, in some instances, international privacy laws

Ensure Appropriate Steps Are Taken to Protect Web Content from Unauthorized Access or Modification

Although information available on public websites is intended to be public (assuming a credible review process and policy is in place), it is still important to ensure that information cannot be modified without authorization. Users of such information rely on its integrity even if the information is not confidential. Content on publicly accessible web servers is inherently more vulnerable than information that is inaccessible from the Internet, and this vulnerability means businesses need to protect public web content through the appropriate configuration of web server resource controls. Examples of resource control practices include:

- Install or enable only necessary services.
- Install web content on a dedicated hard drive or logical partition.
- Limit uploads to directories that are not readable by the web server.
- Define a single directory for all external scripts or programs executed as part of web content.
- Disable the use of hard to symbolic links.
- Define a complete web content access matrix identifying which folders and files in the web server document directory are restricted, which are accessible, and by whom.
- Disable directory listings.
- Deploy user authentication to identify approved users, digital signatures, and other cryptographic mechanisms as appropriate.
- Use intrusion detection systems, intrusion prevent systems, and file integrity checkers to spot intrusions and verify web content.
- Protect each backed server (i.e., database server or directory server) from command injection attacks.

Use Active Content Judiciously After Balancing the Benefits and Risks

Most early websites contained static information, typically in the form of text-based documents. Soon thereafter, interactive elements were introduced to offer new opportunities for user interaction. Unfortunately, these same interactive elements introduced new web-related vulnerabilities. They typically involved dynamically executing code using a large number of inputs from web page URL parameters to hypertext transfer protocol (HTTP) content and, more recently, extensible markup language (XML) content. Different active content technologies pose different related vulnerabilities, and their risks should be weighed against their benefits. Although most websites use some form of active content generators, may also deliver some or all of their content in a static form.

Use Authentication and Cryptographic Technologies as Appropriate to Protect Certain Types of Sensitive Data

Public web servers often support technologies for identifying and authenticating users with differing privileges for accessing information. Some of the technologies are based on cryptographic functions that can provide a secure channel between a web browser client and a web server that supports encryption. Web servers may be configured to use different cryptographic algorithms, providing varying levels of security and performance.

Without proper user authentication in place, businesses cannot selectively restrict access to specific information. All information that resides on subject web server is then accessible by anyone with access to the server. In addition, without some process to authenticate the server, users of the public web server will not be able to determine whether the server is the "authentic" web server or a counterfeit version operated by a cybercriminal.

Even with an encrypted channel and an authentication mechanism, it is possible that attackers may attempt to access the site by brute force. Improper authentication techniques can allow attackers to gather valid usernames or potentially gain access to the website. Strong authentication mechanisms can also protect against phishing attacks, in which hackers may trick users into providing their personal credentials, and pharming, in which traffic to a legitimate website may be redirected to an illegitimate one. An appropriate level of authentication should be implemented based on the sensitivity of the web server's users and content.

Employ Network Infrastructure to Help Protect Public Web Servers

The network infrastructure (e.g., firewalls, routers, intrusion detection systems) that supports the web server plays a critical security role. In most configurations, the network infrastructure will be the first line of defense between a public web server and the Internet. Network design alone, though, can't protect a web server. The frequency, sophistication, and variety of web server attacks perpetrated today support the idea that web server security must be implemented through layered and diverse protection mechanisms, an approach sometimes referred to as "defense-in-depths."

Commit to an Ongoing Process of Maintaining Web Server Security

Maintaining a secure web server requires constant effort, resources, and vigilance. Secure administering a web server on a daily basis is essential. Maintaining the security of a web server will usually involve the following steps:

- Configuring, protecting, and analyzing log files.
- Backup up critical information frequently.
- Maintaining a protected authoritative copy of your organization's web content.
- Establishing and following procedures for recovering from compromise.
- Testing and applying patches in a timely manner.
- Testing security periodically.

E-mail

E-mail has become a critical part of everyday business, from internal management to direct customer support. The benefits associated with e-mail as a primary business tool far outweigh the negatives. However, businesses must be mindful that a successful e-mail platform starts with basic principles of e-mail security to ensure the privacy and protection of customer and business information.

Set Up a Spam E-mail Filter

It has been well documented that spam, phishing attempts, and otherwise unsolicited and unwelcome e-mail often accounts for more than 60 percent of all e-mail that an individual or business receives. E-mail is the primary method for spreading viruses and malware and it is one of the easiest to defend against. Consider using e-mail-filtering services that your e-mail service, hosting provider, or other cloud providers offer. A local e-mail filter application is also an important competent of a solid anti-virus strategy. Ensure that automatic updates are enabled on your e-mail application, e-mail filter and anti-virus programs. Ensure that filters are reviewed regularly so that important e-mail and/or domains are not blocked in error.

Train Employees in Responsible E-mail Usage

The last line of defense for all of your cyber risk efforts lies with the employees who use tools such as e-mail, and their responsible and appropriate use and management of the information under their control. Technology alone can't make a business secure.

Employees must be trained to identify risks associated with e-mail use, how and when to use e-mail appropriate to their work, and when to seek assistance of professionals. Employee awareness training is available in many forms, including printed media, videos, and online training.

Consider requiring security awareness training for all new employees and refresher courses every year. Simple efforts such as monthly newsletters, urgent bulletins when new viruses are detected, and even posters in common areas to remind employees of key security and privacy to-do's create a work environment that is educated in protecting the business.

Protect Sensitive Information Sent Via E-mail

With its proliferation as a primary tool to communicate internally and externally, business e-mail often includes sensitive information. Whether it is company information that could harm the business or regulated data such as personal health information or personally identifiable information, it is important to ensure that such information is only sent and accessed by those who are entitled to see it.

Since e-mail in its native form is not designed to be secure, incidents of misaddressing or other common accidental forwarding can lead to data leakage. Businesses that handle this type of inflation should consider whether such information should be sent via e-mail, or at least consider using e-mail encryption. Encryption is the process of converting data into an unreadable format to prevent disclosure to unauthorized personnel. Only individuals or organizations with access to the encryption key can read the information. Other cloud services offer "Security Web Enabled Drop Boxes" that enable secure data transfer for sensitive information, which is often a better approach to transmitting between companies or customers.

Set a Sensible E-mail Retention Policy

Another important consideration is the management of e-mail that resides on company messaging systems and your users' computers. From the cost of storage and backup to legal and regulatory requirements, companies should document how they will handle e-mail retention and implement basic controls to help them attain those standards. Many industries have specific rules that dictate how long e-mails can or should be retained, but the basic rule of thumb is only as long as it supports your business efforts. Many companies implement a sixty to ninety-day retention standard if not compelled by law to another retention period.

To ensure compliance, companies should consider mandatory archiving at a chosen retention cycle end data and automatic permanent e-mail removal after another set point, such as 180–260 days in archives. In addition, organizations should discourage the use of personal folders on employee computers (most often configurable from the e-mail system level), as this will make it more difficult to manage company standards.

Develop an E-mail Usage Policy

Policies are important for setting expectations with employees or users, and for developing standards to ensure adherence to the company's published policies. Accordingly, the company's policies should be easy to read, understand, define, and enforce. In addition, key areas to address should include what the company e-mail system should and should not be used for, and what data are allowed to be transmitted. Other policy areas should address retention, privacy, and acceptable use.

Depending on the company's business and jurisdiction, there may be a need for e-mail monitoring. The rights of the business and the user should be documented in the policy as well. The policy should be part of the company's general end user-awareness training and reviewed for updates on a yearly basis.

Mobile Devices

If a company uses mobile devices to conduct company business, such as accessing company e-mail or sensitive data, pay close attention to mobile security and the potential threats that can expose and compromise a company's business networks. This section describes the mobile threat environment and the practices that businesses can use to help secure devices such as smartphones, tablets, and Wi-Fi enabled laptops.

Many organizations are finding that employees are most productive when using mobile devices, and the benefits are too great to ignore. But while mobility can increase workplace productivity, allowing employees to bring their own mobile device into the enterprise can create significant security and management challenges.

Data loss and data breaches caused by lost or stolen smartphones create big challenges, as mobile devices are now used to store confidential business information and access to the corporate network. Typically, company security surveys show that the majority of respondents rank loss or theft as their top mobile-device security concern and second in rank is concern about mobile malware. It is important to remember that while the individual employee may be liable for a device, the company is still liable for the data.

Top Threats Targeting Mobile Devices

According to the FCC (2017), the top threats targeting mobile devices are:

- Data loss—An employee or hacker can accesses sensitive information from device or network. This can be unintentional or malicious, and is considered the biggest threat to mobile devices.

- Social Engineering Attacks—A cybercriminal attempts to trick users to disclose sensitive information or install malware. Methods include phishing and targeted attacks.
- Malware—Malicious software includes traditional computer viruses, computer worms, and Trojan horse programs. Specific examples include the Ikee worm, targeting iOS-based devices; and Pjapps malware that can enroll infected Android devices in a collection of hacker-controlled "zombie" devices known as a "botnet."
- Data Integrity Threats—Attempts to corrupt or modify data in order to disrupt operations of a business for financial gain. These can also occur unintentionally.
- Resource Abuse—Attempts to misuse network, device, or identity resources. Examples include sending spam from compromised devices or denial of service attacks using computing resources of compromised devices.
- Web and Network-Based Attacks—Launched by malicious websites or compromised legitimate sites, these target a device's browser and attempt to install malware or steal confidential data that flows through it.

A few simple steps can help ensure company information is protected. These include requiring all mobile devices that connect to the business network be equipped with security software and password protection; and providing general security training to make employees aware of the importance of security practices for mobile devices. More specific practices are detailed below (FCC, 2017).

Use Security Software on All Smartphones
Security software specifically designed for smartphones can stop hackers and prevent cybercriminals from stealing company information or spying on your employees when they use public networks. It can detect and remove viruses and other mobile threats before they cause problems. It can also eliminate annoying text and multimedia spam messages.

Make Sure All Software Is Up-to-Date
Mobile devices must be treated like personal computers in that all software on the devices should be kept current, especially security software. This will protect devices from new variants of malware and viruses that threaten the company's critical information.

Encrypt the Data on Mobile Devices
Business and personal information stored on mobile devices is often sensitive. Encrypting this data is another must. If a device is lost and the SIM card stolen, the thief

will not be able to access the data if the proper encryption technology is loaded on the device.

Have Users Password-Protect Access to Mobile Devices
In addition to encryption and security updates, it is important to use strong passwords to protect data stored on mobile devices. This will go a long way toward keeping a thief from accessing sensitive data if the device is lost or hacked.

Urge Users to Be Aware of Their Surroundings
Whether entering passwords or viewing sensitive or confidential data, users should be aware of who might be looking over their shoulder.

Employ These Strategies for E-mail, Texting, and Social Networking
- *Avoid opening unexpected text messages from unknown senders*—As with e-mail, attackers can use text messages to spread malware, phishing scams, and other threats among mobile device users. The same caution should be applied to opening unsolicited text messages that users have become accustomed to with e-mail.
- *Don't be lured by spammers and phishers*—To shield business networks from cybercriminals, small businesses should deploy appropriate e-mail security solutions, including spam prevention, which protect a company's reputation and manage risks.
- *Click with caution*—Just like on stationary PCs, social networking on mobile devices and laptops should be conducted with care and caution. Users should not open unidentified links, chat with unknown people, or visit unfamiliar sites. It doesn't take much for a user to be tricked into compromising a device and the information on it.

Set Reporting Procedures for Lost or Stolen Equipment
In the case of a loss or theft, employees and management should all know what to do next. Processes to deactivate the device and protect its information from intrusion should be in place. Products are also available for the automation of such processes, allowing small businesses to breathe easier after such incidents.

Ensure All Devices are Wiped Clean Prior to Disposal
Mobile devices have a reset function that allows all data to be wiped. Subscriber identification module (SIM) cards should also be removed.

Employees
Businesses must establish formal recruitment and employment processes to control and preserve the quality of their employees. Many employers have learned the hard

way that hiring someone with a criminal record, falsified credentials, or undesirable background can create a legal and financial nightmare.

Experience has shown that without exercising due diligence in hiring, employers run the risk for making unwise hiring choices that can lead to workplace violence, theft, embezzlement, lawsuits for negligent hiring, and numerous other workplace problems.

Develop a Hiring Process That Properly Vets Candidates

The hiring process should be a collaborative effort among different groups of your organization, including recruitment, human resources, security, legal, and management teams. It is important to have a solid application, resume, interview, and reference-checking process to identify potential gaps and issues that may appear in a background check.

Perform Background Checks and Credentialing

Background checks are essential and must be consistent. Using a background screening company is highly recommended. The standard background screening should include the following checks:

- Employment verification
- Education verification
- Criminal records
- Drug testing
- The U.S. Treasury Office of Foreign Affairs and Control
- Sex offender registries
- Social security traces and validation

Depending on the type of your business, other screening criteria may consist of credit checks, civil checks, and federal criminal checks. Conducting post-hire checks for all employees every two to three years, depending on your industry, is also recommended.

Take Care in Dealing with Third Parties

Employers should properly vet partner companies through which your organization hires third-party consultants. To ensure consistent screening criteria are enforced for third-part consultants, you need to explicitly set the credentialing requirements in your service agreement. State in the agreement that the company's credentialing requirements must be followed.

Set Appropriate Access Controls for Employees

Both client data and internal company data are considered confidential and need particular care when viewed, stored, used, transmitted, or disposed. It is important to analyze the role of each employee and set data access control, based upon role. If a role does not require the employee to ever use sensitive data, the employee's access to the data should be strictly prohibited. However, if the role requires the employee to work with sensitive data, the level of access must be analyzed thoroughly and be assigned in a controlled and tiered manner following "least-privilege" principles, which allow the employee to only access data this is necessary to perform his or her job.

If the organization does not have a system in place to control data access, the following precautions are strongly recommended. Every employee should (FCC, 2017):

- Never access or view client data without a valid business reason. Access should be on a need-to-know basis.
- Never provide confidential data to anyone—client representatives, business partners, or even other employees—unless you are sure of the identity and authority of that person.
- Never use client data for development, testing, training presentations, or any purpose other than providing production service, client-specific testing, or production diagnostics. Only properly sanitized data that can't be traced to a client, client employee, customer, or the organization's employee should be used for such purposes.
- Always use secure transmission methods such as secure e-mail, secure file transfer (from application to application), and encrypted electronic media (e.g., CDs, USB drives, or tapes).
- Always keep confidential data (hard copy and electronic) only as long as it is needed.
- Follow a "clean desk" policy, keeping workspaces uncluttered so that confidential information does not get into the wrong hands.
- Always use only approved document disposal services or shred all hardcopy documents containing confidential information when finished using them. Similarly, use only approved methods that fully remove all data when disposing of, sending out for repair, or preparing to reuse electronic media.

Provide Security Training for Employees

Security awareness training teaches employees to understand system vulnerabilities and threats to business operations that are present when using a computer on a business network.

A strong IT security program must include training IT users on security polity, procedures, and techniques, as well as the various management, operational, and technical controls necessary and available to keep IT resources secure. In addition, IT infrastructure managers must have the skills necessary to carry out their assigned duties effectively. Failure to give attention to the area of security training puts an enterprise at great risk because security of business resources is as much a human issue as it is a technology issue.

Technology users are the largest audience in any organization and are the single most important group of people who can help to reduce unintentional errors and IT vulnerabilities. Users may include employees, contractors, foreign or domestic guest researchers, other personnel, visitors, guests, and other collaborators or associates requiring access. Users must:

- Understand and comply with security policies and procedures.
- Be appropriately trained in the rules of behavior for the systems and applications to which they have access.
- Work with management to meet training needs.
- Keep software and applications updated with security patches.
- Be aware of actions they can take to better protect company information. These actions include: proper password usage, data backup, proper antivirus protection, reporting any suspect incidents or violations of security policy, and following rules established to avoid social engineering attacks, and deter the spread of spam or viruses and worms.

A clear cataloging of what is considered sensitive data versus non-sensitive data is also needed. More often than not, the following data are considered sensitive information that should be handled with precaution:

- Government issued identification numbers (e.g., social security numbers, driver's license numbers)
- Financial account information (bank account numbers, credit card numbers)
- Medical records
- Health insurance information
- Salary information
- Passwords

Training should cover security policies for all means of access and transmission method, include secure databases, e-mail, file transfer, encrypted electronic media, and hard copies.

Employers should constantly emphasize the critical nature of data security. Regulatory scheduled refresher training courses should be established in order to install the data security culture of the organization. Additionally, distribute data privacy and security related news articles in employee training, and send organization-wide communication on notable data privacy related news as reminders to employees.

Operational Security

Although operational security, or OPSEC, has its origins in security information important to military operations, it has applications across the business community today.

In a commercial perspective, OPSEC is the process of denying hackers access to any information about the capabilities or intentions of a business by indentifying, controlling, and protecting evidence of the planning and execution of activities that are essential the success of operations.

OPSEC is a continuous process that consists of five distinct actions:

- Identify information that is critical to the business.
- Analyze the threat to that critical information.
- Analyze the vulnerabilities to the business that would allow a cyber criminal to access critical information.
- Assess the risks to your business if the vulnerabilities are exploited.
- Apply countermeasures to mitigate the risk factors.

In addition to being a five-step process, OPSEC is also a mindset that all business employees should embrace. By educating oneself on OPSEC risks and methodologies, protecting sensitive information that is critical to the success of your business becomes second nature.

This section explains the OPSEC process and provides some general guidelines that are applicable to most businesses. An understanding of the following terms is required before the process can be explained:

- *Critical information*—Specific data about business strategies and operations that are needed by cybercriminals to hamper or harm businesses from successfully operating.
- *OPSEC indicators*—Business operations and publicly available information that can be interpreted or pieced together by a cybercriminal to derive critical information.
- *OPSEC vulnerability*—A condition in which business operations provide OPSEC indicators that may be obtained and accurately evaluated by a cybercriminal to provide a basis for hampering or harming successful business operations.

Identity of Critical Information

The identification of critical information is important in that it focuses the remainder of the OPSEC process on protecting vital information rather than attempting to protect all information relevant to business operations. Given that any business has limited time, personnel, and money for developing secure business practices, it is essential to focus those limited resources on protecting information that is most critical to successful business operations. Examples of critical information include, but should not be limited to, the following (FCC, 2017):

- Customer lists and contact information
- Contracts
- Patents and intellectual property
- Leases and deeds
- Policy manuals
- Articles of incorporation
- Corporate papers
- Laboratory notebooks
- Audiotapes
- Videotapes
- Photographs and slides
- Strategic plans and board meeting minutes

Keep in mind that what is critical information for one business may not be critical for another business. Use the company's mission as a guide for determining what data are truly vital.

Analyze Threats

Analyzing threats involves research and analysis to identify likely cybercriminals who may attempt to obtain crucial information regarding a company's operations. OPSEC planners in businesses should answer the following critical information questions:

- Who might be a cybercriminal (e.g., competitors, politically motivated hackers, etc.)?
- What are cybercriminal's goals?
- What actions might the cybercriminal take?
- What critical information does the cybercriminal already have on the company's operations? (i.e., What is already publicly available?)

Analyze Vulnerabilities

Analyzing vulnerabilities is used to identify the vulnerabilities of a business in protecting critical information. It requires examining each aspect of security that seeks to protect your critical information and then comparing those indicators with the threats identified in the previous step. Common vulnerabilities for businesses include the following:

- Poorly secured mobile devices that have access to critical information
- Lack of policy on what information and networked equipment can be taken home from work or taken abroad on travel
- Storage of critical information on personal e-mail accounts or other non-company networks
- Lack of policy on what business information can be posted to or accessed by social network sites.

Assess Risk

Assessing risk consists of two components. First, OPSEC managers must analyze the vulnerabilities identified in the previous and identify possible OPSEC measures to mitigate each one. Second, specific OPSEC measures must be selected for execution based upon a risk assessment done by the company's senior leadership. Risk assessment requires comparing the estimated cost associated with implementing each possible OPSEC measure to the potential harmful effects on business operations resulting from the exploitation of a particular vulnerability.

OPSEC measure may entail some cost in time, resources, personnel, or interference with normal operations. If the cost to achieve OPSEC protection exceeds the cost of the harm that an intruder could inflict, then the application of the measure is inappropriate. Because the decision not to implement a particular OPSEC measure entails risks, this step requires company's leadership approval.

Payment Cards

If a business accepts payment by credit or debit cards, it is important to have security steps in place to ensure customer information is safe. A business also may have security obligations pursuant to agreements with the bank or payment services processor. These entities can help companies prevent fraud. In addition, free resources and general security tips are available to learn how to keep sensitive information—beyond payment information—safe.

Understand and Catalog Customer and Card Data You Keep

- Make a list of the type of customer and card information you collect and keep—names, addresses, identification information, payment card numbers, magnetic stripe data, bank account details, and social security numbers. It's not only card numbers criminals want; they're looking for all types of personal information, especially if it helps them commit identity fraud.
- Understand where you keep such information and how it is protected.
- Determine who has access to this data and if they need to have access to it.

Evaluate Whether the Company Needs to Keep All the Data It Has Stored

- Once a company knows what information it collects and stores, the company needs to evaluate whether it really needs to keep it. Often businesses may not realize they're logging or otherwise keeping unnecessary data until they conduct an audit. Not keeping sensitive data in storage makes it harder for criminals to steal it.
- It the business has been using card numbers for purposes other than payment transactions, such as a customer loyalty program, the merchant processes should be asked to use alternative data instead. Tokenization, for example, is a technology that masks card numbers and replaces it with an alternate number that can't be used for fraud.

Use Secure Tools and Services

- The payments industry maintains lists of hardware, software, and service providers who have been validated against industry security requirements.
- Small businesses that use integrated payment systems, in which the card terminal is connected to a larger computer system, can check the list of validated payment applications to make sure any software they employ has been tested.
- Have a conversation about security with the business provider if the products or services currently being used are not on the lists.

Control Access to Payment Systems

- Whether a company uses a more complicated payment system or a simple stand-alone terminal, make sure access is controlled.
- Isolate payment systems from other, less secure programs, especially those connected to the Internet. For example, don't use the same computer to process payments and surf the Internet.
- Control or limit access to payment systems to only employees who need access.
- Make sure the company uses a secure system for remote access or eliminate remote access if it is not needed so that criminals can't infiltrate the company system from the Internet.

Use Security Tools and Resources

Companies should work with their bank or processor and ask about the antifraud measures, tools, and services the company can use to ensure criminals can't use stolen card information at the company.

- For e-commerce retailers:
    - The CVV2 code is the three-digit number on the signature panel that can help verify that the customer has physical possession of the card and not just the account number.
    - Retailers can also use an address verification service to ensure that the cardholder has provided the correct billing address associated with the account.
    - Services such as Verified by Visa prompt the cardholder to enter a personal password confirming their identity and provide an extra layer of protection.
- For brick and mortar retailers:
    - Swipe the card and get an electronic authorization for the transaction.
    - Check that the signature matches the card.
    - Ensure your payment terminal is secure and safe form tampering.

THE SECURITY BASICS

- Use strong, unique passwords and change them frequently.
- Use up-to-date firewall and antivirus technologies.
- Do not click on suspicious links you may receive by e-mail or encounter online.

REFERENCES AND RECOMMENDED READING

DHS (2016) *Information Technology Sector—An Annex to the National Infrastructure Protection Plan*. Washington, DC: Department of Homeland Security.

DHS (2009). *National Infrastructure Protection Plan*. Retrieved 11/11/17 @http://www.dhs.gov/ xlibrary/assets/NIPP.Plan.pdf.

DHS (2003). The National Strategy for the Physical Protection of Critical Infrastructures and Key Assets. Accessed @ https://www.dhs.gov/xlibrary/assets/physical_Strat.

HS (2013). Homeland Security Directive 7: Critical Infrastructure Identification, Prioritization, and Protection accessed @ https://www.dihs.gov/xabout/laws/ gc_1214597989952.shtm.

FCC (2017). *Cyber Security Planning Guide.* Federal Communication Commission. Washington, DC.

5

Resilience Measurement Index

Resilience = Anticipation + Absorption + Adaption + Recovery
If an entity is any part of critical infrastructure, responsible persons in charge of the entity must assume they are targets of terrorists or of any other radicalized nutcase. Thus, the question is not when will you be attacked or when your property will be utilized for an attack (remember, 2014 and the 2016 election and the Russian hacking), but instead you have to ask can you, your employees, and your property survive an attack—are you resilient?

—Frank R. Spellman, (1997)

America is no longer protected by vast oceans. We are protected from attack only by vigorous action abroad, and increased vigilance at home.

—President George W. Bush, (2002)

INTRODUCTION[1]

It was not that far in America's distant past that we dealt mostly with the ramifications of natural disasters: Hurricane Katrina in 2005 and Superstorm Sandy in 2012. We also experienced the human-made Northeast blackout event in 2003. All of these events were horrific or at least shocking. Okay, then to this terrible mixture let's add 9/11, the World Trade Center in 2001. This event had even more far-reaching impacts that have (and continue to) directly affected our society's well-being. Even though current efforts that have focused on preventing or mitigating the impact of incidents have achieved admirable results, a more comprehensive approach is needed to the nation's overall resilience. Beyond resilience, which is an absolute must, we must also accomplish, practice, and maintain preparedness, mitigation, response, and recovery programs and capabilities, all of which make resilience a reality. Presidential policy Directive 21 defines sixteen critical infrastructure sectors that are essential to the nation's security, public health and safety, economic viability, and general quality of

KEEP IN MIND!

As noted by that great philosopher (Bob Dylan, of course) in the song: "Times They Are A Changing" . . . recent terrorist events have made this well-worn statement certainly the case. For example, with the manifestation of the Islamic State of Iraq and Syria (ISIS), also known as the Islamic State of Iraq and the Levant (ISIL) and by its Arabic language acronym Daesh and other terrorist groups including inside and outside fanatics there are many out there who would kill us all or at minimum use social media to distort the truth. It is important to point out with the advent of insider threats the message of this book is the same as the other books in this series where the focus has been shifted to the lone wolf (or lone Utah Raptor) terrorist. The fact is there are homegrown terrorists who live among us, plotting, passing on fake news, quivering in the glory of mass murder, blood and guts and beheadings, destruction and the attended glory of making the headlines as martyrs in the sickest sense possible (remember the Mandalay in Las Vegas). Again, remember, these are people who live among us, who shop in our stores, who use the benefits of our free society to grow their hate and to enhance their total disgust for all those things that we value in life.

life (White House, 2013). Because the operations of these critical infrastructure sectors are essential, their protection and resilience is paramount. As the Department of Homeland Security (DHS 2010a) points out "our goal is to ensure a more resilient Nation—one in which individuals, communities, and our economy can adapt to changing conditions as well as withstand and rapidly recover from disruption due to emergencies."

Developing and enhancing resilience of critical infrastructure requires its owners/operators to determine the ability of the system to withstand specific threats, minimize or mitigate potential impacts, and to return to normal operations if degradation occurs. Accordingly, a resilience methodology requires the comprehensive assessment of critical infrastructure systems/assets—from threat to consequence. The methodology needs to support decision-making for risk management, disaster response, and business continuity. Considering these issues, Argonne National Laboratory, in partnership with the U.S. Department of Homeland Security (DHS), has developed an index, the Resilience Measurement Index (RMI), to characterize the resilience of critical infrastructure.

The RMI was formulated to capture the fundamental aspects of resilience for critical infrastructure with respect to all hazards. The RMI methodology supports decision-making related to risk management, disaster response, and maintenance of business continuity. It complements other indices that have been developed—the Protective Measure Index and the Consequences Measurement Index—and thus, in combination with other tools allows critical infrastructure to be compared in terms of resilience, vulnerability, consequences, and ultimately risk. The main objective of the RMI is to measure the ability of a critical infrastructure to reduce the magnitude and/or duration of impacts from disruptive events.

The RMI is based on multiattribute theory and decision analysis principles. Resilience, in the context of critical infrastructure, is defined as the ability of a facility or asset to anticipate, resist, absorb, respond to, adapt to, and recover from a disturbance (Carlson et al., 2012). These six elements are aggregated into four major (Level 1) components: preparedness, mitigation measures, response capabilities, and recovery mechanisms.

The DHS Enhanced Critical Infrastructure Protection Program's Infrastructure Tool provides the Level 1 indices and overall RMI for an asset facility. The indices are based on the aggregation of pertinent components in the Infrastructure Survey Tool (IST). Each of these components has been weighted by subject matter experts to indicate its relative importance to a facility's resilience. The value of the RMI ranges between 0 (low resilience) and 100 (high resilience). Note that a high RMI does not mean that a specific event will not affect the facility or have severe consequences. Conversely, a low RMI does not mean that a disruptive event will automatically lead to a failure of the critical infrastructure and to serious consequences. The RMI instead is used to allow critical infrastructure facilities to compare their level of resilience against the resilience level of other similar facilities (aka benchmarking) nationwide and guide prioritization from improving resilience.

So, you ask, What does all this have to do with the information technology sector? Next question: Where does resiliency fit into the IT world? Both these questions can be summed up easily by answering in two words, respectively: everything and everywhere.

IST RMI Dashboard

All the data and levels of information used for the RMI, as well as the value of its four Level 1 components, are present on an interactive, web-based tool called the IST RMI Dashboard. The dashboard provides a snapshot of the resilience of a critical infrastructure at a specific point in time. The dashboard provides valuable information to owners/operators about their facility's status relative to those of similar assets. The dashboard can be used to create scenarios and assess the implementation of specific resilience measures of procedures that the facility owner/operator might consider. Using a dashboard's interactive "facility scenario" function makes it possible for the facility owner or operator to select possible resilience enhancements and immediately see the resulting modified RMI. Policies, procedures, or operational methods are enhancements with which the facility may increase resilience.

Experience has shown that combining the RMI information with other indices, such as the Protective Measure Index and the Consequences Measurement Index, allows for a comprehensive assessment or risk than can support decision-making about protection, business continuity, and emergency management of critical infrastructure.

THE 411 ON THE RESILIENCE MEASUREMENT INDEX

The goal or the RMI is to find a facility's weakest link. In light of this goal, in 2009, the DHS and its protective security advisors (PSAs) began surveying critical infrastructure using the IST and ultimately produce individual protective measure and vulnerability values through the Protective Measures Index (PMI). This index identifies the protective measures posture of individual facilities at their weakest link, allowing for a survey of the most vulnerable aspects of the facilities.

As critical infrastructure continued to be surveyed using the IST and displayed using the PMI, Argonne National Laboratory, in partnership with the DHS, developed an index for surveying the resilience of critical infrastructure—the Resilience Index (RI).

In the practical usage of the RI it became obvious to the users that the index could be improved by better considering elements contributing to business continuity, continuity of service, cyber risk, and resource dependencies. The first requirement for the enhanced RI was a modification of the IST question set. Modification of the IST provided more information on the elements contributing to dependencies on external providers, business continuity, and emergency management.

The development of this new indicator of resilience, the resilience RMI, was guided by the standards used for the voluntary Private Sector Preparedness Program (PSPrep) and National Security Directive PPD-8. The PSPrep program is based on three main standards (British Standards Institute 25999, NFPA 1600, and ANSI/ASIS SPC.1-2009), which provide a comprehensive management systems approach to organization resilience, preparedness, and business continuity (FEMA, 2013). PPD-8 focuses on national preparedness for strengthening the security and resilience of the nation. It promotes an all-hazards approach based on the identification of core capabilities necessary for communities to be better prepared for significant destructive incidents (DHS, 2011).

Resilience measurement must be organized in a way that is consistent with emergency and risk management processes. To accomplish this, the RMI is based on the same methodologies (multiattribute utility theory [MAUT] and decision analysis) as the RI but organizes the components in terms of preparedness, mitigation measures, response capabilities, and recovery mechanisms.

Combining a pre-incident focus with an enhanced understanding of resilience allows owners/operators to identify improved ways to decrease risk by (1) increasing preparedness for an incident, (2) implementing redundancy to mitigate the effects of an incident, and (3) enhancing emergency action and business continuity planning and implementation to increase the effectiveness of response and recovery procedures. Information provided by the RMI methodology is used by facility owners/operators to better understand how their facilities stack up against similar sector/subsector sites and to help them make risk-informed decisions. This information can also be used for decreasing risk and improving resilience at the regional level. Resilience for the nation includes both critical infrastructure and other components. As stated by Carlson et al. (2012), "the resilience of a community/region is a function of the resilience of its subsystems, including its critical infrastructures, economy, civil society, governance (including emergency services), and supply chains/dependencies." It is important to point out, however, that additional data and methods must be used to capture the resilience of a community/region or the nation.

RISK, VULNERABILITY, AND RESILIENCE
DHS defines risk as "the potential for an unwanted outcome resulting from an incident, event, or occurrence, as determined by its likelihood and the associated consequences" (DHS, 2010b). Risk is thus traditionally defined as a function of three elements: the *threats* to which an asset is susceptible, the *vulnerabilities* of the asset to the threat, and the *consequences* potentially generated by the degradation of the asset (see figure 5.1).

Information Technology Sector Risks[2]
Note that the IT sector is one of the few U.S. critical infrastructures in which terrorists and foreign governments (Russia comes to mind) have executed multiple high-profile attacks directly affecting the public, both in the physical and cyber domain. The following section covers emerging risks to the IT sector and outlines the sector's risk profile.

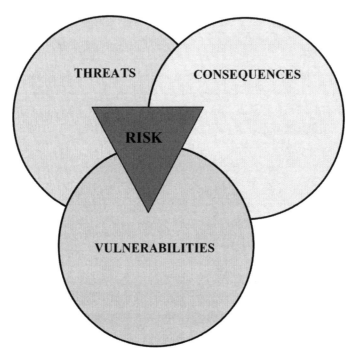

FIGURE 5.1
Risk Elements.

Emerging Issues: Types of Breaches

- **Physical breaches**—A real-world crime such as burglary and equipment theft, as well as any event when a company's equipment is misplaced or lost in transit, is classified as a physical breach. Unauthorized devices may be installed on a system or network, permitting further compromises of data confidentiality and integrity. Physical breaches can also result from reselling, donating, or recycling old equipment that has not been properly cleansed of potentially sensitive information.
- **Increasing interdependencies between sectors**—Cities and regions increasingly rely on complex networks or interconnected infrastructure that comprise and are operated by integrated physical and cyber systems. After a disaster, a failure in one system—such as in the water or energy sectors—could cascade and greatly affect the regions they serve.
- **Increased cyber risks**—Adversaries have successfully executed point-of-sale attacks on large retailers and hotels to gain access to confidential data, which has cost companies and financial institutions hundreds of millions of dollars. Governments have launched targeted cyber espionage of sabotage attacks, and there has been an increase in "hacktivism," or politically motivated cyberattacks. The Federal Bureau of Investigation (FBI) identified North Korea as the source behind recent cyberattacks

that published thousands of confidential company documents online, including personal e-mail correspondences and employee data (Rasmussen, 2015). Building management systems—from heating, ventilations and air conditioning (HVAC) systems, to access control—are increasingly computerized, making a growing portion of operations vulnerable to a cyberattacks or IT outage. Due to the CS sector's dependency on the Internet and IT, the failure or infiltration of cyber systems would create a significant negative economic impact on the sector.

- **Increasing use of social media**—Social media sites allow people to immediately document and disseminate information, making it crucial for the IT sector to respond to incidents quickly and efficiently. Social media brings both risks and benefits; for example, malicious actors could use social media to disrupt events, facilitate attacks, or organize flash mobs, but the sites may also contain valuable information that could aid security efforts during an event or recovery.
- **Network and system security breaches**—Events when computers become infected with malicious code, are accessed by unauthorized individuals remotely, or are used by authorized individuals to perform malicious activity are examples of network and security breaches. This can also include breaches to network routers and firewalls, both within and outside your organization's boundary and control.
- **Data breaches**—The leakage or spillage of sensitive information into insecure channels defines data breaches; they can result from any of the types of events described above. Data breaches can also occur if sensitive information is left improperly exposed by mistake.

Significant Commercial IT Sector Risks

The IT sector operates though a principle of open public access and experiences high-population densities, which can increase the vulnerability to intentional attacks that aim to harm public health and safety, cause property damage, and inflict economic and psychological consequences. In addition, many venues are highly recognizable, increasing the potential attractiveness to an adversary. The key risks affecting the security and resilience of IT sector assets, operations, and workforce include:

- **Cyberattacks**—The sector widely uses the Internet for marketing, merchandising, ticketing, and reservations. A mass communications failure leading to a disruption of the Internet could affect the IT sector as a whole and have cascading economic effects. Cyberattacks could also cause a loss of operations for automated building systems, giving hackers access to automated building systems and internal surveillance footage, and result in the release of private information (e.g., customer credit card accounts, financial information, and internal correspondence).

Threats

Threat is a "natural or man-made occurrence, individual, entity, or action that has or indicates the potential to harm life, information, operations, the environment, and/or property" (DHS, 2010b). Do not confuse the term "hazard" or use it instead of "threat" because, as defined by the DHS lexicon, a *hazard differs from a threat in that a threat is directed at an entity, asset, system, network, or geographic area, while a hazard is not directed* (DHS, 2010b).

Vulnerability

Vulnerability is a *"physical feature or operational attribute that renders an entity open to exploitation or susceptible to a given hazard"* (DHS, 2010b). Consequences are the *"effects of an event, incident, or occurrence"* (DHS, 2010b).

Resilience

If risk is a function of threats and hazards, vulnerabilities, and consequences, the challenge is to define where and how resilience fits into the determination of risk. *Resilience*, as defined by DHS, is the "ability to resist, absorb, recover from or successfully adapt to adversity or a change in conditions" (DHS, 2010b). The DHS lexicon also states that "Resilience can be factored into vulnerability and consequence estimates when measuring risk" (DHS, 2010b). On the basis of this statement, the facility resilience would have an effect on both vulnerability and consequences.

Risk Management

Risk management can be defined as the "process of identifying, analyzing, and communicating risk and accepting, avoiding, transferring or controlling it to an acceptable level at an acceptable cost" (DHS, 2010b). Risk management involves knowing the threats and hazards that could potentially impact a given facility, the impacts on the facility due to its vulnerabilities, and the consequences that might result. On the basis of these characteristics, it is possible to develop specific indicators and metrics to assess the risk to an organization. The main objective is thus to analyze the performance of a facility in terms of protection/vulnerability, resilience, consequence, and, ultimately, risk; and to propose options to improve this performance (see figure 5.2).

How threats, vulnerability, consequences, and resilience fit together in a risk management process is illustrated in the risk management bowtie diagram presented in figure 5.2. Considering a threat or hazard (natural or human-made), the vulnerability and resilience of an organization will impact the potential consequences of an event. The interaction between the elements of risk is complex, and made more so when one considers that transfer of risk between assets in the case of a threat by an intelligent

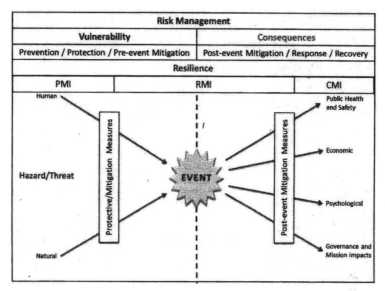

FIGURE 5.2
Risk Management Bowtie Diagram. Source: U.S. Department of Energy
(2013). *Resilience Measurement Index: An indicator of critical infrastructure
resilience.* Washington, DC.

adversary. For example, when protection at a site is increased, vulnerability decreases
and the risk at that site declines, but the risk at another site or sites may increase (Phillips, et al. (2012).

The *Protective Measures Index* (PMI) developed in 2008, was the first index as part
of the DHS Enhanced Critical Infrastructure Protection (ECIP) program. This index
captures the protective measures in place in a given facility (Fisher et al., 2009; Petit
et al., 2011). The fourth edition of this index, launched in January 2013, addresses elements characterizing physical security, security management, security force, information sharing, and security activity background. Therefore, the PMI focuses on the left
side of the risk management bowtie (figure 5.2).

The second index, the *Resilience Measurement Index* (RMI), characterizes the resilience of critical infrastructure at the center part of the bowtie, and mitigates the otherwise maximum consequences depicted on the right side of the bowtie (figure 5.2). The
objectives of this index are to develop a key performance indicator that characterizes
the resilience of the facility and supports the decisions of critical infrastructure own-
ers/operators through the comparison (benchmarking) of like facilities. This index
must be applicable to all types of critical infrastructure sector/subsectors, and must

consider all types of hazards (human-made, natural, and cyber), facility dependencies, and facility capabilities with respect to emergency management.

The Consequences Measurement Index (CMI) is the third index (see figure 5.2); it characterizes the maximum consequence potentially generated by an adverse event at a facility. This index includes information on public health and safety, economic, psychological, and governance and mission impacts form the loss of the facility. This index focuses on the right side of the risks management bowtie shown in figure 5.2.

RESILIENCE MEASUREMENT INDEX METHODOLOGY

Of the three indices described above, it is the RMI that is the focus of our discussion. In this regard, it is interesting to note that the current RMI is a descendent of an earlier index called the RI. Both indices support decision-making in risk management, disaster response, and business continuity. The RI was developed in 2010 using a comprehensive methodology of consistent and uniform data collection and analysis. This index was built using the NAIC definition of critical infrastructure resilience: resilience is the "ability to reduce the magnitude and/or duration of disruptive events" (NIAC, 2009). The effectiveness of a resilient infrastructure or enterprise depends on its "ability to anticipate, absorb, adapt to, and rapidly recover from a potentially disruptive event, whether naturally occurring or human caused" (NIAC, 2009).

The RI characterized the resilience of critical infrastructure in terms of robustness, resourcefulness, and recovery (Fisher et al., 2009; Petit et al., 2012). The main benefit of the RI was to give the critical infrastructure owners/operators a performance indicator of the resilience of their facilities that could support their decisions in risk and resilience management. In early 2012, a review of the index methodology resulted in enhancements to the structure of the RI and the information collected in order to develop a more comprehensive and informative index—the RMI.

The first step in revising the RI was a literature search to determine how to incorporate additional information and provide a better indicator of infrastructure resilience. This work was finished in 2012 and led to the publication of a report titled "Resilience: Theory and Applications" (Carlson et al., 2012). This document outlined the definition of resilience used for developing the RMI:

> Resilience is "the ability of an entity—e.g., asset, organization, community, region—to anticipate, resist, absorb, respond to, adapt to, and recover from a disturbance." (Carlson et al., 2012)

This definition of resilience is broader than the one proposed by NIAC in 2009 by considering not only the capabilities to anticipate, absorb, adapt to, and recover from a disruptive event, but also the notions of resistance and response to the event. The

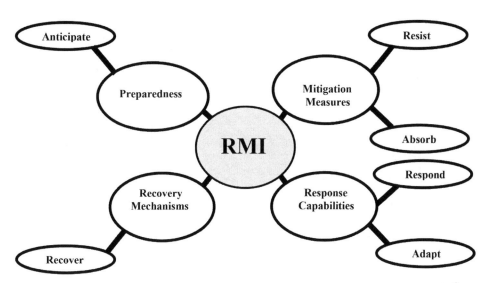

FIGURE 5.3
Relationship between the RMI Components and the Definition of Resilience.

RMI structures the information collected in four categories (Preparedness, Mitigation Measures, Response Capabilities, and Recovery Mechanisms) that characterize the resilience capability of a facility. Figure 5.3 illustrates how the four components constituting the RMI are connected to the six actions that define resilience.

Organization of the Resilience Measurement Index
Based on the definition of resilience presented in the previous section, the RMI organizes the information collected into four groups, also called RMI Level 1 components (Figure 5.4; USDOE, 2013).

The United States Department of Energy's Argonne National Laboratory (2013) points out that the RMI organizes the information collected with the Infrastructure Inventory Tool (IST) into six levels in order of increasing specificity; raw data are gathered at Level 6 and Level 5. They are then combined further through Levels 4, 3, 2, and finally to Level 1. Each of the Level 1 components is defined by the aggregation of Level 2 components that allow analysts to characterize a facility. The RMI is constituted from four Level 1 components, ten Level 2 components, and 29 Level 3 components, as defined by subject matter experts. The Level 1 and Level 2 components are shown in table 5.1.

The following sections present the definition and overview of each Level 1 component and associated Level 2 components that contribute to the RMI calculation.

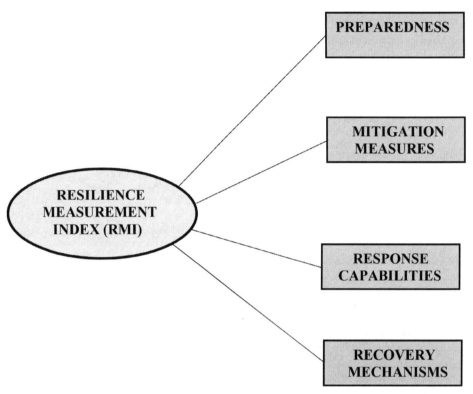

FIGURE 5.4
Level 1 Components of the RMI.

Preparedness

Specific activities undertaken by an entity in anticipation of the threats/hazards, and the possible consequences to which it is subject is known, in the RMI as preparedness. The RMI subdivides into two Level 2 and six Level 3 components as shown in figure 5.5 (USDOE, 2013).

Table 5.1. Major Level 1 and Level 2 Components Constituting the RMI

Preparedness—Level 1	*Mitigation Measures—Level 1*
a. Awareness—Level 2 (2 subcomponents) b. Planning—Level 2 (4)	a. Mitigating Construction—Level 2 (4) b. Alternate Site—Level 2 c. Resources Mitigation Measures—Level 2 (8)
Response Capabilities—Level 1	*Recovery Mechanisms—Level 1*
a Onsite Capabilities—Level 2—(2) b. Offsite Capabilities—Level 2 (3) c. Incident Management and Combined Center Characteristics—Level 2 (2)	a. Restoration Agreements—Level 2 (2) b. Recovery Time—Level 2 (2)

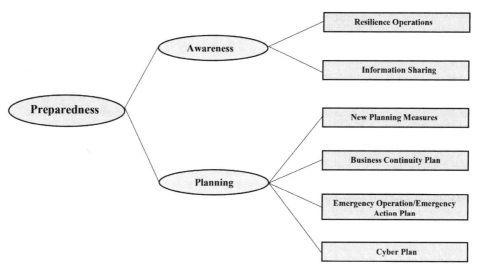

FIGURE 5.5
Level 2 and 3 Components of the RMI Contributing to Preparedness.

It is important to note that specific actions that can be undertaken to enhance awareness related to an asset include the development of hazard-related information, including hazard assessments and information sharing, and the implementation of various measures designed to anticipate potential natural and human-made hazards. This element combines information drawn from responses to questions characterizing resilience operations and information-sharing processes in place at the facility assessed. It also addresses the type of management in place for business continuity, emergency operations, and information technology.

Mitigation planning, response/emergency action planning, and actions undertaken to enhance continuity of operators are planned-related activities. This element combines information drawn from response to questions characterizing the types of plans (business continuity, emergency operations/emergency actions, and cyber) implemented at the facility. For each type of plan, this section of the RMI addresses its characteristics (e.g., level of development and approval), the type of exercises and training defined in the plan, and its content.

Mitigation Measures

Mitigation Measures characterize the facility's capabilities to resist a threat/hazard or to absorb the consequences from the threat/hazard. Mitigation Measures consist of proactive activities; they consist of activities undertaken prior to an event to reduce the severity or consequences of a hazard. Mitigation is meant to capture information on whether the facility's owner or operator recognizes that the facility might be

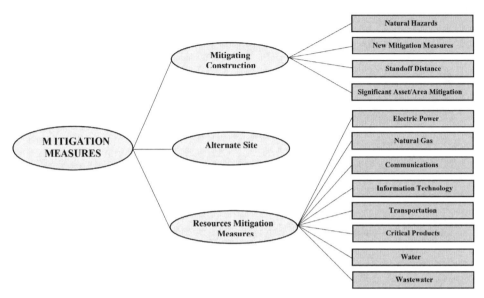

FIGURE 5.6
Level 2 and 3 Components of the RMI Contributing to Mitigation Measures.

susceptible to certain hazards (e.g., hurricanes for facilities in Florida or earthquakes for facilities in California), has determined the possible consequences/impacts, and has undertaken efforts to mitigate the negative impacts those hazards might impose on the facility. In the RMI, Mitigation Measures are subdivided into three Level 2 and twelve Level 3 components (Figure 5.6; USDOE, 2013).

Specific mitigating construction activities include measures to offset naturally occurring adverse events. This component combines information drawn from responses to questions characterizing natural hazards (construction to mitigate impacts, specific plans/procedures for long-term and immediate mitigation measures, deployable mitigation measures), New Mitigation Measures (infrastructure upgrade/redundancy), Standoff Distance (e.g., limiting parking to more than four hundred feet from the facility reduces impacts), and the resilience of Significant Assets/Areas (time before impact and level of degradation) (DHS, 2016; USDOE, 2013).

Mitigation Measures also address the use of an alternative site (i.e., alternate site—Level 2—is an aggregation of questions within the IST. There is no intermediate level or subcomponent between the alternate site level and the questions used for characterizing the alternate site's capabilities). Key features of an alternative site include its characterization and the percentage of the normal level of the main facility's production that the alternative site can maintain. This component combines information drawn from responses to questions characterizing the type of alternative site (full capability, capability to perform essential functions, etc.), its location, equipment, and dependencies.

The RMI's component, which characterizes an entity's dependencies on key resources to support its core operations, is assessed by focusing on the facility's reliance on selected external resources (e.g., electric power, natural gas, communications, information technology, transportation, critical products, water, and wastewater), its susceptibility to disruption of these resources, and any actions that have been undertaken to mitigate the loss of such resources. This component combines information drawn from responses to questions that characterize the resources, alternative resources and backups, and the level of impact to the loss of different resources supporting the facility's core operations.

Response Capabilities

In the RMI, response capabilities are defined as a function of immediate and ongoing activities, tasks, programs, and systems that have been undertaken or developed to respond and adapt to the adverse effects of an event. The Response Capabilities category is subdivided into three Level 2 and seven Level 3 components (figure 5.7).

The Onsite Capabilities component of the RMI captures a facility's capabilities to respond to an accident without needing an immediate response from external first responders. This component is made up of security/safety/emergency management aspects. It combines information drawn from response to questions characterizing the implementation within the last year of new communications and incidence response measures and the immediate onsite response capability for six specific types of

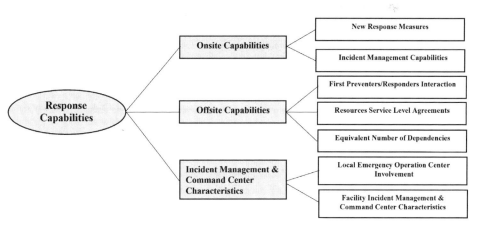

FIGURE 5.7
Level 2 and 3 Components of the RMI Contributing to Response Capabilities.

events (toxic industrial chemical/hazmat release, firefighting, explosive threat, armed response, law enforcement, and medical emergency).

The Offsite Capabilities component groups elements characterizing the interactions with the energy services sector to respond to an event (e.g., fire, medical problem, or law enforcement issue) and support the facility within its boundaries. This component combines information drawn from responses to questions characterizing the interaction with first preventers/responders (law enforcement, emergency medical response, and fire response), and the Resource Service-Level Agreements. The First Preventers/ Responders Interaction section captures the presence of interoperable communication, existing memoranda of understanding, and memoranda of agreement (MOU/ MOA), and orientation visits to the facility. Service Level Agreements with resource providers and the number of dependencies reflect the facility's lack of self-reliance and especially the implementation of contingency/business continuity plans with providers for restoration and the percentage of degradation of normal business functions once a specific resource is lost.

The Incident Management and Command Center Characteristics section groups information that captures the facility's capabilities for managing response, continuity, and recovery operations if an incident occurs. This component combines information drawn from response to questions characterizing the facility's involvement with the local Emergency operation Center and the Facility Incident Management & Command Center characteristic (primary and alternative centers) (USDOE, 2013).

Recovery Mechanisms

The Recovery Mechanisms section includes activities and programs designed to be effective and efficient in returning operating conditions to a level that is acceptable to

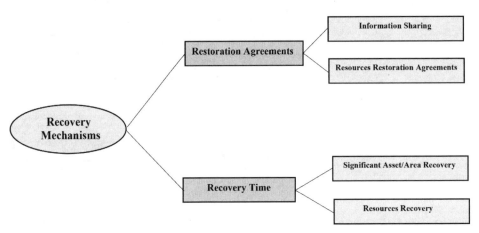

FIGURE 5.8
Level 2 and 3 Components of the RMI Contributing to recovery Mechanisms.

the entity. In the RMI, the Recovery Mechanisms category is subdivided into two Level 2 and four Level 3 components (see Figure 5.8).

Restoration agreements concern information relative to existing MOU/MOA with entities other than emergency responders, as well as procedures/equipment that will support facility restoration. This component combines information drawn from responses characterizing the facility's participation in Information Sharing processes with external organizations and Restoration Resource Agreements (e.g., a priority plan for restoration in case of loss of resource supply).

The Recovery Time section groups information characterizing the time necessary for the facility to recover full operations after the loss of one of its significant components.

NOTES

1. Much of this chapter is based on the U.S. Department of Energy's 2013 Argonne National Laboratory: *Resilience measurement Index: An indicator of Critical infrastructure Resilience.* Washington, DC.

2. Based on material in US DHS (2016) *Information Technology Sector—Specific Plan.* Washington, DC.

REFERENCES AND RECOMMENDED READING

Carlson, L., G. Bassett, W. Buehring, M. Collins, S. Folga, B. Haffenden, F. Petit, J. Phillips, D. Verner, and R. Whitfield (2012). *Resilience Theory and Applications,* Argonne National Laboratory, Decision and Information Sciences Division, ANL/DIS-12-1, Argonne, IL, USA.

DHS (2010a). *Quadrennial Homeland Security Review Report: A Strategic Framework for a Security Homeland (February),* Washington, D.C., available at http://www.dhs.gov/xlibrary/assets/dhs-risk-lexicone-2010.pdf.

DHS (2010b). *DHS Risk Lexicon—2010 edition,* Washington, D.C., available at http://www.dhs.gov/xlibrary/assets/dhs-risk-lexicon-2010.pdf.

DHS (2011). *Presidential Policy Directive/PPD-8: National Preparedness,* Washington, D.C., available at http://www.dhs.gov/presidential-polity-direcitve-8-national-preparedness.

DHS (2016). *Information Technology Sector—An Annex to the National Infrastructure Protection Plan.* Washington, DC: Department of Homeland Security.

FEMA (2013). *The Voluntary Private Sector preparedness Program—PS-Prep™ & Small Business Preparedness,* Washington, D.C., available at http://www.fema.gov/ps-preptm-voluntary-private-secotr-preparedness.

FEMA (2015). *Protecting Critical Infrastructure Against Insider Threats.* Accessed 4/17/15 @ http://emilms.fema.gov/IS0915/IABsummary.htm.

Fisher, R. E., W. A. Buehring, R. G. Whitfield, G. W. Bassett, D. C. Dickinson, R. A. Haffenden, M. S. Klett, and M. A. Lawlor (2009). Constructing Vulnerability and Protective Measures Indices for the Enhanced Critical Infrastructure Protection Program, Argonne National Laboratory, Decision and Information Sciences Division, ANL/DIS-09-4, Argonne, IL, USA.

Haimes, Y. Y. (2004). *Risk Modeling, Assessment, and Management,* 2nd Edition. New York: John Wiley & Sons, p. 699.

Henry, K. (2002). New face of security. *Gov. Security,* Apr., pp. 30–37.

NIAC (2009). Critical Infrastructure Resilience, Final Report and Recommendations, U.S. Department of Homeland Security, Washington, D.C., available to http://www.dhs.gov/ xlibrary/assets/niac/niac_cirtical_infrastructure_resilience.pdf.

NSHS (2006). *National Strategy for Homeland Security.* Accessed 5/13/16 @ www.whitehouse/ homeland.

Perl, R. (2004). *Terrorism and National Security: Issues and Trends.* CRS Issue Brief IB10119. Washington, DC.

Petit, F., L. Eaton, R. Fisher, S. McAraw, and M. Collins (2012). Developing an Index to Assess the Resilience of Critical Infrastructure, International Journal of Risk Assessment and Management (IJRAM), Interscience Publishers, Geneva, Switzerland, Vol. 16, Nos. 1/2/3, pp 28–47.

Petit, R., R. Fisher, W. Buehring, R., Whitfield, and M. Collins (2011). *Protective Measures and Vulnerability Indices for the Enhanced Critical Infrastructure Protection Program,* International Journal of Critical Infrastructures (IJCIS), Interscience Publishers, Geneva, Switzerland, Vol. 7, No. 3, pp. 200-219.

Phillips, et al. (2012). *Maximum Entropy Modeling.* New York: Elsevier Press.

Rasmussen, N. J. (2015). Current Terrorist Threat to the United States, Hearing before the Senate Select Committee on Intelligence, February 12, 2015. http://www.nctc.gov/docs/ Current_Terrorist_Threat_to_the_United _States.pdf.

Sauter, M. A. and Carafano, J.J., (2005). *Homeland Security: A Complete Guide to Understanding, Preventing, and Surviving Terrorism.* NY: McGraw-Hill.

Spellman, F. R., (1997). *A Guide to Compliance for Process Safety Management/Risk Management Planning (PSM/RMP).* Lancaster, PA: Technomic Publishing Company.

The Washington Times (2009). Napolitano tells it like it isn't. Accessed 3/29/09 @www. washingtontimes.com/news/2009/mar/29/tell-it-like-it-is-man-casued-disasters-is-mapolit/.

United States Congress (2005). Annual Country reports on terrorism. 22 USC, Chapter 38, Section 2656f.

USDOE (2013). Argonne National Laboratory. *Resilience Measurement Indeed: And indicator of critical infrastructure resilience.* Washington, DC.

White House (2013). *Presidential Policy Directive—Critical Infrastructure Security and Resilience,* PPD-21, Washington, DC, Available at http://www.whitehouse.gov/the-press-office/2013/02/12/presidential-policy-directive-critical-infrastructure-security-and-resil.

6

Critical Infrastructure Security and Resilience

The flow of providing security protection, from data to understanding:
Data → Information → Knowledge → Understanding
In the prevention of and preparation for terrorism, ending well is the best revenge.

—*F. R. Spellman*

A terrorist act is a Black Swan.
Why?
The event is a surprise (9/11 attack).
The event has had a major effect (changed the world).

After the first recorded instance of the event, it is rationalized by hindsight, as if it could have been expected (recall statements by radical know-it-all pundits and snowflakes); that is, the relevant data were available but unaccounted for in risk mitigations programs (really, are you serious?). [Seriously adapted and severely modified from Taleb, 2007)].

It is more often than not that information technology (IT) properties do not have military defenses and are generally, in many cases, open to the public; thus, they are soft targets. Beyond this obvious explanation the question might be: What makes the IT sector such an attractive terrorism target? The IT sector is an attractive target because of the following:

- The IT sector is a particularly attractive target because it is easy to infiltrate (it is the ultimate soft target because all you need is access to a computer) and like other lifeline functions—which include energy, transportation, and water, and other resources essential to the operations of most critical infrastructure partners and communities financial assets—it is a target of choice.

- IT sector components or assets are spread throughout the nation (the world) with little definition of boundaries.
- Initially, several IT sector assets were designed and constructed with little to no concern for terrorist intrusion or destructive activities.
- Many IT systems are monitored and operated using underprotected computer systems.
- As with many industries attempting to economize, many IT segments and sub-segments assign responsibility for safety and security as a collateral duty to a line employee instead of employing a full-time certified cyber, IT, and safety and security professional.

INFORMATION TECHNOLOGY SECTOR SECURITY GOALS AND ATTRIBUTES

The Department of Homeland Security has identified eight general elements and characteristics of critical infrastructure (including the IT sector) security goals and attributes.

- **Critical Asset Reduction Goal**. Sector resiliency will be most assured if no particular asset can be assessed as more critical than any other. While the ultimate ideal goal would be zero-critical IT assets, the sector will strive to reduce the number of critical assets whenever and wherever possible within fiscal and legal constraints. Sound risk management practices, including asset resiliency, mitigation of risks, and redundancy will be shared and advanced throughout the sector.
- **Cyber Goals and Attributes**. Like physical attributes, these assist the IT sector to evaluate consequences and vulnerabilities, and develop protective strategies. Cyber systems that link and help monitor and control the financial services systems are increasingly recognized as a potential vulnerability. All information that identifies or otherwise describes characteristics of a critical IT asset that is created, held, and maintained by the government or the private sector will be protected from unauthorized disclosure according to established procedures, appropriate to the particular level of information.
- **Volumetric or Throughput Attributes**. These define the extent of any damage, depending on the utilized capacity of the systems, or points where the system may be capacity constrained.
- **Personnel Security Goals and Human Attributes**. Ensure all personnel directly associated with a critical IT asset are vetted for employment suitability, reliability, and trustworthiness using established processes commensurate with requirements of the respective positions held, in conformance with pertinent security policy. Highly trained and skilled personnel are key factors in a comprehensive IT sector security plan. The availability of skilled and experienced technical talent is a concern in the

IT sector. Sustaining essential technical knowledge is critical to maintaining the sector's safety, reliability, and security.

- **Physical Security Goal.** Determine the impact or consequence of critical IT asset loss its mission(s) supported, the known or perceived threat, and the susceptibility to exploitation of vulnerabilities the threat is capable of perpetuating; identify specific IT assets the destruction or disruption of which could result in human casualties or economic disruption similar to the effects of weapons of mass destruction; compile a composite of facility physical security risk assessments.

- **Insider Threat Goal and Attributes**. Responsible parties in charge provide security education and training aids to IT asset owners/operators not having security programs so that they may implement provisions for the vetting of system and network administrators commensurate with the consequences of the loss of sensitive or classified information, production or provisioning capability, and supply chain integrity.

- **Monitoring and Reporting Goals and Attributes**. Ongoing determination of the effectiveness of government threat reporting to officials, owners, and operators responsible for critical IT assets, and to local law enforcement officials and other first responders including, as appropriate, the medical and mass transportation communities.

- **Training and Education Goal and Attributes**. Develop and provide continuous specific security education and training materials for critical IT asset owner/operators.

HOMELAND SECURITY DIRECTIVES

As a result of 9/11, the Homeland Security Department was formed. On matters pertaining to homeland security, Homeland Security Presidential Directives (HSPDs) are issued by the resident. Each directive has specific meaning and purpose and is carried out by the U.S. Department of Homeland Security. Table 6.1 lists HSPDs.

Note: HSPD-7 was revoked by the Presidential Policy Directive 21 (PPD-21) on Critical Infrastructure Security and Resilience on February 12, 2013. PPD-21 states that "Plans developed pursuant to HSPD-7 shall remain in effect until specifically revoked or superseded" (DHS, 2013). Multiple changes came out of PPD-21, including six actions with specific deadlines. One of those actions was to update the National Infrastructure Protection Plan within 240 days.

Note: The significance of Presidential Policy Directive 21 (PPD-21) is that it deals specifically with critical infrastructure security and resilience; it defines security as

Table 6.1.   Homeland Security Presidential Directives

HSPD-1: Organization and Operation of the Homeland Security Council. (White House) Ensures coordination of all homeland security-related activities among executive departments and agencies and promote the effective development and implementation of all homeland security policies.

HSPD-2: Combating Terrorism through Immigration Policies. (White House) Provides for the creation of task force which will work aggressively to prevent aliens who engage in or support terrorist activity from entering the United States and to detain, prosecute, or deport any such aliens who are within the United States.

HSPD-3: Homeland Security Advisory System. (White House) Establishes a comprehensive and effective means to disseminate information regarding the risk of terrorist acts to Federal, State, and local authorities and to the American people.

HSPD-4: National Strategy to Combat Weapons of Mass Destruction. Applies new technologies, increased emphasis on intelligence collection and analysis, strengthens alliance relationships, and establishes new partnerships with former adversaries to counter this threat in all of its dimensions.

HSPD-5: Management of Domestic Incidents. (White House) Enhances the ability of the United States to manage domestic incidents by establishing a single, comprehensive national incident management system.

HSPD-6: Integration and Use of Screening information. (White House) Provides for the establishment of the Terrorist Threat Integration Center.

HSPD-7: Critical Infrastructure Identification, Prioritization, and Protection. (White House) Establishes a national policy for Federal departments and agencies to identify and prioritize United States critical infrastructure and key resources and to protect them from terrorist attacks.

HSPD-8: National Preparedness. (White House) Identifies steps for improved coordination in response to incidents. This directive describes the way Federal departments and agencies will prepare for such a response, including prevention activities during the early stages of a terrorism incident. This directive is a companion to HSPD-5.

HSPD-8 Annex 1: National Planning. Further enhances the preparedness of the United States by formally establishing a standard and comprehensive approach to national planning.

HSPD-9: Defense of United States Agriculture and Food. (White House) Establishes a national policy to defend the agriculture and food system against terrorist attacks, major disasters, and other emergencies.

HSPD-10: Biodefense for the 21st Century. (White House) Provides a comprehensive framework for our nation's Biodefense.

HSPD-11: Comprehensive Terrorist-Related Screening Procedures. (White House) Implements a coordinated and comprehensive approach to terrorist-related screening that supports homeland security, at home and abroad. This directive builds upon HSPD–6.

HSPD-12: Policy for a Common Identification Standard for Federal Employees and Contractors. (White House) Establishes a mandatory, Government-wide standard for secure and reliable forms of identification issued by the Federal Government to its employees and contractors (including contractor employees).

HSPD-13: Maritime Security Policy. Establishes policy guidelines to enhance national and homeland security by protecting U.S. maritime interests.

HSPD-14: Domestic Nuclear Detection established a Domestic Nuclear Detection Office (DNSO) to coordinate efforts to protect the domestic U.S. against dangers from nuclear or radiological materials. EPA supports the detection, response, law enforcement, and information sharing aspects of the DNDO's mission.

HSPD-16: Aviation Strategy. Details a strategic vision or aviation security while recognizing ongoing efforts, and directs the production of a National Strategy for Aviation Security and supporting plans.

HSPD-18: Medical Countermeasures against Weapons of Mass Destruction. (White House) Establishes policy guidelines to draw upon the considerable potential of the scientific community in the public and private sectors to address medical countermeasure requirements relating to CBRN threats.

HSPD-19: Combating Terrorist Use of Explosives in the United States. (White House) Establishes a national policy, and calls for the development of a national strategy and implementation plan, on the prevention and detection of, protection against, and response to terrorist use of explosives in the United States.

HSPD-20: National Continuity Policy. (White House) Establishes a comprehensive national policy on the continuity of federal government structures and operations and a single National Continuity

(continued)

Table 6.1. *(continued)*

Coordinator responsible for coordinating the development and implementation of federal continuity policies.

HSPD-21: Public Health and Medical Preparedness. (White House) Establishes a national strategy that will enable a level of public health and medical preparedness sufficient to address a range of possible disasters.

HSPD-23: Cyber Security requires federal agencies to monitor cyber activity towards federal agencies' computer systems and where necessary, provide action to eliminate sources of hostile action. EPA has a robust security program for both personnel and cyber security as mandate by the directive.

Source: USEPA (2016).

reducing the risk to critical infrastructure by physical means or defense cyber measures to intrusions, attacks, or the effects of natural or manmade disasters. Examples of security measures (DHS, 2016):

- Badge entry at doors
- Using antivirus software
- Fencing around buildings
- Locking computer screens

PRD-21 defines resilience as the ability to prepare for and adapt to changing conditions and withstand and recover rapidly from disruptions. Resilience includes the ability to withstand and recover from deliberate attacks, accidents, or naturally occurring threats or incidents. Examples of resilience measures:

- Developing a business continuity plan
- Having a generator for backup power
- Using building materials that are made more durable

ASSESSING CHALLENGES

The Department of Homeland Security determined that there were many challenges facing the IT sector; in particular it has listed and detailed seven challenges, each of which is covered in this section.

Challenge 1: Advancing the State of the Art in Designing and Testing Secure Applications

Software flaws and inadequate patching and configuration practice are two of the sources of information technology vulnerabilities; therefore, they require two different threads of thinking about research. Current research has shown that across the entire financial services industry, the information protection and risk management community is generally not well equipped to accurately or completely define, specify, estimate, calculate, and measure how to design and test secure application software. Experience has shown that continued mitigation against network vulnerabilities are ongoing and remain important; however, an increasing number of attacks are against software applications, which are not the focus of many financial institutions. The fact is business requirements and risk assessments should drive resource allocations. Risks are driven by complex applications developed in-house and by partners, extension of powerful business applications to vulnerable customers, and increasingly organized criminal attacks (e.g., SQL injections to steal copies of databases, cross-site scripting). To be effective, application security strategies must incorporate development standards and training, automated and manual code reviews, and penetration testing with and without design specifications or source code of the applications being texted. Some financial regulators have issued supervisory guidance on risks associated with web-based applications, urging banks to focus adequate attention on these risks and appropriate risk management practices (U.S. Treasury, 2008).

The testing of financial institution applications for security vulnerabilities stemming from software flaws is often inadequate, incomplete, or nonexistent. Important to IT sector institutions is the gaining of confidence; that is, commercial institutions need to gain the confidence that is needed to deploy business-critical software with some proof of evaluation for obvious application security flaws (e.g., unvalidated user input, buffer-overrun conditions). Without this confidence, financial institutions are forced to develop countermeasures and compensating controls to counter these unknown potential threats and undocumented features of the software. Without explicit security assurance testing and corresponding evidence of testing results, functional testing by development teams and outside software developers is insufficient. IT systems used in commercial institutions need a robust, effective, affordable, and timely security testing methodology and practice to gain the confidence required to deploy application software into sometimes hostile environments for purposes of practical and appropriate risk management.

Commercial institutions, to minimize vulnerability, have urged major software providers to improve the quality of their software development and testing processes for utility software, such as operating systems, but are only beginning to urge application software developers to do the same. Major software companies and outsourcing providers are responding by developing more secure code. However, while there are important and worthwhile efforts, the IT sector industry (and other users of software) remains at risk from fundamental software development practices that produce vulnerable software in the very beginning stages of development. This vulnerable software has, in turn, resulted in a substantial increase in application-level attacks. Risk managers in commercial institutions continue to look for solutions.

The bottom line: the IT sector needs research on how to specify, design, and implement secure software and measure its associated lifecycle costs and the benefits of the various information security technologies and processes. The sector would benefit from better understanding of how to develop, test, and measure secure application software.

Challenge 2: More Secure and Resilient Financial Transaction Systems

Many IT services rely on an information technology infrastructure, including computing hardware, software, and telecommunications networks. Some of this infrastructure is owned and operated by financial institutions and some is provided by third-party service providers in the United States and around the globe. This infrastructure is probed and attacked by a variety of adversaries, including criminal elements and nation-states. These adversaries exploit vulnerabilities in people, processes, and technologies and perpetuate attacks for financial gain to steal proprietary information or to undermine consumer confidence in the financial services industry and the U.S. economy. Threats from adversaries are increasing, raising concerns over the integrity of devices, networks, and applications. The infrastructure is also vulnerable to natural disasters, pandemics, and other outages. The financial services, information technology, and telecommunications industries have responded to these challenges with initiatives to address security, integrity, and resilience; however, significant risks remain in terms of security breaches, fraud (including identity theft), service disruptions, and data integrity.

More secure and resilient financial transaction systems are the key to maintaining the integrity of the many industries. Because the trustworthiness of networks and devices is uncertain they must resist interception and tampering over an increasingly vulnerable environment. One facet is ensuring that networks and devices are "clean" when restoring services after an interruption. Reconstitution of data after an attack requires an additional step: decontamination, which is the process of distinguishing a clean system state (unaffected by the intruder) from the portions of infected system state, and eliminating the causes of those differences. Because system users would prefer as little good data as possible be discarded, this problem is quite difficult. Also of primary importance is the retention and reconstruction of transaction history while simultaneously being fully engaged in business continuity operations and executing a recovery plan. Other sectors have expressed concerns about extending their continuity plans to include vital information found on remote workstations. The possibility of this dislocation of normal corporate boundaries could be strained when relying on a distributed computing model.

As a tool for business continuity planning purposes, remote access is necessary for enhancing productivity. For example, commercial institutions have developed business continuity plans to ensure employees can access networks if core facilities are not available.

The bottom line: the challenge is in finding the right mix of hardware and software that gives employees the ability to conduct their work off-site while still adhering to excessive incremental risk. It should also provide employees the ability to seamlessly move from one location to another while retaining their "session state" and desktop customization (U.S. Treasury, 2008; DHS, 2013).

Challenge 3: Enrollment and Identity Credential Management

A secure IT sector infrastructure requires reliable and unambiguous identification of all parties involved in a transaction and non-repudiation of authorized transactions. Current technologies offer "spot" solutions that secure an aspect of identity management; however, much vulnerability remains. Although strong authentication credentialing technology exists, the initial identification of and linkage to an individual's identity to an authentication credential and the need to replace lost or stolen credentials remain weak links. Many commercial institutions rely on the individual's possession of knowledge that can be stolen, or by biometrics that can be spoofed, and may not scale up to millions of individuals without sacrificing performance. Moreover, the lack of mutual authentication allows for, among other things, the ability for the launching of successful man-in-the middle attacks (i.e., active eavesdropping attacks). Commercial institutions typically rely on "spot" authentication in which the financial institution authenticates customers before a transaction. Research is needed to develop more continuous authentication and credentialing.

Challenge 4: Understanding the Human Insider Threat

IT service institutions grant access to confidential information to authorized parties. To establish and maintain trust in this access-granting process, commercial institutions use a variety of tools and controls to identify, verify, authenticate, and authorize trustworthy individuals and contractors. Measures include background checks, credit history checks, and other historical data checks. The insider threat problem (discussed in detail later) is particularly difficult because of the interplay between technical, legal, managerial, and ethical issues. IT service entities recognize that current measures provide only a "coarse-grained" screening for obvious human threats to begin the access-granting process; individuals are granted access to networks, systems, databases, applications, and ultimately customer and business information based on their job or role in the institution. The process is enforced via a highly complex set of overlapping operational and technical controls, which requires that a large percentage of each financial institution's total information protection budget is dedicated to access management, control, and reporting.

IT Sector and institutions relying on IT services continue to experience damage from the unprofessional, malicious, or criminal activities committed by individuals with authorized access, sometimes in coordination with external individuals, criminal organizations, or terrorists; this trend continues even through pre-employment/engagement checking processes, and the layering of costly operational and technical controls are actively employed. Current approaches suggest adding additional layers—technological or procedural—of surveillance processes to detect, identify, and help stop the unwanted activities of authorized individuals. However, such approaches, while they may reduce undesirable activities, add substantial operating costs to an already costly access management approach.

IT sector and commercial institutions currently have tools that could be useful in determining improper behavior of insiders. Many of these tools are based on physical and logical access but are typically not integrated. Improvements in security information management are needed to detect and prevent improper insider behavior. A critical component of improving security information management is ensuring that appropriate controls are in place to address privacy and other human resource protections.

Challenge 5: Data Centric Protection Strategies
With regard to the IT sector protective measures put in place to build a more secure and resilient infrastructure to protect financial transactions and other important company business, vulnerability still exists because sensitive information can be stolen by criminal elements and other adversaries who attack less secure systems connected to merchants and third-party vendors. Preserving the integrity of each transaction involves identification, authentication, and authorization of each transaction to ensure that counterparties are not criminals or money launderers, and that sensitive information is protected and that loss, copying, or tampering is detected. While business institutions have tools that protect data while it resides in a certain environment, these tools are not effective when the data is taken out of that controlled environment (e.g., when a users cuts and pastes in another form). A key challenge is focusing on metadata to understand when data is accessed, updated, or copied.

Challenge 6: Better Measures of the Value of Security Investments
The IT sector seeks research on the life cycle costs of security technologies that support critical infrastructure protection, and the creation of cost-benefit models that can be adopted within institutions and across the industry. One of the key issues in the adoption of improved protective technologies and processes is the ability of the purchasing organizations to fully understand the costs and benefits of security technologies. Inflation protection organizations, as part of their regular business, can effectively evaluate specific cost elements for various protective programs in terms of operating costs, contracting costs, and the cost of purchasing the needed technology

for an organization. However, information protection organizations typically do not have good estimates of the total life cycle costs of the protective programs on the businesses that are asked to implement, own, and manage these protective programs over the long term. Across the entire IT service sector, the information protection and risk management community is generally not well-equipped to accurately or completely define, estimate, calculate, measure, or communicate the benefits that result from protective programs. Further exacerbating this issue is that the "benefits" of security are often intangible and often related more to loss avoidance, making traditional return-on-investment calculations difficult. There needs to be a stronger correlation between security investment and the reduction of risk and subsequent loss. Some methods used today to justify security investments may not align or be equivalent with methodologies under generally accepted accounting principles. Research is needed to establish a baseline risk and to understand changes from the baseline that result from investment. This research also could benefit the broader risk management community.

Challenge 7: Development of Practical Standards

Practical standards and suggested practices is one of the prevailing techniques for closing the gap between state-of-the-art and state-of-the-practice. In an attempt to further the protection of the IT service sector critical infrastructures, numerous documents outlining suggested practices have been developed, most addressing a closely circumscribed segment of various IT service systems and practices. Unfortunately, the problem is that, to date, the industry has been unable to quantitatively correlate best practices with reduced risk. If such a relationship could be determined and quantified, financial institutions would have the tools needed to justify risk management and risk reduction measures. This analysis could, in turn, assist the industry in agreeing on a common and consistent set of practices. A related question is how practitioners and regulators should adopt or consider these in developing robust and resilient infrastructures vis-à-vis the confusion caused by so many different best practices guides and standards.

ASSESSING CONSEQUENCES

The potential physical and cyber consequences of any incident, including terror attacks and natural or human-made disasters, are the primary consideration in risk assessment. In the context of this text, consequence is measured as the range of loss or damage that can be expected. The consequences that are considered for the national-level comparative risk assessment are based on the criteria as set forth in HSPD-7. These criteria can be divided into four main categories:

- **Human Impact**: Effect on human life and physical well-being (e.g., fatalities, injures).
- **Economic Impact**: Direct and indirect effects on the economy (e.g., costs resulting from disruption of products or services, costs to respond to and recover from the disruption, costs to rebuild the asset, and long-term costs due to environmental damage).
- **Impact on Public Confidence**: Effect on public morale and confidence in national economic and political institutions.
- **Impact on Government Capability**: Effect on the government's ability to maintain order, deliver minimum essential public services, ensure public health and safety, and carry out national security-related missions.

Moreover, HSPD-7 is important to the IT sector in that it required the Department of Homeland Security to "serve as the focal point for the security of cyberspace" with a mission that included "analysis, warning, information sharing, vulnerability reduction, mitigation, and aiding national recovery efforts for critical infrastructure information systems." This directive established a national policy for federal departments and agencies to indentify and prioritize U.S. critical infrastructure and key resources and to protect them from terrorist attacks. In addition, it required heads of all federal agencies to "develop . . . plans for protecting the physical and cyber critical infrastructure and key resources that they own or operate." Hence, the federal government began to directly address issues of cyber security within the federal government systems (FCC, 2017).

DID YOU KNOW?

The DHS has the mission to provide a common baseline of security across the federal civilian executive branch and to help agencies manage their cyber risk. The common baseline is provided in part through the EINSTEIN system. EINSTEIN services two key roles in federal government cybersecurity. First, EINSTEIN detects and blocks cyber attacks from compromising federal agencies. Second, EINSTEIN provides DHS with the situational awareness to use threat information detected in one agency to protect the rest of the government and to help the private sector protect itself (DHS, 2017b).

As a result of HSPD-7, the Department of Homeland Security established the National Cybersecurity Division. The objectives of this division are "to build and maintain an effective national cyberspace response system, and to implement a cyber-risk management program for protection of critical infrastructure." The primary operational arms of the division are first the Cybersecurity Preparedness and National Cyber Alert System, and secondly the US Computer Emergency Response Team (US-CERT). The National Cyber Alert System was created by US-CERT and the Department of Homeland Security to help protect computers. One of US-CERT's overarching goals is to ensure that individuals and agencies have access to timely information through tips and alerts about security topics and events. US-CERT has become the national first line of defense for the war of cybersecurity. CERT's Cyber Risk Management Program assesses risk, prioritizes resources, and executes protective measures in order to secure the cyber infrastructure. It includes such things as current risk assessments and vulnerabilities that are maintained in their vulnerability database, the National Cyber Alert System, for information dissemination, and a number of other references for cybersecurity measures.

In addition to the importance of HSPD-7 providing guidance and direction in cybersecurity and IT service sector protection objectives, as a further shot in the security arm, so to speak, HSPD-23 was signed in January 2008 by President Bush; this directive was necessary due to increased cyber activity on an international scale and attacks targeted at U.S. computers and networks—including computer-controlled systems. HSPD-7 established a Comprehensive National Cybersecurity initiative. Although the document is classified, public sources have indicated that in addition to establishing the National Cyber Security Center within the Department of Homeland Security, the initiative had twelve other objectives (FCC, 2017):

- Move toward managing a single federal enterprise network
- Deploy intrinsic detection systems
- Develop and deploy intrusion prevention tools
- Review and potentially redirect research and funding
- Connect current government cyber operations centers
- Develop a government-wide cyber intelligence plan
- Increase the security of classified networks
- Expand cyber education
- Define enduring leap-ahead technologies
- Define enduring deterrent technologies and programs
- Develop multipronged approaches to supply chain risk management
- Define the role of cybersecurity in private sector domains

DID YOU KNOW?

The federal enterprise network depends on IT systems and computer networks for essential operations. These systems face large and diverse cyber threats that range from unsophisticated hackers to technically competent intruders using state-of-the-art intrusion techniques. Many malicious attacks are designed to steal information and disrupt, deny access to, degrade, or destroy critical information systems (DHS, 2017a).

REFERENCES AND RECOMMENDED READINGS

Crayton, J. W. (1983). Terrorism and the Psychology of the Self, pages 33-41 in Lawrence Zelic Freedman and Yonah Alexander, eds., *Perspectives on Terrorism*. Wilmington, DE: Scholarly Resources.

DHS (2003). The National Strategy for the Physical Protection of Critical Infrastructures and Key Assets. Accessed @ https://www.dhs.gov/xlibrary/assets/physical_Strat.

DHS (2013). Homeland Security Directive 7: Critical Infrastructure Identification, Prioritization, and Protection accessed @ https://www.dihs.gov/xabout/laws/gc_1214597989952.shtm.

DHS (2016). What is security and resilience? Accessed @ https://www.dhs.gov/what-security and-resilience.

DHS (2016) *Information Technology Sector—An Annex to the National Infrastructure Protection Plan*. Washington, DC: Department of Homeland Security.

DHS (2017a). *Securing Federal Networks*. Accessed 4/15/17 @ https:/www.dhs.gov/topic/securing-federal-networks.

DHS (2017b). *EINSTEIN*. Accessed 4/14/17 @ https://www.dhs.gov/einstein.

FCC (2017). Public Safety Tech Topic #20—Cyber Security and Communications. Accessed 4/14/17 @ https://www.fcc.gov/help/public-safety-tech-topic-20-cyber-security-and-communiicaitons

FEMA (2015). *Protecting Critical Infrastructure Against Insider Threats*. Accessed 4/17/15 @ http://emilms.fema.gov/IS0915/IABsummary.htm.

Ferracuti, F. (1982). A Sociopsychiatric Interpretation of Terrorism. *The Annals of the American Academy of Political and Social Science,* 463, September, 129–41.

FR (2007). *Federal Register* 17688-17745.

Hudson, R. A. (1999). *The Sociology and Psychology of Terrorism: Who becomes a Terrorist and Why?* Washington, DC: Library of Congress.

Lees, Frank (1996). *Loss Prevention in the Process Industries* 3:A5.1-A5.11. New York: Butterworth-Heinemann.

Long, D. E. (1990). *The Anatomy of Terrorism.* New York: Free Press.

Margolin, J. (1977). *Psychological Perspectives on Terrorism.* In Y. Alexander & S. M. Finger (eds.). "Terrorism: Interdisciplinary Perspectives." New York: John Jay Press.

Olson, M. (1971). *The Logic of Collective Action.* Boston: Harvard University Press.

OMB (1998). *Federal Conformity Assessment Activities, Circular A-119.* Washington, DC: White House.

Pearlstein, R. (1991). *The Mind of the Political Terrorist.* Wilmington, DE: Scholarly Resources, Inc.

Spellman, F. R. (1999). *Process Safety Management.* Lancaster, PA: Technomic Publishing Co.

Sullivant, J. (2007). *Strategies for protecting national critical infrastructure assets: A focus on Problem-Solving.* New York: Wiley & Sons.

USEPA (2016). *Homeland Security Presidential Directives.* Accessed @ https://www.epa.gov/ emeergency-resposne/horelamnd -security-presidential-directives.

U.S. Treasury (2008). *Guidance on Application Security.* Accessed http://www.occ.treas.gov/ ftp/bulletin/2008-16.html.

Wilkinson, P. (1974). *Political Terrorism.* London: Macmillan.

7

Vulnerability Assessment

In God we trust, all others we monitor.

—Intercept Operator's motto

One result of the events of 9/11 was the Department of Homeland Security's (DHS) directive to establish a Critical Infrastructure Protection Task Force to ensure that activities to protect and secure vital infrastructure are comprehensive and carried out expeditiously. Another is the heightened concern among citizens in the United States over the security of their energy infrastructure (i.e., the uninterrupted supply of electrical power and fuel to power vehicles, homes, and vital communications systems). As mentioned, along with other critical infrastructure, the IT service sector is classified as "vulnerable" in the sense that inherent weaknesses in its operating environment could be exploited to cause harm to the system. There is also the possibility of a cascading effect—a chain of events—due to a terrorist act affecting IT sector providers, which could cause corresponding damage (collateral damage) to other nearby users. In addition to significant damage to the nation's IT service sector, entities using and needing IT services to function can result in loss of life due to a lack of proper emergency response; shutdown of other industries; loss of electronic communication operational control networks could cause catastrophic environmental damage to rivers, lakes, and wetlands; and other long-term public health impacts.

Public and private members who utilize IT sector services conduct risk assessments. These assessments look at issues and potential vulnerabilities both within individual organizations and sector-wide. Since risk management is part of business operations culture, both regulators and private organizations have a long history of conducting regular risk assessments. In the private sector some of these risk assessments are mandated through regulation and validated by the examination process. Further, private sector institutions conduct voluntary risk assessments to meet their business needs as part of their continuity planning and/or in conjunction with trade associations' recommendations and self-regulatory requirements (DHS, 2007).

ASSESSING VULNERABILITIES

The IT services sector conducts ongoing vulnerability assessments. What is a vulnerability assessment? For the purpose of this text and according to FEMA (2008), vulnerability is defined as any weakness that can be exploited by an aggressor to make an asset susceptible to hazard damage. In addition, according to the Department of Homeland Security (DHS 2009), vulnerabilities are physical features or operational attributes that render an entity open to exploitation or susceptible to a given hazard. Vulnerabilities may be associated with physical (e.g., a broken fence), cyber (e.g., lack of a firewall), or a human (e.g., insider threats; untrained guards) factors.

Vulnerability assessments estimate the odds that a characteristic, of, or flaw in, an infrastructure could make it susceptible to destruction, disruption, or exploitation based on its design, location, security posture, processes, or operations. Vulnerabilities typically are identified through internal assessments and information sharing with customers, vendors, and suppliers.

A vulnerability assessment methodology was developed as part of the complete IT services sector-specific plan risk assessment methodology. The methodology examined physical, cyber, and human vulnerabilities and considered relevant national preparedness threat scenarios. The process varied depending on the architecture elements being studied and included subject matter expert interviews, site visits, and modeling and analysis.

The vulnerabilities of IT services architecture elements may vary depending on whether they are operational or implementation specific. Operational vulnerabilities may include those that result from the inherent principles of network design, unanticipated network congestion caused by external factors, or collateral consequences from major disasters or events. Implementation-specific vulnerabilities may be very particular in nature—from bugs in application software and protocol deficiencies to backdoors in vendor equipment firmware or software. The magnitude of the implementation vulnerabilities also varies depending on the exposure of the vulnerable equipment. While embedded firmware, for example, may have only limited exposures to configuration and maintenance functions, systems such as the Domain Name Service require a high degree of exposure in order to provide service to customers (DHS, 2010).

Conducting vulnerability assessments is conducted on many levels. These vulnerability assessments include examinations into the potential risks resulting from cross-sector dependency, sector-specific vulnerabilities, and dependencies on key assets, systems, technologies, and processes. Moreover, DHS has instituted a process to provide awareness training to financial services asset owner/operators. The purpose of awareness training is to provide IT sector personnel with information about the place of their asset within the overall IT services mission requirements and acquisition process so they will understand their rules and importance to the entities at the corporate an site levels (DHS, 2010). The training focuses on:

- Protection of IT interests
- Protection of federal interests
- Importance of facilities fostering relationships with local responders and federal, state, and local law enforcement/civil authorities for business recovery planning.

Awareness training also informs the asset owner/operators of the protection measures applied to their proprietary and business-sensitive information provided by and to the IT service sector. Once critical IT assets are identified and prioritized, the next step is to conduct standardized assessments. DHS, working through and with various agencies, has established a standardized mission assurance assessment for application to critical IT service assets. These assessments consider impact, vulnerability, and threat/hazard (whether from natural disaster, technological failure, human error, criminal activity, or terrorist attack). This approach to risk assessment ensures consideration of relevant factors for each IT service asset and a relative prioritization of risks to support military operations.

INSIDER THREAT VULNERABILITY

The insider threat to an IT service organization and hostile and criminal cyber activities is not about rocket science; instead it is about malicious software (malware) and the variety of forms of hostile or intrusive software, including computer viruses, worms, Trojan horses, ransomware, spyware, adware, scareware, and others. One does not need to be a super genius to understand what insider threat really is. The truth is the insider threat is . . . a human, a person, a mammal, Homo sapiens, a breathing organism, a heartbeat. The point is to protect an organization from insider threats. The organization must "use tools to monitor the traffic in or out of the networks and be able to focus that monitoring on specific people who do something concerning or suspicious; moreover, nontechnical employee behavior must be monitored" (INSA, 2017).

"Behavior must be monitored" . . . yes, for sure. What monitoring really comes down to, however, is awareness. An important part of any successful vulnerability assessment process is awareness. Security and risk managers (and all employees in general) working in or with the critical infrastructure sectors must be aware of the potential for insider threat vulnerability. Again, the key word is *awareness*. Awareness means that personnel within the critical infrastructure sectors must know how to identify and take action against insider threats. To achieve this critical goal, safety and security personnel must be provided with an overview of and be cognizant of common characteristics and indicators associated with malicious insiders and effective measures to counter insider threats.

Protecting against Insider Threats (FEMA, 2015)

As mentioned earlier, when analyzing threats to our nation's critical infrastructure, we tend to focus on malicious actions from boat or plane loads of outside actors. Of equal concern (and even more so in the author's view) are threats from an insider—someone we have given legitimate access to information, systems, and resources. The measures we take to detect and protect against external threats may not be sufficient to address threats from insiders.

A malicious insider has access and inside knowledge of the organization and uses that knowledge with the intent to cause harm. The insider may be a current employee, a former employee, a service provider, or, especially in the current era, a planted person inside who has been brainwashed and turned into a terrorist waiting for the moment of maximum impact to people and property.

Given the importance of our nation's critical infrastructure, the actions taken by a malicious employee or service proceed could have devastating consequences. Let's look at some actual examples.

- A service provider employee at a nuclear facility stole two five-gallon containers of low-enriched uranium dioxide and then attempted to extort $100,000 by threatening to disperse the material in an unnamed U.S. city.
- A power company field engineer, angry with his supervisor, disabled protection systems at a substation and forced the shutdown of the entire network. More than 800,000 customers lost power as a result.
- Two municipal employees used their access credentials to sabotage the system controlling the traffic lights of a major city, causing widespread traffic delays. The damage took four days to repair.
- A disgruntled supermarket meat packaging employee intentionally contaminated hamburger meat with a pesticide, causing various levels of illness in 92 consumers.

Insider threats endanger the integrity and security of our workplaces and our communities. This section helps you become aware of threat indicators and actions you can take. As stated earlier, and it can't be overstated, awareness is the first step to keeping our nation and workplaces safe.

Insider Threat Defined

The President's National Infrastructure Advisory Council (2008) defines the insider threat as follows:

> The insider threat to critical infrastructure is one or more individuals with the access or inside knowledge of a company, organization, or enterprise that would allow them to exploit the vulnerabilities of the entity's security, systems, services, products, or facilities with the intent to cause harm.

A person who takes advantage of access or inside knowledge in such a manner commonly is referred to as a "malicious insider."

The Scope of Insider Threats

Insider threats can be accomplished through either physical or cyber means and may involve any of the following:

- **Physical or information-technology sabotage**—Involves modification or damage to an organization's facilities, property, assets, inventory, or systems with the purpose of harming or threatening harm to an individual, the organization, or the organization's operations.
- **Theft of intellectual property**—Involves removal or transfer of an organization's intellectual property outside the organization through physical or electronic means (also known as economic espionage).

DID YOU KNOW?

The FBI testified in June 2012 that in the preceding year, economic espionage losses in the U.S. economy totaled more than $13 billion. In the previous four years, the number of arrests the FBI made had doubled; indictments increased by a factor of five; and convictions increased by a factor of eight (FBI, 2012). In another survey, security professionals found that 43.2 percent of respondents attributed some loss at their organization to insiders. Forty-six percent of responders said the damage caused by insider attacks was more damaging than outside attacks (CSI, 2011).

- **Theft of economic fraud**—Involves acquisition of an organization's financial or other assets through theft or fraud.
- **National security espionage**—Involves obtaining information or assets with a potential impact on national security through clandestine activities.

Common Characteristics and Traits of Malicious Insiders

Based on research conducted by the Software Engineering Institute at Carnegie Mellon University and the U.S. Secret Service National Threat Assessment Center, malicious insiders often are perceived or known to be difficult or high-maintenance employees who are:

- Obviously unhappy or extremely resentful
- Having financial, performance, or behavioral problems
- At risk (or perceived to be) for layoff or termination

Keep in mind that not all malicious insiders fit this characterization. Insiders involved in national security espionage, for example, may exhibit few outward signs. In the majority of cases, however, management and/or human resources personnel were well aware of the employees and their issues prior to an incident.

Personal Factors Associated with Insiders

The following motives and personal situations frequently are linked with malicious insiders:

- Personal or Behavioral Problems
  - Vulnerable to blackmail
  - Experiencing family or financial problems
  - Prone to compulsive or destructive behavior
  - Subject to ego or self-image issues
- Personal Desires
  - Seeking adventure or thrill
  - Seeking approval and returned favors
  - Professing allegiance
- Workplace Issues
  - Experiencing problems at work
  - Feeling anger or need for revenge

Organizational Factors That Embolden Malicious Insiders

The following organizational factors have been known to encourage or present opportunities to potential malicious insiders.

- Access and Availability
  - Ease of access to materials and information
  - Ability to exit the facility or network with materials or information
- Policies and Procedures
  - Undefined or inadequate policies and procedures
  - Inadequate training
  - Lack of training
- Time Pressure and Consequences
  - Rushed employees
  - Perception of lack of consequences

Insider Activities and Behavior You May See

Insider threats may be detected through particular activities and behavior on the part of the insider. This section identifies those indicators. These activities and behaviors often will appear unusual or suspicious. Keep in mind there may be several explanations for a particular activity or behavior identified here, but when combined with other factors, certain activity or behavior point toward a possible insider threat. A combination or confluence of indicators should not be ignored.

Types of Insider Activities and Behavior

Unusual or suspicious insider activities and behavior can be described using the following categories:

- Inappropriate Interest or Acquisition
- Unauthorized or Unusual Computer Use
- Unusual Hours, Contacts, or Travel
- Secretive or Peculiar Behavior
- Personal or Financial Issues

Employer Actions

- Clearly communicating and consistently enforcing security policies and controls
- Ensuring that proprietary information and materials are adequately, if not robustly, protect
- Routinely monitoring computer networks for suspicious activity

- Ensuring security (to include computer network security) personnel have the tools they need
- Consulting with legal and law enforcement experts as needed to ensure compliance with the law

Employee Actions

Today, critical infrastructure organizations employ a number of security measures to reduce the risk of insider threats. The measures involving employees include, but are not limited to:

- Using appropriate screening processes to select new employees.
- Educating employees about security or other protocols.
- Encouraging and providing nonthreatening, convenient ways for employees to report suspicious behavior in a confidential manner.
- Becoming familiar with behavior and activities associated with malicious insiders.
- Documenting and evaluating incidents of suspicious or disruptive behavior.
- Consulting with legal and law enforcement experts as needed to ensure compliance with the law.

THE VULNERABILITY ASSESSMENT[1]

A *vulnerability assessment* (VA) involves an in-depth analysis of the facility's functions, systems, and site characteristics to identify facility weaknesses and lack of redundancy, and determine mitigations or corrective actions that can be designed and implemented to reduce the vulnerabilities. A VA can be a stand-alone process or part of a full risk assessment. During this assessment, the analysis of site assets is based on: (a) the identified threat; (b) the criticality of the assets; and (c) the level of protection chosen (i.e., based on willingness or unwillingness to accept risk).

It is important to point out that post-9/11 all sectors have taken great strides to protect their critical infrastructure. For instance, government and industry have developed VA methodologies for critical infrastructure systems and trained thousands of auditors and others to conduct them.

The actual complexity of VA will range based upon the design and operation of the financial services asset. The nature and extent of the VA will differ among systems based on a number of factors, including system size, potential population, and safety evaluations which also vary based on knowledge and types of threats, available security technologies, and applicable local, state, and federal regulations. Preferably, a VA is "performance-based," meaning that it evaluates the risk to the financial services assets based on the effectiveness (performance) of existing and planned measures to counteract adversarial actions. According to the US EPA (2002), the common elements of vulnerability assessments are as follows:

- Characterization of the IT service sector, including its mission and objectives.
- Identification and prioritization of adverse consequences to avoid.
- Determination of critical assets that might be subject to malevolent acts that could result in undesired consequences.
- Assessment of the likelihood (qualitative probability) of such malevolent acts from adversaries.
- Evaluation of existing countermeasures.
- Analysis of current risk and development of a prioritized plan for risk reduction.

Benefits of Assessments

IT service sector members should routinely perform vulnerability assessments to better understand threats and vulnerabilities, determine acceptable levels of risk, and stimulate action to mitigate identified vulnerabilities. These assessments are based upon the extensive knowledge of regulators and guidance issued, and takes into account physical, cyber, and human vulnerabilities, available redundancy, and the sector's reliance on sector-sector assets, systems and processes, and cross-sector reliance on these factors. Consequence assessments include direct economic impacts and national confidence impacts, and are based on expert judgment and exercises. The direct benefits of performing a vulnerability assessment include:

- **Build and broaden awareness**—the assessment process directs senior management's attention to security. Security issues, risks, vulnerabilities, mitigation options, and best practices are brought to the surface. Awareness is one of the least expensive and most effective methods for improving the organization's overall security posture.
- **Establish or evaluate against a baseline**—if a baseline has been previously established, an assessment is an opportunity for a checkup to gauge the improvement or deterioration of an organization's security posture. If no previous baseline has been performed (or the work was not uniform or comprehensive), an assessment is an opportunity to integrate and unify previous efforts, define common metrics, and establish a definitive baseline. The baseline also can be compared against best practices to provide perspective on an organization's security posture.
- **Identify vulnerabilities and develop responses**—generating lists of vulnerabilities and potential responses is usually a core activity and outcome of an assessment. Sometimes, due to budget, time, complexity, and risk considerations, the response selected for many of the vulnerabilities may be non-action, but after completing the

assessment process these decisions will be conscious ones, with a documented decision process and item-by-item rationale available for revisiting issues at scheduled intervals. This information can help drive or motivate the development of a risk management process.

- **Categorize key assets and drive the risk management process**—an assessment can be a vehicle for reaching corporate-wide consensus on a hierarchy of key assets. This ranking, combined with threat, vulnerability, and risk analysis, is at the heart of any risk management process. For many organizations, the Y2K was the first time a company-wide inventory and ranking of key assets was attempted. An assessment allows any organization to revisit that list from a broader and more comprehensive perspective.

- **Develop and build internal skills and expertise**—a security assessment, when not implemented in an "audit" mode, can serve as an excellent opportunity to build security skills and expertise within an organization. A well-structured assessment can have elements that serve as a forum for cross-cutting groups to come together and share issues, experiences, and expertise. External assessors can be instructed to emphasize "teaching and collaborating" rather than "evaluating" (the traditional role). Whatever the organization's current level of sophistication, a long-term goal should be to move the organization toward a capability for self-assessment.

- **Promote action**—although disparate security efforts may be underway in an organization, an assessment can crystallize and focus management's attention and resources on solving specific and systemic security problems. Often, the people in the trenches are well aware of security issues (and even potential solutions) but are unable to convert their awareness to action. An assessment provides an outlet for their concerns and the potential to surface these issues at appropriate levels (legal, financial, executive) and achieve action. A well-designed and executed assessment not only identifies vulnerabilities and makes recommendations, it also gains executive buy-in, identifies key players, and establishes a set of cross-cutting groups that can convert those recommendations into action.

- **Kick off an ongoing security effort**—an assessment can be used as a catalyst to involve people throughout the organization in security issues, build cross-cutting teams, establish permanent forums and councils, and harness the momentum generated by the assessment to build an ongoing institutional security effort. The assessment can lead to the creation of either an actual or a virtual (matrixed) security organization.

Vulnerability Assessment Process

Table 7.1 provides an overview of the elements included in the assessment methodology. The elements included in this overview are based on actual in-field experience and lessons learned.

Table 7.1. Basic Elements in Vulnerability Assessments

Element	Points to Consider

1. **Characterization of the communications entity, including its mission and objectives**	• What are the important missions of the system to be assessed? Define the highest priority services provided by the utility. Identify the industry's customers:
	
	  ** General public
	  ** Government
	  ** Military
	  ** Industrial
	  ** Critical care
	  ** Retail operations
	  ** Firefighting
	
	• What are the most important facilities, processes, and assets of the system for achieving the mission objectives and avoiding undesired consequences? Describe the:
	  ** Industry facilities
	  ** Operating procedures
	  ** Management practices that are necessary to achieve the mission objectives
	  ** How the industry operates
	  ** Treatment processes
	  ** Storage methods and capacity
	  ** Energy use and storage
	  ** Distribution system
	
	In assessing those assets that are critical, consider critical customers, dependence on other infrastructures (e.g., chemical, transportation, communications), contractual obligations, single points of failure, chemical hazards and other aspects of the industry's operations, or availability of industry utilities that may increase or decrease the criticality of specific facilities, processes, and assets.

2. **Identification and prioritization of adverse consequences to avoid**	• Take into account the impacts that could substantially disrupt the ability of the system to provide a safe and reliable supply of materials. IT service sector systems should use the vulnerability assessment process to determine how to reduce risk associated with the consequences of significant concern.
	• Ranges of consequences or impacts for each of these events should be identified and defined. Factors to be considered in assessing the consequences may include:
	  ** Magnitude of service disruption
	  ** Economic impact (such as replacement and installation costs for damaged critical assets or loss of revenue due to service outage)
	  ** Number of illnesses or deaths resulting from an event
	  ** Impact on public confidence in the material supply
	  ** Chronic problems arising from specific events
	  ** Other indicators of the impact of each event as determined by the financial service sector.
	
	Risk reduction recommendations at the conclusion of the vulnerability assessment strive to prevent or reduce each of these consequences.

(continued)

Table 7.1. *(continued)*

Element	Points to Consider
3. Determination of critical assets that might be subject to malevolent acts that could result in undesired consequences	• What are the malevolent acts that could reasonably cause undesired consequences?
	** Electronic, computer, or other automated systems that are utilized by the financial sector entities (e.g., Supervisory Control and Data Acquisition (SCADA)
	** The use, storage, or handling of various financial services supplies
	** The operation and maintenance of such systems
4. Assessment of the likelihood (qualitative probability) of such malevolent acts from adversaries	• Determine the possible modes of attack that might result in consequences of significant concern based on critical assets of the financial service sector entity. The objective of this step of the assessment is to move beyond what is merely possible and determine the likelihood of a particular attack scenario. This is a very difficult task as there is often insufficient information to determine the likelihood of a particular event with any degree of certainty.
	• The threats (the kind of adversary and the mode of attack) selected for consideration during a vulnerability assessment will dictate, to a great extent, the risk reduction measures that should be designed to counter the threat(s). Some vulnerability assessment methodologies refer to this as a "Design Basis Threat" (DBT) where the threat serves as the basis for the design of countermeasures, as well as the benchmark against which vulnerabilities are assessed. It should be noted that there is no single DBT or threat profile for all financial systems in the United States. Differences in geographic location, size of the utility, previous attacks in the local area and many other factors will influence the threat(s) that the IT service sector entity should consider in their assessments. IT service sector entities should consult with the local FBI and/or other law enforcement agencies, public officials, and others to determine the threats upon which their risk reduction measures should be based.
5. Evaluation of existing countermeasures (Depending on countermeasures already in place, some critical assets may already be sufficiently protect. This step will aid in identification of the areas of greatest concern and help to focus priorities for risk reduction.)	• What capabilities does the system currently employ for detection, delay and response?
	** Identify and evaluate current detection capabilities such as intrusion detection systems, energy quality monitoring, operational alarms, guard post orders, and employee security awareness programs.
	** Identify current delay mechanisms such as locks and key control, fencing, structure integrity of critical assets, and vehicle access checkpoints.
	** Identify existing policies and procedures for evaluation and response to intrusion and system malfunction alarms, and cyber system intrusions.

Element	Points to Consider

It is important to determine the performance characteristics. Poorly operated and maintained security technologies provide little or no protection.

- What cyber protection system features does the facility have in place? Assess what protective measures are in-place for the SCADA and business-related computer information systems such as:
  - ** Firewalls
  - ** Modem access
  - ** Internet and other external connections, including wireless data and voice communications
  - ** Security polices and protocols

It is important to identify whether vendors have access rights and/or "backdoors" to conduct system diagnostics remotely.

- What security policies and procedures exist, and what is the compliance record for them? Identify existing policies and procedures concerning:
  - ** Personal security
  - ** Physical security
  - ** Key and access badge control
  - ** Control of system configuration and operational data
  - ** Vendor deliveries
  - ** Security training and exercise records

6. Analysis of current risk and development of a prioritized plan for risk reduction

- Information gathered on threat, critical assets, IT service sector operations, consequences, and existing countermeasures should be analyzed to determine the current level of risk. The utility should then determine whether current risks are acceptable or risk reduction measures should be pursued.
- Recommended actions should measurably reduce risks by reducing vulnerabilities and/or consequences through improved deterrence, delay, detection, and/or response capabilities or by improving operational policies or procedures. Selection of specific risk reduction actions should be completed prior to considering the cost of the recommended action(s). Facilities should carefully consider both short- and long-term solutions. An analysis of the cost of short- and long-term risk reduction actions may impact which actions the utility chooses to achieve its security goals.
- Facilities may also want to consider security improvements. Security and general infrastructure may provide significant multiple benefits. For example, improved treatment processes or system redundancies can both reduce vulnerabilities and enhance day-to-day operation.
- Generally, strategies for reducing vulnerabilities fall into two broad categories:
  - ** Sound business practices—affect policies, procedures, and training to improve the overall security-related culture at the chemical facility. For example, it is important to ensure rapid communication capabilities exist between public health authorities and local law enforcement and emergency responders.
  - ** Security upgrades—improve capabilities for detection, delay, or response.

In Table 7.1, step 3 deals with identification of asset criticality. This is an important step in any vulnerability assessment. Identifying assets criticality serves several functions:

- It enables more careful consideration of factors that affect risk, including threats, vulnerabilities, and consequences of loss or compromise of the asset.
- It enables more focused and thorough consideration of loss or compromise of the asset.
- It enables leaders to develop robust methods for managing consequences of asset loss (restoration).
- It provides a means to increase awareness of a broad range of employees to protect truly critical assets and to differentiate in policies and procedures the heightened protection they require.

As previously indicated, identifying the criticality of assets is used primarily to focus the vulnerability analysis efforts. It also assists with the ranking of various recommendations for reducing vulnerabilities. As an example, let's take a look at the criticality of electric power assets and operations included in the normal operation of financial service sector assets:

- Physical
  - Generators
  - Substations
  - Transformers
  - Transmission lines
  - Distribution lines
  - Control center
  - Warehouses
  - Office buildings
  - Internal and external infrastructure dependencies
- Cyber
  - SCADA systems
  - Networks
  - Databases
  - Business systems
  - Telecommunications
- Interdependencies
  - Single-point nodes of failures
  - Critical infrastructure components of high reliance

VULNERABILITY ASSESSMENT METHODOLOGY

Vulnerability assessment methodology consists of ten elements. Each element along with a description of each is listed below (US DOE, 2002).

1. Network architecture
2. Threat environment
3. Penetration testing
4. Physical security
5. Physical asset analysis
6. Operations security
7. Policies and procedures
8. Impact analysis
9. Infrastructure interdependencies
10. Risk characterization

Network Architecture

This element provides an analysis of the information assurance features of the information network(s) associated with the organization's critical information systems. Information examined should include network topology and connectivity (including subnets), principal information assets, interface and communication protocols, function and linage of major software and hardware components (especially those associated with information security such as intrusion detectors), and policies and procedures that govern security features of the network.

Procedures for information assurance in the system, including authentication of access and management of access authorization, should be reviewed. The assessment should identify any obvious concerns related to architectural vulnerabilities, as well as operating procedures. Existing security plans should be evaluated, and the results of any prior testing should be analyzed. Results from the network architecture assessment should include potential recommendations for changes in the information architecture, functional areas and categories where testing is needed, and suggestions regarding system design that would enable more effective information and information system protection.

Three techniques are often used in conducting the network architecture assessment:

1. Analysis of network and system documentation during and after the site visit
2. Interview with facility staff, managers, and chief information officer
3. Tours and physical inspections of key facilities

Threat Environment

Development of a clear understanding of the threat environment is a fundamental element of risk management. When combined with an appreciation of the value of the information assets and systems, and the impact of unauthorized access and subsequent malicious activity, an understanding of threats provides a basis for better defining the level of investment needed to prevent such access.

The threat of a terrorist attack to IT service sector infrastructure is real and could come from several areas, including physical, cyber, and interdependency. In addition, threats could come from individuals or organizations motivated by financial gain or persons who derive pleasure from such penetration (e.g., recreational hackers, disgruntled employees). Other possible sources of threats are those who want to accomplish extremist goals (e.g., environmental terrorists, antinuclear advocates) or embarrass one or more organizations.

This element should include a characterization of these and other threats, identification of trends in these threats, and ways in which vulnerabilities are exploited. To the largest extent possible, characterization of the threat environment should be localized, that is, within the organization's service area.

Penetration Testing

The purpose of network penetration testing is to utilize active scanning and penetration tools to identity vulnerabilities that a determined adversary could easily exploit. Penetration testing can be customized to meet the specific needs and concerns of the financial service sector unit. In general, penetration testing should include a test plan and details on the rules of engagement (ROE). It should also include a general characterization of the access points of the critical information systems and include a general characterization of the access points to the critical information systems and communication interface connections, modem network connections, access points to principal network routers, and other external connections. Finally, penetration testing should include identified vulnerabilities and, in particular, whether access could be gained to the control network or specific subsystem or devices that have a critical role in assuring continuity of service.

Penetration testing consists of an overall process of establishing the ground rules or ROE for the test; establishing a white cell for continuous communication; developing a format or methodology for the test; conducting the test; and generating a final report that details methods, findings, and recommendations.

Penetration testing methodology consists of three phases: reconnaissance, scenario development, and exploitation. A one-time penetration test can provide the utility with valuable feedback; however, it is far more effective if performed on a regular basis. Repeated testing is recommended because new threats develop continuously, and the networks, computers, and architecture of the financial service sector unit or utility are likely to change over time.

Physical Security

A critical dependency for the IT service sector as well as the other sectors is related to the physical security of the facilities. The purpose of physical security assessment is to examine and evaluate the systems in place (or being planned) and to identify potential improvements in this area for the sites evaluated. Physical security systems include access controls, barriers locks and keys, badges and passes, intrusion detection devices and associated alarm reporting and display, closed-circuit television (assessment and surveillance), communications equipment (telephone, two-way radio, intercom, cellular), lighting (interior and exterior), power sources (line, battery, generator), inventory control, postings (signs), security system wiring, and protective force. Physical security systems are reviewed for design, installation operation, maintenance, and testing.

The physical security assessment should focus on those sites directly related to the critical facilities, including information systems and assets required for operation. Typically included are facilities that house critical equipment or information assets or networks dedicated to the operation of electric, oil, or gas transmission, storage, or delivery systems. Other facilities can be included on the basis of criteria specified by the organization being assessed. Appropriate levels of physical security are contingent upon the value of company assets, the potential threats to these assets, and the cost associated with protecting the assets. Once the cost of implementing/maintaining physical security programs is known, it can be compared to the value of the company assets, thus providing the necessary information for risk management decisions. The focus of the physical security assessment task is determined by prioritizing the company assets; that is, the most critical assets receive the majority of the assessment activity.

At the start of the assessment, survey personnel should develop a prioritized listing of company assets. This list should be discussed with company personnel to identify areas of security strengths and weaknesses. During these initial interviews, assessment areas that would provide the most benefit to the company should be identified; once known, they should become the major focus of the assessment activities.

The physical security assessment of each focus area usually consists of the following:

- Physical security program (general)
- Physical security program (planning)
- Barriers
- Access controls/badges
- Locks/keys

- Intrusion detection systems
- Communications equipment
- Protective force/local law enforcement agency

The key to reviewing the above topics is not to just identify if they exist but to determine the appropriate level that is necessary and consistent with the value of the asset being protected. The physical security assessment worksheets provide guidance on appropriate levels of protection.

Once the focus and content of the assessment task have been identified, the approach to conduct the assessment can be either at the "implementation level" or at the "organizational level." The approach taken depends on the maturity of the security program.

For example, a company with a solid security infrastructure (staffing plans/procedures, funding) should receive a cursory review of these items; however, facilities where the security programs are being implemented should receive a detailed review. The security staff can act upon deficiencies found at the facilities, once reported.

For companies with an insufficient security organization, the majority of time spent on the assessment should take place at the organizational level to identify the appropriate staffing/funding necessary to implement security programs to protect company assets. Research into specific facility deficiencies should be limited to finding just enough examples to support any staffing/funding recommendations.

Physical Asset Analysis

The purpose of the physical asset analysis is to examine the systems and physical operational assets to ascertain whether vulnerabilities exist. Included in this element is an examination of asset utilization, system redundancies, and emergency operating procedures. Consideration should also be given to the topology and operating practices for electric and gas transmission, processing, storage, and delivery, looking specifically for those elements that either singly or in concert with other factors provide a high potential for disrupting service. This portion of the assessment determines company and industry trends regarding these physical assets. Historic trends, such as asset utilization, maintenance, new infrastructure investments, spare parts, SCADA linkages, and field personnel are part of the scoping element.

The proposed methodology for physical assets is based on a macrolevel approach. The analysis can be performed with company data, public data, or both. Some companies might not have readily available data or might be reluctant to share that data.

Key output from analysis should be graphs that show trends. The historic data analysis should be supplemented with on-site interviews and visits. Items to focus on during a site visit include the following:

- Trends in field testing
- Trends in maintenance expenditures
- Trends in infrastructure investments
- Historic infrastructure outages
- Critical system components and potential system bottlenecks
- Overall system operation controls
- Use and dependency of SCADA systems
- Linkages of operation staff with physical and IT security
- Adequate policies and procedures
- Communications with other regional financial assets
- Communications with external infrastructure providers
- Adequate organizational structure

Operations Security

Operations security (OPSEC) is the systematic process of denying potential adversaries (including competitors or their agents) information about capabilities and intentions of the host organization. OPSEC involves identifying, controlling, and protecting generally nonsensitive activities concerning planning and execution of sensitive activities. The OPSEC assessment reviews the processes and practices employed for denying adversary access to sensitive and nonsensitive information that might inappropriately aid or abet an individual's or organization's disproportionate influence over system operation. This assessment should include a review of security training and awareness programs, discussions with key staff, and tours of appropriate principal facilities. Information that might be available through public access should also be reviewed.

Policies and Procedures

The policies and procedures by which security is administered (1) provide the basis for identifying and resolving issues; (2) establish the standards of reference for policy implementation; and (3) define and communicate roles, responsibilities, authorities, and accountabilities for all individuals and organizations that interface with critical systems. They are the backbone for decisions and day-to-day security operations. Security policies and procedures become particularly important at times when multiple parties must interact to effect a desired level of security and when substantial legal ramifications cold result from policy violations. Policies and procedures should be reviewed to determine whether they (1) address the key factors affecting security; (2) enable effective compliance, implementation, and enforcement; (3) reference or conform to established standards; (4) provide clear and comprehensive guidance; and (5) effectively address roles, responsibilities, accountabilities, and authorities.

The objective of the policies and procedures assessment task is to develop a comprehensive understanding of how a facility protects its critical assets through the development and implementation of policies and procedures. Understanding and assessing this area provide a means of identifying strengths and areas for improvements that can be achieved through:

- Modification of current policies and procedures
- Implementation of current policies and procedures
- Development and implementation of new policies and procedures
- Assurance of compliance with policies and procedures
- Cancellation of policies and procedures that are no longer relevant, or are inappropriate for the facility's current strategy and operations

Impact Analysis

A detailed analysis should be conducted to determine the influence that exploitation of unauthorized access to critical facilities or information systems might have on an organization's operations (e.g., market and/or physical operations). In general, such an analysis would required thorough understanding of (1) the applications and their information processing, (2) decisions influenced by this information, (3) independent checks and balances that might exist regarding information upon which decisions are made, (4) factors that might mitigate the impact of unauthorized access, and (5) secondary impacts of such access. Similarly, the physical chain of events following disruption, including the primary, secondary, and tertiary impacts of disruption, should be examined.

The purpose of the impact analysis is to help estimate the impact that detrimental impacts could have on financial service sector units. The impact analysis provides an introduction to risk characterization by providing quantitative estimates of these impacts so that the IT service sector unit can implement a risk management program and weigh the risks and costs of various mitigation measures.

Infrastructure Interdependencies

The term "infrastructure interdependencies" refers to the physical and electronic (cyber) linkages within communications and among our nation's critical infrastructures—energy (electric power, oil, natural gas), telecommunications, transportation, water supply systems, banking and finance, emergency services, and government services. This task identifies the direct infrastructure linkages between and among the infrastructures that support critical facilities as recognized by the organization. Performance of this task requires a detailed understanding of an organization's functions, internal infrastructures, and how they link to external infrastructures.

The purpose of the infrastructure interdependencies assessment is to examine and evaluate the infrastructures (internal and external) that support critical facility functions, along with their associated interdependencies and vulnerabilities.

Risk Characterization

Risk characterization provides a framework for prioritizing recommendations across all task areas. The recommendations for each task area are judged against a set of criteria to help prioritize the recommendations and assist the organization in determining the appropriate course of action. It provides a framework for assessing vulnerabilities, threats, and potential impacts (determined in the other tasks). In addition, the existing risk analysis and management process at the organization should be reviewed and, if appropriate, utilized for prioritizing recommendations. The degree to which corporate risk management includes security factors is also evaluated.

Vulnerability Assessment Procedures

Vulnerability assessment procedures can be conducted for IT service sector assets using various methodologies. For example, the checklist analysis is an effective technology. In addition, Pareto analysis (80/20 principle), relative ranking, pre-removal risk assessment (PRRA), change analysis, failure mode and effects analysis (FMEA), fault tree analysis, event tree analysis, what-if analysis and Hazard and Operability (HAZOP) can be used in conducting the assessment.

Based on personal experience, the what-if analysis and HAZOP seem to be the most user-friendly methodologies to use. A sample what-if analysis procedural outline is presented below, followed by a brief explanation and outline for conducting HAZOP.

What-If Analysis Procedure/Sample What-If Questions

The steps in a What-If Checklist analysis are as follows:

1. Select the team (personnel experienced in the process).
2. Assemble information (piping and instrumentation drawings (P&IDs), process flow diagrams (PFDs), operating procedures, equipment drawings, etc.).
3. Develop a list of what-if questions.
4. Assemble your team in a room where each team member can view the information.
5. Ask each what-if question in turn and determine:
   - What can cause the deviation from design intent that is expressed by the question?
   - What adverse consequences might follow?
   - What are the existing design and procedural safeguards?
   - Are these safeguards adequate?

- If these safeguards are not adequate, what additional safeguards does the team recommend?

6. As the discussion proceeds, record the answers to these questions in tabular format.

7. Do not restrict yourself to the list of questions that you developed before the project started. The team is free to ask additional questions at any time.

8. When you have finished the what-if questions, proceed to examine the checklist. The purpose of this checklist is to ensure that the team has not forgotten anything. While you are reviewing the checklist, other what-if questions may occur to you.

9. Make sure that you follow up all recommendations and action items that arise from the hazards evaluation.

HAZOP Analysis

The HAZOP analysis technique uses a systematic process to (1) identify possible deviations from normal operations and (2) ensure that safeguards are in place to help prevent accidents. The HAZOP uses special adjectives (such as speed, flow, pressure, etc.) and combined process conditions (such as "more," "less," "no," etc.) to systematically consider all credible deviations from normal conditions. The adjectives, called guide words, are a unique feature of HAZOP analysis.

In this approach, each guide word is combined with relevant process parameters and applied at each point (study node, process section, or operating step) in the process that is being examined.

The following is an example of creating deviations using guide words and process parameters:

Guide Words		Parameter		Deviation
NO	+	FLOW	=	NO FLOW
MORE	+	PRESSURE	=	HIGH PRESSURE
AS WELL AS	+	ONE PHASE	=	TWO PHASE
OTHER THAN	+	OPERATION	=	MAINTENANCE
MORE	+	LEVEL	=	HIGH LEVEL

Table 7.2.

Guide Words	Meaning
No	Negation of the Design Intent
Less	Quantitative Decrease
More	Quantitative Increase
Part Of	Other Material Present by Intent
As Well As	Other Materials Present Unintentionally
Reverse	Logical Opposite of the Intent
Other Than	Complete Substitution

Table 7.3. Common HAZOP Analysis Process Parameters

Flow	Time	Frequency	Mixing
Pressure	Composition	Viscosity	Addition
Temperature	pH	Voltage	Separation
Level	Speed	Information	Reaction

Guide words are applied to both the more general parameters (e.g., react, mix) and the more specific parameters (e.g., pressure, temperature). With the general parameters, it is not unusual to have more than one deviation from the application of one guide word. For example, "more reaction" could mean either that a reaction takes place at a faster rate, or that a greater quantity of product results. On the other hand, some combination of guide words and parameters will yield no sensible deviation (e.g., "as well as" with "pressure").

HAZOP Procedure
1. Select the team.
2. Assemble information (P&IDs, PFDs, operating procedures, equipment drawings, etc.).
3. Assemble your team in a room where each team member can view P&IDs.
4. Divide the system you are reviewing into nodes (you can present the nodes or the team can choose them as you go along).
5. Apply appropriate deviations to each node. For each deviation, address the following questions:
   - What can cause the deviation from design intent?
   - What adverse consequences might follow?
   - What are the existing design and procedural safeguards?
   - Are these safeguards adequate?
   - If these safeguards are not adequate, what does the team recommend?
6. As the discussion proceeds, record the answers to these questions in tabular format.

VULNERABILITY ASSESSMENT: CHECKLIST PROCEDURE
In performing the vulnerability assessment of any IT service sector unit or facility, one of the simplest methodologies to employ is the checklist. The Building Vulnerability Assessment Checklist developed by the Department of Veterans Affairs (VA) and is part of EEMA 426, *Reference Manual to Mitigate Potential Terrorist Attacks Against Buildings* is the reference manual that is recommended in this book and is available on the Internet at http://www.fema.gov/media-library-data/2013072. It is an excellent guide for conducting a viable Checklist-Type Vulnerability Assessment. This Checklist will help you to prepare your threat assessment because it allows a consistent se-

curity evaluation of designs at various levels. The checklist can be used as a screening tool for preliminary design vulnerability assessment and supports the preparation of all steps for use by the assessment teams during preparation for interviews with facility representatives to help assure that all relevant aspects of the financial services assets are considered in the survey.

The bottom line: through the vulnerability assessments, the IT service sector has determined that some of its greatest challenges are its dependence on the telecommunications network and the power grid.

NOTE

1. Much of the information in this section is from the US Department of Energy (DOE 2002) *Vulnerability Assessment Methodology: Electric Power Infrastructure*. Washington, DC; US Army Research Laboratory (2000) *Vulnerability Risk Assessment, ARL-TR-1045*. Washington, DC: DOD; U.S. Dept of Justice, (2002) *A method to Assess the Vulnerability of U.S. Chemical Facilities*. Washington, DC.

REFERENCES AND RECOMMENDED READING

CBO (2004). *Homeland Security and the Private Sector*. Accessed 5/2/168 @www.cbo.gov/ft. docs.

CSI (2011). *2010/2011. Computer Crime and Security Survey*. Orlando, FL: Computer Security Institute.

DHS (2009). *National Infrastructure Protection Plan*. Retrieved 5/11/17 @http://www.dhs.gov/xlibrary/assets/NIPP.Plan.pdf.

DHS (2003). The National Strategy for the Physical Protection of Critical Infrastructures and Key Assets. Accessed @ https://www.dhs.gov/xlibrary/assets/physical_Strat.

DHS (2007). *Critical Infrastructure Vulnerability Assessments*. Washington, DC: Department of Homeland Security.

DHS (2013). Homeland Security Directive 7: Critical Infrastructure Identification, Prioritization, and Protection accessed @ https://www.dihs.gov/xabout/laws/gc_1214597989952.shtm.

DHS (2016). What is security and resilience? Accessed @ https//www.dhs.gov/what-security and-resilience.

DHS (2016). *Information Technology Sector—An Annex to the National Infrastructure Protection Plan*. Washington, DC: Department of Homeland Security.

DoDD (2010). DoD Policy and Responsibility for Critical Infractions –DODD 3020.40. Washington, DC: U.S. Department of Defense.

FBI (2012). Insider Espionage. Report before the House Committee on Homeland Security Subcommittee on Counter Terrorism and Intelligence. Washington, DC: Federal Bureau of Investigation.

FEMA (2008). *FEMA452: Risk Assessment A How to Guide.* Accessed 5/01/16 @fema.gov/ library/file?type=published/filetofile.

FEMA (2015). *Protecting Critical Infrastructure Against Insider Threats.* Accessed 4/17/15 @ http://emilms.fema.gov/IS0915/IABsummary.htm.

INSA (2017). *Building a Stronger Intelligence Community.* Arlington, VA: Intelligence and National Security alliance. Accessed @ www.insooline.org.

National Infrastructure Advisory Council (2008). *First Report and Recommendations on the Insider Threat to Critical Infrastructure.* Washington, DC.

President's National Infrastructure Advisory Council (2008). *The Insider Threat to Critical Infrastructure.* Washington, DC.

Spellman, F. R. (1997). *A Guide to Compliance for PSM/RMP.* Lancaster, PA: Technomic Publishing Company.

U.S. Department of Energy (2010). *Energy Sector-Specific Plan: An Annex to the National Infrastructure Protection Plan.* Washington, DC: USDOE.

US DOE (2002). *Vulnerability Assessment Methodology: Electric Power Infrastructure.* Washington, DC.

US EPA (2002). *Vulnerability Assessment Fact Sheet.* EPA 816-F-02-025. @ www.epa.gov/ ogwdw/security/index.html

8

Incident Response and Reporting

"We're in uncharted territory."

—Rudi Giuliani (9/11/01)

In many of the volumes of this infrastructure series, I do not hesitate to use the above statement because it is not only germane but also truthful. In light of this, when New York mayor Rudi Giuliani made the above statement to Police Commissioner Bernard Kerik at the World Trade Center Site, September 11, 2001, to a point and to a degree, one of the first (and not to be forgotten) gross understatements of the twenty-first century had been uttered. Indeed, for citizens of the United States, 9/11 placed our level of consciousness, awareness, fear, and questions of what to do next in "uncharted territory." Actually, when you get right down to it, 9/11 generated more questions than anything else. Many are still asking the following questions today:

Why?

Why would anyone have the audacity to attack the United States?

What kind of cold-blooded killers would even think of conducting such an event?

Who were those Islamic radicals who perpetrated 9/11?

What were the terrorists' goal(s)?

Why were we not ready for such an attack?

Why had we not foreseen such an event?

Why were our emergency responders so undermanned, ill-prepared, and ill-equipped to handle such a disaster?

What took the military fighter planes so long to respond?

What did our government really know (if anything) before the events occurred?

Could anyone have prevented it?

Bottom line questions: Why us? Hell, why anyone?

Why?

These and several other questions continue to resonate today; no doubt they will continue to haunt us for some time to come.

Maybe we ask post-9/11-related questions because of who we are, what we are, and what we are not. That is, because we are Americans, we are free and uninhibited thinkers who think what we say and say what we think—isn't America great! Most Americans are soft-hearted and sympathetic to those in need—compassion is the very nature and soul of being American. Americans are not born terrorists; they are not born into a terrorist regime; they are not raised with fear in their hearts—they are not afraid every time they leave their homes and go about their daily business. Suicide bombers and other like terrorists are those that occupy some other faraway place; definitely not the United States, and they are definitely not American. Right?

Notwithstanding exceptions to the rule, such as Timothy McVeigh (a so-called red-blooded American, born and raised in the United States) and the domestic terrorist who mailed the anthrax, terrorism was foreign to us.

Today, from a safety/security point of view, based on the events of 9/11 and the anthrax events, we should no longer be asking why. Instead, we should not waste our time, money, and energy asking why or in pointing a finger of blame at our government, military, 9/11 emergency responders, and/or the terrorists. We should stop asking why and shift our mindset to asking what-if. The point is we need to stop feeling sorry for ourselves and except the fact that there are folks out there who do not share our view of the American way of life. Earlier, in regard to security preparedness, we pointed to the need to ask what-if questions. Simply, what-if analysis is a proactive approach used to prevent or mitigate certain disasters, extreme events—those human- or nature-generated. Obviously, asking and properly answering what-if questions has little affect on preventing the actions of Mother Nature, such as earthquakes, tornadoes, hurricanes (Katrina type-events), and others. On the other hand, it is true that what-if questions, when properly posed and answered (with results), can reduce the death toll and overall damage caused by these natural disasters. We are certainly aware that these natural events are possible, probable, and likely, and their effects can be horrendous—beyond tragic. The irony is apparent, however, especially when we ask: How many of us are actually willing to move away from or out of earthquake zones, hurricane and tornado allies, and floodplains to live somewhere else?

The fact is we do not possess a crystal ball to foretell the future. What-if questions prepare us to react and respond to certain contingencies. And respond we must, because there are certain events we simply can't prevent. The best response to an event we can't prevent is summed up by the Boy Scouts motto: Be Prepared!

INFORMATION TECHNOLOGY SERVICE SECTOR CONTINGENCY PLANNING

Incident response and emergency response planning or contingency planning for extreme events has long been standard practice for emergency planners and safety professionals in industrial systems operations. For many years, prudent practices have required consideration of the potential impact of severe natural events (forces of nature), including earthquakes, tornadoes, volcanoes, floods, hurricanes, and blizzards. These possibilities have been included in IT service sector industry infrastructure emergency preparedness and disaster response planning. In addition, many IT sector production and cyber distribution facilities have considered the potential consequences of man-made disasters such as operator error and manufacturer's industrial equipment defects. Currently, IT sector managers and operators must also consider violence in the workplace. Moreover, at present, as this text has pointed out, there is a new focus of concern: the potential effects of intentional acts by domestic (homegrown—in-house) or international (foreign) terrorists.

As a result, the security paradigm has not necessarily changed but instead has been radically adjusted—reasonable, necessary, and sensible accommodation for and mitigation of just about any emergency situation imaginable have been and continue to be made. Because we cannot foresee all future domestic or intentional acts of terrorism, we must be prepared to shift from the proactive to reactive mode on short notice—in some cases, on very short notice. Accordingly, we must be prepared to respond to, react to, and mitigate what we can't prevent. Unfortunately, there is more we can't prevent than we can prevent. In light of this, in this section we present in outline form a reactive mitigation procedure, the template example for a standard Information Technology Service Sector Crisis Communications Plan, dealings with natural and man-made disasters, which could also be applied in response to acts of terrorism.

CRISIS COMMUNICATIONS PLAN

Note: The following criteria have not been established as anything other than guidelines and are offered not as definitive or official regulations or procedures but rather as informed advice (based on more than 30 years of safety, industrial hygiene, emergency contingency planning and security experience) insofar as to the subject matter specific to both public and private sectors.

Note: This emergency action plan applies to locations and facilities that are occupied by IT sector personnel performing their designated work activities.

The fact is well-known: When an emergency occurs, the need to communicate is immediate. The goals of a crisis communications plan are to document and understand the steps needed to:

- Rapidly restore IT processing activities after an emergency.
- Minimize IT Sector equipment damage.
- Minimize impact and loss to customers.
- Minimize negative impacts on public health and employee safety.
- Minimize adverse effects on the environment.
- Provide emergency public information concerning customer service.

Although we are concerned with the IT sector in this text, the USEPA developed *Large Water System Emergency Response Outline: Guidance to Assist Community Water Systems in Complying with the Public Health and Bioterrorism Preparedness and Response Act of 2002* (dated July 2003), with minor adjustments, can be applied as a template for any critical infrastructure sector, including the financial service sector. This template provides guidance and recommendations to aid facilities in the preparation of emergency response plans under the PL 107-188. The template is provided below.

Crisis Communications Plan Template

1. Introduction
   Safe and reliable operation is vital to every industrial operation. Crisis Communications Plan (CCP) is an essential part of managing a IT sector process or entity. The introduction should identify the requirement to have a documented CCP, the goal(s) of the plan (e.g., be able to quickly identify an emergency and initiate timely and effective response action, be able to quickly respond and repair damages to minimize system downtime), and how access to the plan is limited. Plans should be numbered for control. Recipients should sign and date a statement that includes their (1) CCP number, (2) agreement not to reproduce the CCP, and (3) they have read the CCP.

CCPs do not necessarily need to be one document. They may consist of an overview document, individual Emergency Action Procedures, check lists, additions to existing operations manuals, appendices, etc. There may be separate, more detailed plans for specific incidents. There may be plans that do not include particularly sensitive information and those that do. Existing applicable documents should be referenced in the CCP.

2. Emergency Planning Process
   1. Planning Partnerships
      The planning process should include those parties who will need to help the IT sector in an emergency situation (e.g., first responders, law enforcement, public health officials, nearby utilities, local emergency planning committees, testing labs, etc.). Partnerships should track from the IT sector operation up through local, state, regional, and federal agencies, as applicable and appropriate, and could also document compliance with governmental requirements.
   2. General Emergency Response Policies, Procedures, Actions, Documents
      A short synopsis of the overall emergency management structure, how other industrial emergency response, contingency, and risk management plans fit into the CCP for IT sector emergencies, and applicable policies, procedures, actions plans, and reference documents should be cited. Policies should include interconnect agreements with adjacent communities and just how the CCP may affect them.
   3. Scenarios
      Use your Vulnerability Assessment (VA) findings to identify specific emergency action steps required for response, recovery, and remediation for applicable incident types. In Section V of this plan, specific emergency actions procedures addressing each of the incident types should be addressed.
   4. Emergency Response Plan—Policies
      A. System Specific Information
         In an emergency, IT sector industries need to have basic information for system personnel and external parties such as law enforcement, emergency responders, repair contractors/vendors, the media, and others. The information needs to be clearly formatted and readily accessible so system staff can find and distribute it quickly to those who may be involved in responding to the emergency. Basic information that may be presented in the emergency response plan are the system's ID number, system name, system address or location, directions to the system, population served, number of service connections, system owner, and information about the person in charge of managing the emergency. Distribution maps, detailed plant drawings, site plans, source/storage/production energy locations, and operations manuals may be attached to this plan as appendices or referenced.

    B. PWS ID, Owner, Contact Person

    C. Population served and service connections

    D. System Components

        Conduits and constructed conveyances

        Physical barriers

        Electronic, computer, or other automated systems that are utilized by the IT Sector

        Emergency power generators (onsite and portable)

        The operation and maintenance of such system components

5. Chain-of-Command Chart developed in Coordination with Local Emergency Planning Committee (internal and/or External Emergency Responders, or both)

    A. Contact Name

    B. Organization and Emergency Response Responsibility

    C. Telephone number(s) (hardwire, cell phones, faxes, e-mail)

    D. State 24-hour Emergency Communications Center Telephone

6. Communications Procedures: Who, What, When

During most emergencies, it will be necessary to quickly notify a variety of parties both internal and external to the financial service sector entity. Using the Chain-of-Command Chart and all appropriate personnel from the lists below, indicate who activates the plan, the order in which notification occurs, and the members of the Emergency Response Team. All contact information should be available for routine updating and readily available. The following lists are not intended to be all inclusive—they should be adapted to your specific needs.

    A. Internal Notification Lists

        Operations Dispatch

        IT Sector Manager

        Data (IT) Manager

        Maintenance Manager

        Other

    B. Local Notification

        Head of local government (i.e., Mayor, City Manager, Chairman of Board, etc.)

        Public Safety Officials—Fire, Local Law Enforcement (LLE), Police, EMS, Safety if a malevolent act is suspected LLE should be immediately notified and in turn will notify the FBI, if required. The FBI is the primary agency for investigating sabotage.

        Other Government Entities: Health, Schools, Parks, Finance, Electric, etc.

C. External Notification Lists
   State Department of Environmental Quality (DEQ)
   USEPA/USDOE/DHS/FCC
   State Police
   State Health Department (lab)
   Critical customers (Special considerations for hospitals, federal, state and
       country government centers, etc).
   Service Aid
   Mutual Aid
   Commercial customers not previously notified

D. Public/Media Notification: When and How to Communicate
   Effective communications is a key element of emergency response, and a
   media or communications plan is essential to good communications. Be
   prepared by organizing basic facts about the crisis and your chemical system. Develop key messages to use with the media that are clear, brief, and
   accurate. Make sure your messages are carefully planned and have been
   coordinated with local and state officials. Considerations should be given
   to establishing protocols for both field and office staff to respectfully defer
   questions to the utility spokesperson.
       Be prepared to list geographic boundaries of the affected area, (e.g., west
   of highway a, east of highway b, north of highway c, and south of highway d
   to ensure the public clearly understand the system boundaries).

E. Personnel Safety
   This should provide direction as to how operations staff, emergency responders, and the public should respond to a potential toxic chemical
   release, including facility evacuation, personnel accountability, proper Personnel Protective Equipment as dictated by the Risk Management Program,
   and whether the nearby public should be "in-place sheltered" or evacuated.

F. Equipment
   The ERP should identify equipment that can obviate or significantly lessen
   the impact of terrorist attacks or other intentional actions on the public
   health and protect the safety and supply of communities and individuals.
   The IT sector facility should maintain an updated inventory of current
   equipment and repair parts for normal maintenance work.
       Because of the potential for extensive or catastrophic damage that could
   result from a malevolent act, additional equipment sources should be identified for the acquisition and installation of equipment and repair parts
   in excess of normal usage. A certain number of "long-lead" procurement
   equipment should be inventoried and the vendor information for such

unique and critical equipment maintained. In addition, mutual aid agreements with other industries, and the equipment available under the agreement, should be addressed. Inventories of current equipment, repair parts, and associated vendors should be indicated.

G. Property Protection

A determination should be made as to what IT sector producing, processing, distribution operation/facility should be immediately "locked down," specific access control procedures implemented, initial security perimeter established, a possible secondary malevolent event considered. The initial act may be a divisionary act.

H. Training, Exercises, and Drills

Emergency response training is essential. The purpose of the training program is to inform employees of what is expected of them during an emergency situation. The level of training on a CCP directly affects how well a financial service sector facility's employees can respond to an emergency. This may take the form of orientation scenarios, table-top workshops, functional exercises, etc.

I. Assessment

To evaluate the overall CCP's effectiveness and to ensure that procedures and practices developed under the CCP are adequate and are being implemented, IT sector industry staff should audit the program on a periodic basis.

7. Emergency Action Procedures (EAPs)

These are detailed procedures used in the event of an operation emergency or malevolent act. EAPs may be applicable across many different emergencies and are typically common core elements of the overall municipality Emergency Response Plan (ERP) (e.g., responsibilities, notifications lists, security procedures, etc.) and can be referenced.

a. Event classification/severity of emergency

b. Responsibilities of emergency director

c. Responsibilities of incident commander

d. Emergency Operations Center (EOC) activation

e. Division internal communications and reporting

f. External communications and notifications

g. Emergency telephone list (division internal contacts)

h. Emergency telephone list (off-site responders, agencies, state 24-hour emergency phone number, and others to be notified)

i. Mutual Aid Agreements

j. Contact list of available emergency contractor services/equipment

    k. Emergency equipment list (including inventory for each facility)

    l. Security and access control during emergencies

    m. Facility evacuation and lockdown and personnel accountability

    n. Treatment and transport of injured personnel (including electrocution and petrochemical exposure)

    o. Petrochemical records—to compare against historical results for baseline

    p. List of available labs for emergency use

    q. Emergency sampling and analysis (petrochemical)

    r. Water use restrictions during emergencies

    s. Alternate temporary chemical supplies during emergencies

    t. Isolation plans for chemical supply, treatment, storage, and distribution systems

    u. Mitigation plans for neutralizing, flushing, and collecting spilled chemicals

    v. Protection of vital records during emergencies

    w. Record keeping and reporting (FCC, FEMA, DHS, DOT, OSHA, EPA, and other requirements; it is important to maintain accurate financial records of expenses associated with the emergency event for possible federal reimbursement)

    x. Emergency program training, drills/and tabletop exercises

    y. Assessment of emergency management plan and procedures

    z. Crime scene preservation training and plans

        aa. Communication Plans:

            Police

            Fire

            Local government

            Media

        bb. Administration and logistics, including EOC, when established

        cc. Equipment needs/maintenance of equipment

        dd. Recovery and restoration of operations

        ee. Emergency event closeout and recovery

8. Incident-Specific Emergency Action Procedures (EAPs)

Incident-Specific EAPs are action procedures that identify specific steps in responding to an operational emergency of malevolent act.

    a. General response to terrorist threats (other than bomb threat and incident-specific threats)

    b. Incident-specific response to man-made or technological emergencies

       Contamination event (articulated threat with unspecified materials)

       Contamination threat at a major event

Notification from health officials of potential contamination

Intrusion through supervisory control and data acquisition (SCADA)

c. Significant structural damage resulting from intentional act

d. Customer complaints

e. Severe weather response (snow, ice, temperature, lightning)

f. Flood response

g. Hurricane and/or tornado response

h. Fire response

i. Explosion response

j. Major vehicle accident response

k. Electrical power outage response

l. Water supply interruption response

m. Transportation accident response—barge, plane, train, semi-trailer/tanker

n. Contaminated/tampered with water treatment chemicals

o. Earthquake response

p. Disgruntled employee response (i.e., workplace violence)

q. Vandal response

r. Bomb threat response

s. Civil disturbance/riot/strike

t. Armed intruder response

u. Suspicious mail handling and reporting

9. Next Steps

a. Plan review and approval

b. Practice and plan to update (as necessary, once every year recommended)

Training requirements

Who is responsible for conducting training, exercises, and emergency drills?

Update and assessment requirements

Incident-specific requirements

c. Annexes

Facility and location information

Facility maps

Facility drawings

Facility descriptions/layout

10. References and Links

a. Department of Homeland Security—http://www.dhs/gov/dhspublic

b. Environmental Protection Agency—http://www.epa.gov

c. Federal Emergency Management Agency—http://ww.fema.gov

d. Local Emergency Planning Committees—http://www.epa.gov/ceppo/ep clist.htm

THE BOTTOM LINE

Because industrial emergencies (in less than extreme conditions) can seriously affect the surrounding community and environment, and because poor planning and/or panic can only make a bad situation worse, and can also lead to additional injury and death, your role as IT sector manager in emergency response is doubly important. A crisis out of hand can easily devastate a community—and your organization is (or should be) an active member of your community. By ensuring less than effective emergency response, IT site managers endanger not only themselves and their organizations but also endanger their organization's community and standing as well.

The real bottom line is that even well-implemented cybersecurity structures and plans may not prevent all breaches of a business' data defenses, so it is imperative to have procedures in place to respond to security breaches when they occur.

REFERENCES AND RECOMMENDED READING

Brauer, R. L. (1994). *Safety and Health for Engineers.* New York: Van Nostrand Reinhold.

CoVan J. (1995). *Safety Engineering.* New York: John Wiley and Sons.

DHS (2009). *National Infrastructure Protection Plan.* Retrieved 05/11/17 @http://www.dhs.gov/ xlibrary/assets/NIPP.Plan.pdf.

DHS (2003). The National Strategy for the Physical Protection of Critical Infrastructures and Key Assets. Accessed @ https://www.dhs.gov/xlibrary/assets/physical_Strat.

DHS (2013). Homeland Security Directive 7: Critical Infrastructure Identification, Prioritization, and Protection accessed @ https://www.dihs.gov/xabout/laws/ gc_1214597989952.shtm.

DHS (2016). *Information Technology Sector—An Annex to the National Infrastructure Protection Plan.* Washington, DC: Department of Homeland Security.

Healy, R. J. (1969). *Emergency and Disaster Planning.* New York: Wiley.

Office of the Federal Register, 29 CFR 1910.120. Washington, DC: Office of the Federal Register, 1987.

Planning Guide and Checklist for Hazardous Materials Contingency Plans. FEMA-10, Federal Emergency Management Agency, Washington, DC, July 1981.

Safety and Health Requirements Manual, rev. ed. EM 385-1-1, U.S. Army Corps of Engineers, Washington, DC, October 1987.

Smith, A. J. (1980). *Managing Hazardous Substances Accidents.* New York: McGraw-Hill.

Spellman, F. R. (1997). *A Guide to Compliance for Process Safety Management Planning (PSM/ RMP).* Lancaster, PA: Technomic Publishing Company.

USDOE (2008). *Emergency Support Function #12—Energy Annex*. Washington, DC: U.S. Department of Energy.

U.S. Department of Energy (2010). *Energy Sector-Specific Plan: An Annex to the National Infrastructure Protection Plan*. Washington, DC: USDOE.

USEPA (2002). *Water Utility Response, Recovery & Remediation Guidance for Man-made and/or Technological Emergencies*. Washington, DC: United States Environmental Protection Agency.

USEPA (2003). *Large Water System Emergency Response Plan Outline: Guidance to Assist Community Water Systems in Complying with the Public Health Security and Bioterrorism Preparedness and Response Act of 2002*. EPA 810-F-03-007 accessed 6/2006 @ www.epa. gov/safewater/security. Washington, DC: United States Environmental Protection Agency.

9

Security Techniques and Hardware

Protection of employees and members of the public who visit any facility is a complex and challenging responsibility. It is also one of the company's top priorities.

If your facility still uses keyed locks, does anyone in your facility control those keys? Does anyone in your facility know who has keys? Does anyone know how many keys have been issued? Is there a recorded record of each key that has been issued?

> I know your password . . . therefore, you belong to me.

CYBER PHYSICAL SECURITY PROVISIONS

Whenever we walk into any business or other pedestrian entry IT entity, we usually pay little attention to our surroundings. Why? Well, we become used to the surroundings and the ambience through our continued usage of such a place or from the perusal of such services. And, more than likely we are in a hurry, as usual, and surroundings are not that important to us; instead, the business at hand is much more important.

Let's say, on the other hand, we are part of that group of people who take it all in, no matter where or when. Well, if this is the case, when we walk into the business building there are a few things that stand out to us. First, it is usually busy, crowded, and hectic. The standard cashier greets us as we stand to pay for whatever goods we plan to buy. While the cashier totals our purchases we might glance to our right or left or above the place we are standing; there we would probably notice the CCTV security cameras here and there with some pointed right at us. And we presume that the teller behind the teller window is in close proximity and easy reach of an alarm or panic button, which will sound the alarm and hopefully send security and the police scrambling to respond.

These security devices are obvious to us or at least we assume they are present. However, it is what we do not see, anticipate, expect, comprehend, or assume is present (or should be) that is really what the emphasis is about herein. Note that there are many devices and security systems that are available to protect IT sector assets not open to pedestrian traffic and fewer available to IT facilities or facilities that use IT services that are open to pedestrian traffic (malls, stores, music halls, sports stadium, businesses, etc.). In locations where a variety of security devices are viable, many of are not readily visible to most people. However, again, keep in mind that some of the devices and security techniques discussed in the following are only viable in IT assets that are not open to pedestrian traffic.

The bottom line: the physical security of any facility depends on a number of security decisions that can be identified through a comprehensive risk-management process. The objective of risk management is to identify an achievable level of protection for a company that is as comprehensive as closely as possible to the level of risk without exceeding the risk. The achievable level of protection that should be sought and pursued dealing with minimizing and safeguarding printed materials with sensitive information; ensuring mail security; disposing of trash securely; disposal of electronic equipment securely; and training employees in physical facility security procedures. In this chapter our focus is on the latter, on facility security procedures. The point is we can't expect IT sector equipment and operations to be secure unless the physical structure housing such items and functions are secure.

THE MULTIPLE-BARRIER APPROACH

Ideally, in a perfect world, all IT sector physical sites/facilities/assets would be secured in a layered fashion (aka the multiple barrier approach). Layered security systems are vital. Using the protection "in depth" principle, requiring that an adversary defeat several protective barriers or security layers to accomplish its goal, the financial service sector physical infrastructure can be made more secure. Protection in depth is a term commonly used by the military to describe security measures that reinforce one another, masking the defense mechanisms from view of intruders, and allowing the defender time to respond to intrusion or attack.

A prime example of the use of the multibarrier approach to ensure security and safety is demonstrated by the practices of the bottled water industry. In the aftermath of 9/11 and the increased emphasis on homeland security, a shifted paradigm of national security and vulnerability awareness has emerged. Recall that in the immediate aftermath of the 9/11 tragedies, emergency responders and others responded quickly and worked to exhaustion. In addition to the emergency responders, bottled water companies responded immediately by donating several million bottles of water to the crews at the crash sites in New York, at the Pentagon, and in Pennsylvania. International Bottled Water Association (IBWA 2004) reports that "within hours of the first attack, bottled water was delivered where it mattered most; to emergency personnel on the scene who required ample water to stay hydrated as they worked to rescue victims and clean up debris" (p. 2).

Bottled water companies continued to provide bottled water to responders and rescuers at the 9/11 sites throughout the post-event(s) process(es). These patriotic actions by the bottled water companies, however, beg the question: How do we ensure the safety and security of the bottled water provided to anyone? IBWA (2004) has the answer: using a multibarrier approach, along with other principles, will enhance the safety and security of bottled water. IBWA (2004) describes its multibarrier approach as follows:

> **A multi-barrier approach**—Bottled water products are produced utilizing a multi-barrier approach, from source to finished product, that helps prevent possible harmful contaminants (physical, chemical or microbiological) from adulterating the finished product as well as storage, production, and transportation equipment. Measures in a multi-barrier approach may include source protection, source monitoring, reverse osmosis, distillation, filtration, ozonation or ultraviolet (UV) light. Many of the steps in a multi-barrier system may be effective in safeguarding bottled water from microbiological and other contamination. Piping in and out of plants, as well as storage silos and water tankers are also protected and maintained through sanitation procedures. In addition, bottled water products are bottled in a controlled, sanitary environment to prevent contamination during the filling operation. (p. 3)

In IT sector infrastructure security protection in depth is used to describe a layered security approach that is not open to pedestrian traffic. A protection in depth strategy uses several forms of security techniques and/or devices against an intruder and does not rely on one single defensive mechanism to protect infrastructure. By implementing multiple layers of security, a hole or flaw in one layer is covered by the other layers. An intruder will have to intrude through each layer without being detected in the process—the layered approach implies that no matter how an intruder attempts to accomplish his goal, he will encounter effective elements of the physical protection system.

For example, as depicted in figure 9.1, an effective security layering approach requires that an adversary penetrate multiple, separate barriers to gain entry to a critical TARGET at an IT sector facility. As shown in Figure 9.1, protection in depth (multiple layers of security) helps to ensure that the security system remains effective in the event of a failure or an intruder bypassing a single layer of security.

Again, as shown in figure 9.1, layered security starts with the outer perimeter (the fence—the first line of physical security) of the facility and goes inward to the facility, the buildings, structures, other individual assets, and finally to the contents of those buildings—the TARGETs.

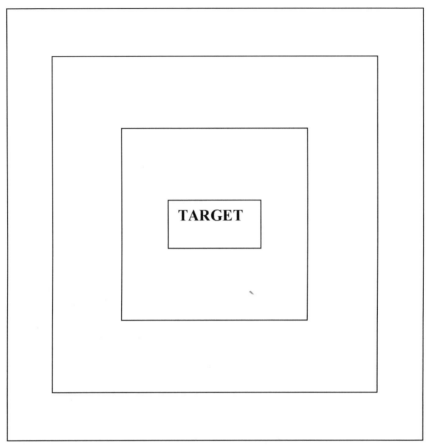

FIGURE 9.1
Layered approach to security for non-pedestrian traffic IT facilities.

The area between the outer perimeter and structures or buildings is known as the site. This open site area provides an incomparable opportunity for early identification of an unauthorized intruder and initiation of early warning/response. This open space area is commonly used to calculate the standoff distance; that is, it is the distance between the outside perimeter (public areas to the fence) to TARGET or critical assets (buildings/structures) inside the perimeter (inside the fence line—the restricted access area).

The open area, between perimeter fence and TARGET (e.g., operations center), if properly outfitted with various security devices, can also provide layered protection against intruders. For example, lighting is a deterrent. Based on personal experience, an open area within the plant site that is almost as well lighted at night as would be expected during daylight hours is the rule of thumb. In addition, strategically placed motion detectors along with crash barriers at perimeter gate openings and in front of vital structures are also recommended. Armed, mobile guards who roam the interior of the plant site on a regular basis provide the ultimate in site area security.

The next layer of physical security is the outside wall of the target structure(s) itself. Notwithstanding door, window, and/or skylight entry, walls prevent most intruders from easy entry. If doors can only be entered using card reader access, security is shored up or enhanced to an extent. The same can be said for windows and skylights that are fashioned small enough to prohibit normal human entry. These same "weak" spots in buildings can be bastioned with break-proof or reinforced security glass.

The final layer of security is provided by properly designed interior features of buildings. Examples of these types of features include internal doors and walls, equipment cages, and backup or redundant equipment.

In the preceding discussion, the conditions described referred to perfect world conditions; that is, to those conditions that we "would want" (i.e., the security manager's proverbial wish list) to be incorporated into the design and installation of new financial service sector infrastructure. Since 9/11, however, many of the peripheral (fence line) measures described above have become more difficult to incorporate into financial service sector infrastructure. This is not to say that IT sector sites and facilities do not have fence lines or fences; many of them do. These fences are designed to keep vandals, thieves, and trespassers out. The problem is not only the fact that many of these facilities were constructed several years ago before urban encroachment literally encircled the many sites, allowing, at present, little room for security stand backs or setbacks to be incorporated into electrical power stations, plants, and/or critical equipment locations. Based on personal observation, many of these fences face busy city streets or closely abut structures outside the fence line. The point is that when one sits down to plan a security upgrade, these factors must be taken into account.

The fly in the ointment for the IT sector assets is accessibility. People who use IT services in person need to enter the facilities to conduct their business. Thus, the multiple barrier approach to security in a mall, for example, is unrealistic, at best.

Managers of IT sector infrastructure have four primary security areas to manage. These security areas are listed and described below.

- Physical Security—in the IT sector, where practicable, physical security techniques and practices has the most effect at "fenced" locations. At such locations, a systems approach is best, where detection, assessment, communication, and response are planned and supported by resources, procedures, and policies.
- Cyber/Information Technology Security—only the use of key operating systems that have been properly vetted and scrubbed of alleged Chinese and/or Russian Trojan

horses hacked into the North American electrical grid is important. The only positive way to ensure the security of the North American grid is to disconnect its cyber and other digital systems from the Internet. This step is impractical at the present time, but points to the need to conduct frequent audits of the system and install firewall protection in digital components and other systems to prevent hacking. Frequent third-party penetration testing is advised.

- Employment Screening—mitigates the threat from the enemy at the water cooler (inside the organization). We are always amazed whenever we conduct security audits for various companies. Often, a simple check such as reviewing an employee's driving record often reveals that the employee has no license, is driving on a suspended license, or has a horrific driving record. Hiring standards and pre-employment background investigations may help ensure the trustworthiness and reliability of personnel who have unescorted access to critical facilities.

- Protecting Potentially Sensitive Information—the old saying that goes—a secret can best be held between three people so long as two of the three are dead—makes the point that reducing the likelihood that information could be used by those intent on disrupting operations or causing death destruction in IT service sector sites is crucial. Information should only be shared within an organization on a need-to-know basis only.

For existing facilities, security upgrades should be based on the results generated from the vulnerability assessment, which characterizes and prioritizes those assets that may be targeted. Those vulnerabilities identified must be protected.

In the following sections, various security hardware and/or devices are described. These devices serve the main purpose of providing security against physical and/or digital intrusion. That is, they are designed to delay and deny intrusion and are normally coupled with detection and assessment technology. Possible additional security measures, based on the vulnerability assessment that may be recommended (covered in this text) include the following (NAERC, 2002):

- Electronic security
- Closing non-essential perimeter and internal portals
- Physical barriers such as bollards or Jersey walls
- Fencing
- Lighting
- Security surveys
- Vulnerability assessments
- Availability of security resources

- General personnel and security officer training
- Law enforcement liaison
- Ensure availability of essential spare parts (machines, repair parts, wire, pipe, valves, transformers, etc.) for critical facilities

Keep in mind, however, and as mentioned previously, no matter the type of security device or system employed, financial service sector systems cannot be made immune to all possible intrusions or attacks. Whenever a facility safety/security manager tells us that he or she has secured their site 100 percent, we are reminded of Schneier's (2000) view of security: "You can't defend. You can't prevent. The only thing you can do is detect and respond." Simply, when it comes to making "anything" absolutely secure from intrusion or attack, there is inherently, or otherwise, no silver bullet.

In the next section, security hardware devices are discussed in detail. Before we describe these hardware devices, keep in mind that in addition to security hardware devices to help protect and monitor IT services sector assets there are a few employee practices and actions that can be taken to protect IT services assets. For example, when a commercial asset computer system fails and must be disposed of, how is it disposed of? Is there a procedure or practice in place to prevent the valuable information on the system's hard drive from being pulled from a trash heap or from a dumpster dive and used by potential enemies? Are shredders used? Are they state of the art shredders that prevent scraps from being reassembled by enemies? Are building cleaning crews properly vetted and supervised? Do you have a team that routinely inspects suspended ceilings for bugs, cameras, and listening recorders? Do you have key stroke reader capability; that is, can you record what messages are being sent by employees? Do you routinely check hard-wired phone lines? Have you removed all door signs that tell anyone what is on the other side of the room? Have you trained your employees to be slightly suspicious of just about anything and everything? Have you opened your manholes lately to see what is inside?

All of these practices just mentioned do not require security hardware such as barriers, motion detectors, fences, locks, biometric systems, video cameras, armed guards, electrified fences, and so forth. What they require instead is common sense, awareness, and alert and engaged supervisors and employees. The point is what is heard at the water cooler is sometimes more significant than any security alarm apparatus can provide.

Again, keep in mind that many of the security hardware devices described in the following are only applicable to non-pedestrian facilities only; we simply cannot barricade or fence in, for example, sports arenas and shopping malls.

SECURITY HARDWARE DEVICES[1]

USEPA (2005) groups infrastructure security devices or products described below into four general categories:

- Physical asset monitoring and control devices
- Cyber protection devices
- Communication/integration
- Environmental monitoring devices

Physical Asset Monitoring and Control Devices

Aboveground, Outdoor Equipment Enclosures

IT services sector facilities and sites can consist of multiple structural components spread over a wide area and typically include a centralized production, storage, and distribution centers, as well component supply facilities that are typically distributed at multiple locations throughout the area. One of the primary reasons for constructing structural components that house operational equipment aboveground eliminates the safety risks associated with confined space entry, which is often required for the maintenance of equipment located below ground. In addition, space restrictions often limit the amount of equipment that can be located inside, and there are concerns that some types of equipment (such as backflow prevention devices—to prevent chemicals and fuel wastes from entering plant and offsite potable water systems) can, under certain circumstances, discharge fuel slurry or waste mixtures that could flood pits, vaults, or equipment rooms. In regard to electrical power, electrical substations are not usually suited for underground installation. Therefore, many pieces of critical electrical manufacturing equipment are located outdoors and aboveground in configurations that are properly fenced, insulated, or isolated to prevent accidental electrical shock or short circuits/fires in equipment.

Experience demonstrates that many different system components can be and are often installed outdoors and aboveground, many of them controlled by wireless communication devices. Examples of the types of components that could be included in commercial facilities or its ancillaries are:

- Backflow prevention devices
- Air release and control valves
- Pressure vacuum breakers
- Oil and gas pumps and motors
- Petrochemical storage and feed equipment
- Meters
- Sampling equipment

- Instrumentation
- Electrical substations
- Oil and natural gas pipelines

One of the most effective security measures for protecting aboveground equipment, where feasible, is to place it inside a building or exterior fenced structure. When/where this is not possible, enclosing the equipment or parts of the equipment using some sort of commercial or homemade add-on structure may help to prevent tampering with the equipment. These types of add-on structures or enclosures, which are designed to protect people and animals from electrocution and to protect equipment both from the elements and from unauthorized access or tampering, typically consist of a box-like fenced structure that is placed over or around the entire component, or over/around critical parts of the component (i.e., valves, etc.), and is then secured to delay or prevent intruders from tampering with the equipment. The enclosures are typically locked or otherwise anchored to a solid foundation, which makes it difficult for unauthorized personnel to remove the enclosure and access the equipment.

Standardized aboveground enclosures are available in a wide variety of materials, sizes, and configurations. Many options and security features are also available for each type of enclosure, and this allows system operators the flexibility to customize an enclosure for a specific application and/or price range. In addition, most manufacturers can custom-design enclosures if standard, off-the-shelf enclosures do not meet a user's needs.

Many of these enclosures are designed to meet certain standards. For example, the American Society of Sanitary Engineers (ASSE) has developed Standard #1060, *Performance Requirements for Outdoor Enclosures for Backflow Prevention Assemblies*. If an enclosure will be used to house backflow preventer, this standard specifies the acceptable construction materials for the enclosure, as well as the performance requirements that the enclosure should meet, including specifications for freeze protection, drainage, air inlets, access for maintenance, and hinge requirements. ASSE #1060 also states that the enclosure should be lockable to enhance security.

Electrical substation and electrical equipment enclosures must meet the requirements and recommendations of various OHSA standards, National Fire Protection Association (NFPA), National Electrical Codes (NEC), Institute of Electrical and Electronic Engineers (IEEE), and local code requirements.

Equipment enclosures can generally be categorized into one of four main configurations, which include:

- One piece, drop over enclosures
- Hinged or removable top enclosures

- Sectional enclosures
- Shelters with access locks

All enclosures, including those with integral floors, must be secured to a foundation to prevent them from being moved or removed. Un- or poorly-anchored enclosures may be blown off the equipment being protected, or may be defeated by intruders. In either case, this may result in the equipment beneath the enclosure becoming exposed and damaged. Therefore, ensuring that the enclosure is securely anchored will increase the security of the protected equipment.

The three basic types of foundations that can be used to anchor the aboveground equipment enclosure are concrete footers, concrete slabs-on-grade, or manufactured fiberglass pads. The most common types of foundations utilized for equipment enclosures are standard or slab-on-grade footers; however, local climate and soil conditions may dictate whether either of these types of foundations can be used. These foundations can be either precast or poured in place at the installation site. Once the foundation is installed and properly cured, the equipment enclosure is bolted or anchored to the foundation to secure it in place.

An alternative foundation, specifically for use with smaller Hot Box® enclosures, is a manufactured fiberglass pad known as the Glass Pad™. The Glass Pad™ has the center cut out so that it can be dropped directly over the piece of equipment being enclosed. Once the pad is set level on the ground, it is backfilled over a two-inch flange located around its base. The enclosure is then placed on top of the foundation, and is locked in place with either a staple- or a slotted-anchor, depending on the enclosure configuration.

One of the primary attributes of a security enclosure is its strength and resistance to breaking and penetration. Accordingly, the materials from which the enclosure is constructed will be important in determining the strength of the enclosure, and thus its usefulness for security applications. Enclosures are typically manufactured for either fiberglass or aluminum. With the exception of the one piece, drop-over enclosure, which is typically fabricated from fiberglass, each configuration described above can be constructed from either material. In addition, enclosures can be custom-manufactured from polyurethane, galvanized steel, or stainless steel. Galvanized or stainless steel is often offered as an exterior layer, or "skin," for an aluminum enclosure. Although they are typically utilized in underground applications, precast concrete structures can also be used as aboveground equipment enclosures. However, precast structures are much heavier and more difficult to maneuver than are their fiberglass and aluminum counterparts. Concrete is also brittle, and that can be a security concern, however, products can be applied to concrete structures to add strength and minimize security risks (i.e., epoxy coating). Because precast concrete structures can be purchased from any concrete producers, this document does not identify specific vendors for these types of products.

In addition to the construction materials, enclosure walls can be configured or reinforced to give them added strength. Adding insulation is one option that can strengthen the structural characteristics of an enclosure; however, some manufacturers offer additional features to add strength to exterior walls. For example, while most enclosures are fabricated with a flat wall construction, some vendors manufacture fiberglass shelters with ribbed exterior walls. These ribs increase the structural integrity of the wall and allow the fabrication of standard shelters up to twenty feet in length. Another vendor has developed a proprietary process that uses a series of integrated fiberglass beams that are placed throughout a foam inner core to tie together the interior and exterior walls and roof. Yet another vendor constructs aluminum enclosures with horizontal and vertical redwood beams for structural support.

Other security features that can be implemented on aboveground, outdoor equipment enclosures include locks, mounting brackets, tamper-resistant doors, and exterior lighting.

Active Security Barriers (Crash Barriers)

Terrorist vehicle attacks are on the rise. Consider the Halloween 2017 truck attack in New York City that killed eight and injured many. There are steps we can take to lessen the possibility of many of these attacks. For example, active security barriers (also known as crash barriers) are large structures that are placed in roadways at entrance and exit points to protect facilities to control vehicle access to these areas. These barriers are placed perpendicular to traffic to block the roadway so that the only way that traffic can pass the barrier is for the barrier to be moved out of the roadway. These types of barriers are typically constructed from sturdy materials, such as concrete or steel, such that vehicles cannot penetrate them. They are also designed at a certain height off the roadway so that vehicles cannot go over them.

The key difference between active security barriers, which include wedges, crash beams, gates, retractable bollards, and portable barricades and passive security barriers, which include non-moveable bollards, jersey barriers, and planters, is that active security barriers are designed so that they can be raised and lowered or moved out of the roadway easily to allow authorized vehicles to pass. Many of these types of barriers are designed so that they can be opened and closed automatically (i.e., mechanized gates, hydraulic wedge barriers), while others are easy to open and close manually (swing crash beams, manual gates). In contrast to active barriers, passive barriers are permanent, non-movable barriers, and thus they are typically used to protect the perimeter of a protected facility, such as sidewalks and other areas that do not require vehicular traffic to pass. Several of the major types of active security barriers such as wedge barriers, crash beams, gates, bollards, and portable/removable barricades are described below.

Wedge barriers are plated, rectangular steel buttresses approximately 2-3 feet high that can be raised and lowered from the roadway. When they are in the open position, they are flush with the roadway and vehicles can pass over them. However, when they are in the closed (armed) position, they project up from the road at a 45 degree angle, with the upper end pointing toward the oncoming vehicle and the base of the barrier away from the vehicle. Generally, wedge barriers are constructed from heavy gauge steel or concrete that contains an impact-dampening iron rebar core that is strong and resistant to breaking or cracking, thereby allowing them to withstand the impact from a vehicle attempting to crash through them. In addition, both of these materials help to transfer the energy of the impact over the barrier's entire volume, thus helping to prevent the barrier from being sheared off its base. In addition, because the barrier is angled away from traffic, the force of any vehicle impacting the barrier is distributed over the entire surface of the barrier and is not concentrated at the base, which helps prevent the barrier from breaking off at the base. Finally, the angle of the barrier helps hang up any vehicles attempting to drive over it.

Wedge barriers can be fixed or portable. Fixed wedge barriers can be mounted on the surface of the roadway ("surface-mounted wedges") or in a shallow mount in the road's surface, or they can be installed completely below the road surface. Surface-mounted wedge barricades operate by rising from a flat position on the surface of the roadway, while shallow-mount wedge barriers rise from their resting position just below the road surface. In contrast, below-surface wedge barriers operate by rising from beneath the road surface. Both the shallow-mounted and surface-mounted barriers require little or no excavation, and thus do not interfere with buried utilities. All three barrier mounting types project above the road surface and block traffic when they are raised into the armed position. Once they are disarmed and lowered, they are flush with the road thereby allowing traffic to pass. Portable wedge barriers can be moved into place after the barrier has been set into place.

Installing rising wedge barriers requires preparation of the road surface. Installing surface-mounted wedges does not require that the road be excavated, however, the road surface must intact and strong enough to allow the bolts anchoring the wedge to the road surface to attach properly. Shallow-mount and below-surface wedge barricades require excavation of a pit that is large enough to accommodate the wedge structure, as well as any arming/disarming mechanisms. Generally, the bottom of the excavation pit is lined with gravel to allow for drainage. Areas not sheltered from rain or surface runoff can be installed with a gravity drain or self priming pump. Table 9.1 lists the pros and cons of wedge barriers.

Table 9.1.   Pros and Cons of Wedge Barriers

Pros	Cons
Can be surface-mounted or completely installed below the roadway surface.	Installation below the surface of the roadway will require construction that may interfere with buried utilities.
Wedge barriers have a quick response time (normally 3.5-10.5 seconds, but barrier can be 1–3 seconds) in emergency situations. Because emergency activation of the barrier causes more wear and tear on the system than does normal activation, it is recommended for use only in true emergency situations.	Regular maintenance is needed to keep wedge fully operational.
Surface or shallow-mount wedge barricades can be utilized in locations with a high water table and/or corrosive soils.	Improper use of the system may result in authorized vehicles being hung up by the barrier and damaged. Guards must be trained to use the system properly to ensure that this does not happen. Safety technologies may also be installed to reduce the risk of the wedge activating under an authorized vehicle.
All three wedge barrier designs have a high crash rating, thereby allowing them to be employed for higher security applications.	
These types of barrier are extremely visible, which may deter potential intruders.	

Source: USEPA, 2005.

Crash beam barriers consist of aluminum beams that can be opened or closed across the roadway. While there are several different crash beam designs, every crash beam system consists of an aluminum beam that is supported on each side by a solid footing or buttress, which is typically constructed from concrete, steel, or some other strong material. Beams typically contain an interior steel cable (typically at least one inch in diameter) to give the beam added strength and rigidity. The beam is connected by a heavy-duty hinge or other mechanism to one of the footings so that it can swing or rotate out of the roadway when it is open, and can swing back across the road when it is in the closed (armed) position, blocking the road and inhibiting access by unauthorized vehicles. The non-hinged end of the beam can be locked into its footing, thus providing anchoring for the beam on both sides of the road and increasing the beam's resistance to any vehicles attempting to penetrate it. In addition, if the crash beam is hit by a vehicle, the aluminum beam transfers the impact energy to the interior cable, which in turn transfers the impact energy through the footings and into their foundation, thereby minimizing the chance that the impact will snap the beam and allow the intruding vehicle to pass through.

Crash beam barriers can employ drop-arm, cantilever, or swing beam designs. Drop-arm crash beams operate by raising and lowering the beam vertically across the road. Cantilever crash beams are projecting structures that are opened and closed by extending the beam from the hinge buttress to the receiving buttress located on the opposite side of the road. In the swing beam design, the beam is hinged to the buttress such that it swings horizontally across the road. Generally, swing beam and cantilever designs are used at locations where a vertical lift beam is impractical. For example, the swing beam or cantilever designs are utilized at entrances and exits with overhangs, trees, or buildings that would physically block the operation of the drop-arm beam design.

Installing any of these crash beam barriers involves the excavation of a pit approximately 48 inches deep for both the hinge and the receiver footings. Due to the depth of excavation, the site should be inspected for underground utilities before digging begins. Table 9.2 lists the pros and cons of crash beams.

In contrast to wedge barriers and crash beams, which are typically installed separately from a fence line, *gates* are often integrated units of a perimeter fence or wall around a facility.

Gates are basically movable pieces of fencing that can be opened and closed across a road. When the gate is in the closed (armed) position, the leaves of the gate lock into steel buttresses that are embedded in concrete foundations located on both sides of the roadway, thereby blocking access to the roadway. Generally, gate barricades are constructed from a combination of heavy gauge steel and aluminum that can absorb an impact from vehicles attempting to ram through them. Any remaining impact en-

Table 9.2. Pros and Cons of Crash Beams

Pros	Cons
Requires little maintenance, while providing long-term durability.	Crash beams have a slower response time (normally 9.5–15.3 seconds, but can be reduced to 7–10 seconds in emergency situations) than do other types of active security barriers, such as wedge barriers. Because emergency activation of the barrier causes more wear and tear on the system than does normal activation, it is recommended for use only in true emergency situations.
No excavation is required to the roadway itself to install crash beams.	All three crash beam designs possess a low crash rating relative to other types of barriers, such as wedge barriers, and thus they typically are used for lower security applications. Certain crash barriers may not be visible to oncoming traffic and therefore may require additional lighting and/or other warning markings to reduce the potential for traffic to accidentally run into the beam.

Source: USEPA, 2005.

ergy not absorbed by the gate material is transferred to the steel buttresses and their concrete foundation.

Gates can utilize a cantilever, linear, or swing design. Cantilever gates are projecting structures that operate by extending the gate from the hinge footing across the roadway to the receiver footing. A linear gate is designed to slide across the road on tracks via a rack and pinion drive mechanism. Swing gates are hinged so that they can swing horizontally across the road.

Installation of the cantilever, linear, or swing gate designs described above involve the excavation of a pit approximately 48 inches deep for both the hinge and receiver footings to which the gates are attached. Due to the depth of excavation, the site should be inspected for underground utilities before digging begins. Table 9.3 lists the pros and cons of gates.

Bollards are vertical barriers at least 3 feet tall and 0.4 to 2 feet in diameter that are typically set 4 to 5 feet apart from each other so that they block vehicles from passing between them. Smaller bollards, usually 4 inches diameter and pipe filled with concrete, are installed in parking areas to prevent vehicles from striking walls or windows or to protect walkway areas. Bollards can either be fixed in place, removable, or retractable. Fixed and removable bollards are passive barriers that are typically used along building perimeters or on sidewalks to prevent vehicles from them, while allowing pedestrians to pass them. In contrast to passive bollards, retractable bollards are active security barriers that can easily be raised and lowered to allow vehicles to pass

Table 9.3.   Pros and Cons of Gates

Pros	Cons
All three gate designs possesses an intermediate crash rating, thereby allowing them to be utilized for medium to higher security applications.	Gates have a slower response time intermediate crash rating, thereby (normally 10-15 seconds, but can be reduced to 7-10 seconds in emergency situations) than do other types of active security barriers, such as wedge barriers. Because emergency activation of the barrier causes more wear and tear on the system than does normal activation, it is recommended for use only in true emergency situations.
Requires very little maintenance.	
Can be tailored to blend in with perimeter fencing.	
Gate construction requires no roadway excavation.	
Cantilever gates are useful for roads with high crowns or drainage gutters.	
These types of barriers are extremely visible, which may deter intruders.	
Gates can also be used to control pedestrian traffic.	

Source: USEPA, 2005.

between them. Thus, they can be used in driveways or on roads to control vehicular access. When the bollards are raised, they protect above the road surface and block the roadway; when they are lowered, they sit flush with the road surface, and thus allow traffic to pass over them. Retractable bollards are typically constructed from steel or other materials that have a low weight-to-volume ratio so that they require low power to raise and lower. Steel is also more resistant to breaking than is a more brittle material, such as concrete, and is better able to withstand direct vehicular impact without breaking apart.

Retractable bollards are installed in a trench dug across a roadway—typically at an entrance or gate. Installing retractable bollards requires preparing the road surface. Depending on the vendor, bollards can be installed either in a continuous slab of concrete, or in individual excavations with concrete poured in place. The required excavation for a bollard is typically slightly wider and slightly deeper than the bollard height when extended aboveground. The bottom of the excavation is typically lined with gravel to allow drainage. The bollards are then connected to a control panel that controls the raising and lowering of the bollards. Installation typically requires mechanical, electrical, and concrete work; if utility personnel with these skills are available, then the utility can install the bollards themselves. Table 9.4 lists the pros and cons of retractable bollards.

Portable/removable barriers, which can include removable crash beams and wedge barriers, are mobile obstacles that can be moved in and out of position on a roadway. For example, a crash beam may be completely removed and stored off-site when it is not needed. An additional example would be wedge barriers that are equipped with wheels that can be removed after the barricade is towed into place.

When portable barricades are needed, they can be moved into position rapidly. To provide them with added strength and stability, they are typically anchored to buttress boxes that are located on either side of the road. These buttress boxes, which may or

Table 9.4. Pros and Cons of Retractable Bollards

Pros	Cons
Bollards have a quick response time (normally 3 to 10 seconds, but can be reduced to 1-3 seconds in emergency situations).	Bollard installations will require construction below the surface of the roadway, which may interfere with buried utilities.
Bollards have an intermediate crash rating, which allows them to be utilized for medium to higher security applications.	Some maintenance is needed to ensure the barrier is free to move up and down.
	The distance between bollards must be decreased (i.e., more bollards must be installed along the same perimeter) to make these systems effective against small vehicles (i.e., motorcycles).

Source: USEPA, 2005.

may not be permanent, are usually filled with sand, water, cement, gravel, or concrete to make them heavy and aid in stabilizing the portable barrier. In addition, these buttresses can help dissipate any impact energy from vehicles crashing into the barrier itself.

Because these barriers are not anchored into the roadway, they do not require excavation or other related construction for installation. In contrast, they can be assembled and made operational in a short period of time. The primary shortcoming to this type of design is that these barriers may move if they are hit by vehicles. Therefore, it is important to carefully assess the placement and anchoring of these types of barriers to ensure that they can withstand the types of impacts that may be anticipated at that location. Table 9.5 lists the pros and cons of portable/removable barricades.

Because the primary threat to active security barriers is that vehicles will attempt to crash through them, their most important attributes are their size, strength, and crash resistance. Other important features for an active security barrier are the mechanisms by which the barrier is raised and lowered to allow authorized vehicle entry, and other factors, such as weather resistance and safety features.

Alarms

An *alarm system* is a type of electronic monitoring system that is used to detect and respond to specific types of events—such as unauthorized access to an asset, or a possible fire. In chemical processing systems, alarms are also used to alert operators when process operating or monitoring conditions go out of preset parameters (i.e., process alarms). These types of alarms are primarily integrated with process monitoring and reporting systems (i.e., SCADA systems). Note that this discussion does not focus on alarm systems that are not related to a facility's processes.

Alarm systems can be integrated with fire detection systems, intrusion detection systems (IDSs), access control systems, or closed circuit television (CCTV) systems, such that these systems automatically respond when the alarm is triggered. For example, a smoke detector alarm can be set up to automatically notify the fire department

Table 9.5. Pros and Cons of Portable/Removable Barricades

Pros	Cons
Installing portable barricades requires no foundation or roadway excavation.	Portable barriers may move slightly when hit by a vehicle, resulting in a lower crash resistance.
Can be moved in and out of position in a short period of time.	Portable barricades typically require 7.75 to16.25 seconds to move into place, and thus they are considered to have a medium response time when compared with other active barriers.
Wedge barriers equipped with wheels can be easily towed into place.	
Minimal maintenance is needed to keep barriers fully operational.	

Source: USEPA, 2005.

when smoke is detected; or an intrusion alarm can automatically trigger cameras to turn on in a remote location so that personnel can monitor that location.

An alarm system consists of sensors that detect different types of events; an arming station that is used to turn the system on and off; a control panel that receives information, processes it, and transmits the alarm; and an annunciator that generates a visual and/or audible response to the alarm. When a sensor is tripped it sends a signal to a control panel, which triggers a visual or audible alarm and/or notifies a central monitoring station. A more complete description of each of the components of an alarm system is provided below.

Detection devices (also called *sensors*), are designed to detect a specific type of event (such as smoke, intrusion, etc.). Depending on the type of event they are designed to detect, sensors can be located inside or outside of the facility or other asset. When an event is detected, the sensors use some type of communication method (such as wireless radio transmitters, conductors, or cables) to send signals to the control panel to generate the alarm. For example, a smoke detector sends a signal to a control panel when it detects smoke.

Alarms use either normally closed (NC) or normally open (NO) electric loops, or "circuits," to generate alarm signals. These two types of circuits are discussed separately below.

In NC loops or circuits, all of the system's sensors and switches are connected in series. The contacts are "at rest" in the closed (on) position, and current continually passes through the system. However, when an event triggers the sensor, the loop is opened, breaking the flow of current through the system and triggering the alarm. NC switches are used more often than are NO switches because the alarm will be activated if the loop or circuit is broken or cut, thereby reducing the potential for circumventing the alarm. This is known as a "supervised" system.

In NO loops or circuits, all of the system's sensors and switches are connected in parallel. The contacts are "at rest" in the open (off) position, and no current passes through the system. However, when an event triggers the sensor, the loop is closed. This allows current to flow through the loop, powering the alarm. NO systems are not "supervised" because the alarm will not be activated if the loop or circuit is broken or cut. However, adding an end-of-line resistor to an NO loop will cause the system to alarm if tampering is detected.

An *arming station*, which is the main user interface with the security system, allows the user to arm (turn on), disarm (turn off), and communicate with the system. How a specific system is armed will depend on how it is used. For example, while IDSs can be armed for continuous operation (24 hours/day), they are usually armed and disarmed according to the work schedule at a specific location so that personnel going about their daily activities do not set off the alarms. In contrast, fire protection systems are typically armed 24hours/day.

A *control panel* receives information from the sensors and sends it to an appropriate location, such as to a central operations station or to a 24-hour monitoring facility. Once the alarm signal is received at the central monitoring location, personnel monitoring for alarms can respond (such as by sending security teams to investigate or by dispatching the fire department).

An *annunciator* responds to the detection of an event by emitting a signal. This signal may be visual, audible, electronic, or a combination of these three. For example, fire alarm signals will always be connected to audible annunciators, whereas intrusion alarms may not be.

Alarms can be reported locally, remotely, or both locally and remotely. Local and remotely- (centrally-) reported alarms are discussed in more detail below.

A *local alarm* emits a signal at the location of the event (typically using a bell or siren). A "local only" alarm emits a signal at the location of the event but does not transmit the alarm signal to any other location (i.e., it does not transmit the alarm to a central monitoring location). Typically, the purpose of a "local only" alarm is to frighten away intruders, and possibly to attract the attention of someone who might notify the proper authorities. Because no signal is sent to a central monitoring location, personnel can only respond to a local alarm if they are in the area and can hear and/or see the alarm signal.

Fire alarm systems must have local alarms, including both audible and visual signals. Most fire alarm signal and response requirements are codified in the National Fire Alarm Code, National Fire Protection Association (NFPA) 72. NFPA 72 discusses the application, installation, performance, and maintenance of protective signaling systems and their components. In contrast to fire alarms, which require a local signal when fire is detected, many IDSs do not have a local alert device because monitoring personnel do not wish to inform potential intruders that they have been detected. Instead, these types of systems silently alert monitoring personnel that an intrusion has been detected, thus allowing monitoring personnel to respond.

In contrast to systems that are set up to transmit "local only" alarms when the sensors are triggered, systems can also be set up to transmit signals to a *central location*, such as to a control room or guard post at the utility, or to a police or fire station. Most fire/smoke alarms are set up to signal both at the location of the event and at a fire station or central monitoring station. Many insurance companies require that facilities install certified systems that include alarm communication to a central station. For example, systems certified by the Underwriters Laboratory (UL) require that the alarm be reported to a central monitoring station.

The main differences between alarm systems lie in the types of event detection devices used in different systems. *Intrusion sensors*, for example, consist of two main categories: perimeter sensors and interior (space) sensors. *Perimeter intrusion sensors* are typically applied on fences, doors, walls, windows, etc. and are designed to detect an intruder before he/she accesses a protected asset (i.e., perimeter intrusion sensors are used to detect intruders attempting to enter through a door, window, etc.). In contrast, *interior intrusion sensors* are designed to detect an intruder who has already accessed the protected asset (i.e., interior intrusion sensors are used to detect intruders once they are already within a protected room or building). These two types of detection devices can be complementary, and they are often used together to enhance security for an asset. For example, a typical intrusion alarm system might employ a perimeter glass-break detector that protects against intruders accessing a room through a window, as well as an ultrasonic interior sensor that detects intruders that have gotten into the room without using the window. Table 9.6 lists and describes types of perimeter and interior sensors.

Fire detection/fire alarm systems consist of different types of fire detection devices and fire alarm systems available. These systems may detect fire, heat, smoke, or a combination of any of these. For example, a typical fire alarm system might consist of heat sensors, which are located throughout a facility and that detect high temperatures or a certain change in temperature over a fixed time period. A different system might be outfitted with both smoke and heat detection devices. A summary of several different types of fire/smoke/heat detection sensors is provided in table 9.7.

Once a sensor in an alarm system detects an event, it must communicate an alarm signal. The two basic types of alarm communication systems are hardwired and wireless. Hardwired systems rely on wire that is run from the control panel to each of the detection devices and annunciators. Wireless systems transmit signals from a transmitter to a receiver through the air—primarily using radio or other waves. Hardwired systems are usually lower-cost, more reliable (they are not affected by terrain or environmental factors), and significantly easier to troubleshoot than are wireless systems. However, a major disadvantage of hardwired systems is that it may not be possible to hardwire all locations (e.g., it may be difficult to hardwire remote locations). In addition, running wires to their required locations can be both time-consuming and costly. The major advantage to using wireless systems is that they can often be installed in areas where hardwired systems are not feasible. However, wireless components can be much more expensive when compared to hardwired systems. In addition, in the past, it has been difficult to perform self-diagnostics on wireless systems to confirm that they are communicating properly with the controller. Presently, the majority of wireless systems incorporate supervising circuitry, which allows the subscriber to know immediately if there is a problem with the system (such as a broken detection device or a low battery), or if a protected door or window has been left open.

Table 9.6. Perimeter and Interior Sensors

Type of Perimeter Sensor	Description
Foil	Foil is a thin, fragile, lead-based metallic tape that is applied to glass windows and doors. The tape is applied to the window or door and electric wiring connects this tape to a control panel. The tape functions as a conductor and completes the electric circuit with the control panel. When an intruder breaks the door or window, the fragile foil breaks, opening the circuit and triggering an alarm condition.
Magnetic switches (reed switches)	The most widely-used perimeter sensor. They are typically used to protect doors, as well as windows that can be opened (windows that cannot be opened are more typically protected by foil alarms).
Glass break detectors	Placed on glass and sense vibrations in the glass when it is disturbed. The two most common types of glass-break detectors are shock sensors and audio discriminators.

Type of Interior Sensor	Description
Passive infrared (PIR)	Presently, the most popular and cost effective interior sensors. PIR detectors monitor infrared radiation (energy in the form of heat) and detect rapid changes in temperature within a protected area. Because infrared radiation is emitted by all living things, these types of sensors can be very effective.
Quad PIRs	Consists of two dual-element sensors combined in one housing. Each sensor has a separate lens and a separate processing circuitry, which allows each lens to be set up to generate a different protection pattern.
Ultrasonic detectors	Emits high frequency sound waves, and senses movement in a protected area by sensing changes in these waves. The sensor emits sound waves that stabilize and set a baseline condition in the area to be protected. Any subsequent movement within the protected area by a would-be intruder will cause a change in these waves, thus creating an alarm condition.
Microwave detectors	Emits ultra-high frequency radio waves, and the detector senses any changes in these waves as they are reflected throughout the protected space. Microwaves can penetrate through walls, and thus a unit placed in one location may be able to protect multiple rooms.
Dual technology devices	Incorporates two different types of sensor technology (such as PIR and microwave technology) together in one housing. When both technologies sense an intrusion, an alarm is triggered.

Source: USEPA, 2005.

Table 9.7. Fire/Smoke/Heat Detection Sensors

Detector Type	Description
Thermal detector	Senses when temperatures exceed a set threshold (fixed temperature detectors) or when the rate of change of temperature increases over a fixed time period (rate-of-rise detectors).
Duct detector	Located within the haring and ventilation ducts of the facility. This sensor detects the presence of smoke within the system's return or supply ducts. A sampling tube can be added to the detector to help span the width of the duct.
Smoke detectors	Senses invisible and/or visible products of combustion. The two principle types of smoke detectors are photoelectric and ionization detectors. The major differences between these devices are described below: • Photoelectric smoke detectors react to visible particles of smoke. These detectors are more sensitive to the cooler smoke with large smoke particles that is typical of smoldering fires. • Ionization smoke detectors are sensitive to the presence of ions produced by the chemical reactions that take place with few smoke particle, such as those typically produced by fast burning/flaming fires.
Multisensor detectors	A combination of photoelectric and thermal detectors. The photoelectric sensor serves to detect smoldering fires, while the thermal detector senses the heat given off from fast burning/flaming fires.
Carbon monoxide (CO) detectors	Used to indicate the outbreak of fire by sensing the level of carbon monoxide in the air. The detector has an electrochemical cell which senses carbon monoxide, but not some or other products of combustion.
Beam detectors	Designed to protect large, open spaces such as industrial warehouses. These detectors consist of three parts: the transmitter, which projects a beam of infrared light; the receiver, which registers the light and produces an electrical signal; and the interface, which processes the signal and generates alarm of fault signals. In the event of a fire, smoke particles obstruct the beam of light. Once a preset threshold is exceeded, the detector will go into alarm.
Flame detectors	Senses either ultraviolet (UV) or infrared (IR) radiation emitted by a fire.
Air-sampling detectors	Actively and continuously samples the air from a protected space and are able to sense the pre-combustion stages of incipient fire.

Source: USEPA, 2005.

Backflow Prevention Devices

Backflow prevention devices are designed to prevent backflow, which is the reversal of the normal and intended direction of water flow in a water system. Backflow is a potential problem in a petrochemical processing system because if incorrectly cross-connected to potable water it can spread contaminated water back through a distribution system. For example, backflow at uncontrolled cross-connections (cross-connections are any actual or potential connection between the public water supply and a source of chemical contamination) or pollution can allow pollutants or contaminants to enter the potable water system. More specifically, backflow from private plumbing systems, industrial areas, hospitals, and other hazardous contaminant-containing systems, into public water mains and wells poses serious public health risks and security problems. Cross-contamination from private plumbing systems can contain biological hazards (such as bacteria or viruses) or toxic substances that can contaminate and sicken an entire population in the event of backflow. The majority of historical incidences of backflow have been accidental, but growing concern that contaminants could be intentionally backfed into a system is prompting increased awareness for private homes, businesses, industries, and areas most vulnerable to intentional strikes. Therefore, backflow prevention is a major tool for the protection of water systems.

Backflow may occur under two types of conditions: backpressure and backsiphonage. *Backpressure* is the reverse from normal flow direction within a piping system that is the result of the downstream pressure being higher than the supply pressure. These reductions in the supply pressure occur whenever the amount of water being used exceeds the amount of water supplied, such as during water line flushing, fire fighting, or breaks in water mains. *Backsiphonage* is the reverse from normal flow direction within a piping system that is caused by negative pressure in the supply piping (i.e., the reversal of normal flow in a system caused by a vacuum or partial vacuum within the water supply piping). Backsiphonage can occur where there is a high velocity in a pipe line; when there is a line repair or break that is lower than a service point; or when there is lowered main pressure due to high water withdrawal rate, such as during fire fighting or water main flushing.

To prevent backflow, various types of backflow preventers are appropriate for use. The primary types of backflow preventers are:

- Air Gap Drains
- Double Check Valves
- Reduced Pressure Principle Assemblies
- Pressure Vacuum Breakers

Biometric Security Systems

Biometrics involves measuring the unique physical characteristics or traits of the human body. In ancient times biometrics involved the judging of one's accent, body hair or face to determine friend or foe. Presently, it is well-known that any aspect of the body that is measurably different from person to person—for example fingerprints or eye characteristics—can serve as a unique biometric identifier for that individual. Biometric systems recognizing fingerprints, palm shape, eyes, face, voice, and signature comprise the bulk of the current biometric systems.

Biometric security systems use biometric technology combined with some type of locking mechanisms to control access to specific assets. In order to access an asset controlled by a biometric security system, an individual's biometric trait must be matched with an existing profile stored in a database. If there is a match between the two, the locking mechanisms (which could be a physical lock, such as at a doorway, an electronic lock, such as at a computer terminal or some other type of lock) is disengaged, and the individual is given access to the asset.

A biometric security system is typically comprised of the following components:

- A sensor, which measures/records of a biometric characteristic or trait
- A control panel, which serves as the connection point between various system components. The control panel communicates information back and forth between the sensor and the host computer, and controls access to the asset by engaging or disengaging the system lock based on internal logic and information from the host computer.
- A host computer, which processes and stores the biometric trait in a database
- Specialized software, which compares an individual image taken by the sensor with a stored profile or profiles
- A locking mechanism, which is controlled by the biometric system
- A power source to power the system

Biometric Hand and Finger Geometry Recognition

Hand and finger geometry recognition is the process of identifying an individual through the unique "geometry" (shape, thickness, length, width, etc.) of that individual's hand or fingers. Hand geometry recognition has been employed since the early 1980s and is among the most widely-used biometric technologies for controlling access to important assets. It is easy to install and use, and is appropriate for use in any location requiring use of two finger highly-accurate, non-intrusion biometric security. For example, it is currently used in numerous workplaces, day care facilities, hospitals, universities, airports, refineries, and power plants.

A newer option within hand geometry recognition technology is finger geometry recognition (not to be confused with fingerprint recognition). Finger geometry recognition relies on the same scanning methods and technologies as does hand geometry recognition, but the scanner only scans two of the user's fingers, as opposed to his entire hand. Finger geometry recognition has been in commercial use since the mid 1990s and is mainly used in time and attendance applications (i.e., to track when individuals have entered and exited a location). To date the only large-scale commercial use of two finger geometry for controlling access is at Disney World, where season pass holders use the geometry of their index and middle finger to gain access to the facilities.

To use a hand or finger geometry unit, an individual presents his or her hand or fingers to the biometric unit for "scanning." The scanner consists of a charged coupled device (CCD), which is essentially a high resolution digital camera; a reflective platen on which the hand is placed; and a mirror or mirrors that help capture different angles of the hand or fingers. The camera "scans" individual geometric characteristics of the hand or fingers by taking multiple images while the user's hand rests on the reflective platen. The camera also captures "depth," or three-dimensional information, through light reflected from the mirrors and the reflective platen. This live image is then compared to a "template" that was previously established for that individual when they were "enrolled" in the system. If the live scan of the individual matches the stored template, the individual is "verified," and is given access to that asset. Typically, verification takes about 2 seconds. In access control applications, the scanner is usually connected to some sort of electronic lock, which unlocks the door, turnstile, or other entry barrier when the user is verified. The user can then proceed through the entrance. In time and attendance applications, the time that an individual checks in and out of a location is stored for later use.

As discussed above, hand and finger geometry recognition systems can be used in several different types of applications, including access control and time and attendance tracking. While time and attendance tracking can be used for security, it is primarily used for operations and payroll purposes (i.e., clocking in and clocking out). In contrast, access control applications are more likely to be security-related. Biometric systems are widely used for access control, and can be used on various types of assets, including entryways, computers, vehicles, etc. However, because of their size, hand/finger recognition systems are primarily used in entryway access control applications.

Biometric Overview-Iris Recognition
The iris, which is the colored or pigmented area of the eye surrounded by the sclera (the white portion of the eye), is a muscular membrane that controls the amount of light entering the eye by contracting or expanding the pupil (the dark center of the

eye). The dense, unique patterns of connective tissue in the human iris were first noted in 1936, but it was not unitl 1994, when algorithms for iris recognition were created and patented, that commercial applications using biometric iris recognition began to be used extensively. There are now two vendors producing iris recognition technology: both the original developer of these algorithms, as well as a second company, which has developed and patented a different set of algorithms for iris recognition.

The iris is an ideal characteristic for identifying individuals because it is formed in utero, and its unique patterns stabilize around eight months after birth. No two irises are alike; neither an individual's right or left irises, nor the irises of identical twins. The iris is protected by the cornea (the clear covering over the eye), and therefore it is not subject to the aging or physical changes (and potential variation) that are common to some other biometric measures, such as the hand, fingerprints, and the face. Although some limited changes can occur naturally over time, these changes generally occur in the iris' melanin and therefore affect only the eye's color and not its unique patterns (in addition, because iris scanning uses only black and white images, color changes would not affect the scan anyway). Thus, barring specific injuries or certain rate surgeries directly affecting the iris, the iris' unique patterns remain relatively unchanged over an individual's lifetime.

Iris recognition systems employ a monochromatic or black and white video camera that uses both visible and near infrared light to take video of an individual's iris. Video is used rather than still photography as an extra security procedure. The video is used to confirm the normal continuous fluctuations of the pupil as the eye focuses, which ensures that the scan is of a living human being and not a photograph or some other attempted hoax. A high resolution image of the iris is then captured or extracted from the video, using a device often referred to as a "frame grabber." The unique characteristics identified in this image are then converted into a numeric code, which is stored as a "template" for that user.

Card Identification/Access/Tracking Systems

A card reader system is a type of electronic identification system that is used to identify a card and then perform an action associated with that card. Depending on the system, the card may identify where a person is or where they were at a certain time; or it may authorize another action, such as disengaging a lock. For example, a security guard may use his card at card readers located throughout a facility to indicate that he has checked a certain location at a certain time. The reader will store the information and/or send it to a central location where it can be checked later to ensure that the guard has patrolled the area. Other card reader systems can be associated with a lock so that the cardholder must have their card read and accepted by the reader before the lock disengages.

A complete card reader system typically consists of the following components:

- Access cards that are carried by the user
- Card readers, which read the card signals and send the information to control units
- Control units, which control the response of the card reader to the card
- A power source

A "card" may be a typical card or another type of device, such as a key fob or wand. These cards store electronic information, which can range from a simple code (i.e., the alphanumeric code on a Proximity card) to individualized personal data (i.e., biometric data on a Smartcard). The card reader reads the information stored on the card and sends it to the control unit, which determines the appropriate action to take when a card is presented. For example, in a card access system the control unit compares the information on the card versus stored access authorization information to determine if the card holder is authorized to proceed through the door. If the information stored in the card reader system indicates that the key is authorized to allow entrance through the doorway, the system disengages the lock and the key holder can proceed through the door.

There are many different types of card reader systems on the market. The primary differences between card reader systems are different in the way that data is encoded on the cards and in the way this data is transferred between the card and the card reader and in the types of applications for which they are best suited. However, all card systems are similar in the way that the card reader and control unit interact to respond to the card.

While card readers are similar in the way that the card reader and control unit interact to control access, they are different in the way data is encoded on the cards and the way these data are transferred between the card and the card reader. There are several types of technologies available for card reader systems. These include:

- Proximity
- Wiegand
- Smartcard
- Magnetic stripe
- Bar code
- Infrared
- Barium ferrite
- Hollerith
- Mixed technologies

Table 9.8 below summarizes various aspects of card reader technologies. The determination for the level of security rate (low, moderate, or high) is based on the level of technology a given card reader system has and how simple it is to duplicate that technology, and thus bypass the security. Vulnerability ratings were based on whether the card reader can be damaged easily due to frequent use or difficult working conditions (i.e., weather conditions if the reader is located outside). Often this is influenced by the number of moving parts in the system—the more moving parts, the greater the system's potential susceptibility to damage. The life cycle rating is based on the durability of a given card reader system over its entire operational period. Systems requiring frequent physical contact between the reader and the card often have a shorter life cycle due to the wear and tear to which the equipment is exposed. For many card reader systems, the vulnerability rating and life cycle ratings have a reciprocal relation-

Table 9.8. Card Reader Technology

Types of Card Readers	Technology	Life Cycle	Vulnerability	Level of Security
Proximity	Embedded radio frequency circuits encoded with unique information	Long	Virtually none	Moderate-high
Wiegand	Short lengths of small-diameter, special alloy wire with unique magnetic properties	Long	Low susceptibility to damage; high durability due to embedded wires	Moderate-expensive
Magnetic Stripe	Electromagnetic charges to encode information on a piece of tape attached to back of card	Moderate	Moderately susceptible to damage due to frequency of use	Low-Moderate
Bar Code	Series of narrow and wide bars and spaces	Short	High; easily damaged	Low
Hollerith	Holes punched in a plastic or paper card and read optically	Short	High; easily damaged from frequent	Low
Infrared	An encoded shadow pattern within the card, read using an infrared scanner	Moderate	IR scanners are optical and thus, vulnerable to contamination	High
Barium Ferrite	Uses small bits of magnetized barium ferrite, placed inside a plastic card. The polarity and location of the "spots" determines the coding	Moderate	Low susceptibility to damage; durable since spots are embedded in the material	Moderate-High
Smartcards	Patterns or series of narrow and wide bars and spaces	Short	High susceptibility to damage, low durability	Highest

Source: USEPA, 2005.

ship. For instance, if a given system has a high vulnerability rating it will almost always have a shorter life cycle.

Card reader technology can be implemented for facilities of any size and with any number of users. However, because individual systems vary in the complexity of their technology and in the level of security they can provide to a facility, individual users must determine the appropriate system for their needs. Some important features to consider when selecting a card reader system include:

- The technological sophistication and security level of the card system
- The size and security needs of the facility
- The frequency with which the card system will be used. For systems that will experience a high frequency of use it is important to consider a system that has a longer life cycle and lower vulnerability rating, thus making it more cost effective to implement.
- The conditions in which the system will be used (i.e., will it be used on the interior or exterior of buildings, does it require light or humidity controls, etc.). Most card reader systems can operate under normal environmental conditions, and therefore this would be a mitigating factor only in extreme conditions.
- System costs

Exterior Intrusion-Buried Sensors

Buried sensors are electronic devices that are designed to detect potential intruders. The sensors are buried along the perimeters of sensitive assets and are able to detect intruder activity both above and below ground. Some of these systems are composed of individual, stand-alone sensor units, while other sensors consist of buried cables.

There are four types of buried sensors that rely on different types of triggers. These are: pressure or seismic; magnetic field; ported coaxial cable; and fiber-optic cables. These four sensors are all covert and terrain-following, meaning they are hidden from view and follow the contour of the terrain. The four types of sensors are described in more detail below. Table 9.9 presents the distinctions between the four types of buried sensors.

Exterior Intrusion Sensors

An exterior intrusion sensor is a detection device that is used in an outdoor environment to detect intrusions into a protected area. These devices are designed to detect an intruder and then communicate an alarm signal to an alarm system. The alarm system can respond to the intrusion in many different ways, such as by triggering an audible or visual alarm signal, or by sending an electronic signal to a central monitoring location that notifies security personnel of the intrusion.

Table 9.9. Types of Buried Sensors

Type	Description
Pressure or Seismic	Responds to disturbances in the soil.
Magnetic Field	Responds to a change in the local magnetic field caused by the movement of nearby metallic material.
Ported Coaxial Cables	Responds to motion of a material with a high dielectric constant or high conductivity near the cables.
Fiber-Optic Cables	Responds to a change in the shape of the fiber that can be sensed using sophisticated sensors and computer signal processing.

Source: Adapted from Garcia (2001).

Intrusion sensors can be used to protect many kinds of assets. Intrusion sensors that protect physical space are classified according to whether they protect indoor, or "interior" space (i.e., an entire building or room within a building), or outdoor, or "exterior" space (i.e., a fence line or perimeter). Interior intrusion sensors are designed to protect the interior space of a facility by detecting an intruder who is attempting to enter, or who has already entered a room or building. In contrast, exterior intrusion sensors are designed to detect an intrusion into a protected outdoor/exterior area. Exterior protected areas are typically arranged as zones or exclusion areas placed so that the intruder is detected early in the intrusion attempt before the intruder can gain access to more valuable assets (e.g., into a building located within the protected area). Early detection creates additional time for security forces to respond to the alarm.

Exterior intrusion sensors are classified according to how the sensor detects the intrusion within the protected area. The three classes of exterior sensor technology include:

- Buried line sensors
- Fence-associated sensors
- Freestanding sensors

1. Buried Line Sensors—As the name suggests, buried line sensors are buried underground and designed to detect disturbances within the ground—such as disturbances caused by an intruder digging, crawling, walking, or running on the monitored ground. Because they sense ground disturbances, these types of sensors are able to detect intruder activity both on the surface and below ground. Individual types of exterior buried line sensors function in different ways, including detecting motion, pressure, or vibrations within the protected ground, or by detecting changes in some type of field (e.g., magnetic field) that the sensors generate within the protected ground. Specific types of buried line sensors include pressure

or seismic sensors, magnetic field sensors, ported coaxial cables, and fiber-optic cables. Details on each of these sensor types are:

- *Buried-line pressure* or *seismic sensors* detect physical disturbances to the ground—such as vibrations or soil compression—caused by intruders walking, driving, digging, or otherwise physically contacting the protected ground. These sensors detect disturbances from all directions and, therefore, can protect an area radially outward from their location. However, because detection may weaken as a function of distance from the disturbance, choosing the correct burial depth from the design area will be crucial. In general, sensors buried at a shallow depth protect a relatively small area but have a high probability of detecting intrusion within that area, while sensors buried at a deeper depth protect a wider area but have a lower probability of detecting intrusion into that area.

- *Buried line magnetic field sensors* detect changes in a local magnetic field that are caused by the movement of metallic objects within that field. This type of sensor can detect ferric metal objects worn or carried by an intruder entering a protected area on foot as well as vehicles being driven into the protected area.

- *Buried line ported coaxial cable sensors* detect the motion of any object (i.e., human body, metal, etc.) possessing high conductivity and located within close proximity to the cables. An intruder entering into the protected space creates an active disturbance in the electric field, thereby triggering an alarm condition.

- *Buried line fiber-optic cable sensors* detect changes in the attenuation of light signals transmitted within the cable. When the soil around the cable is compressed the cable is distorted, and the light signal transmitted through the cable changes, initiating an alarm. This type of sensor is easy to install because it can be buried at a shallow burial depth (only a few centimeters) and still be effective.

2. Fence-Associated Sensors—Fence-associated sensors are either attached to an existing fence or are installed in such a way as to create a fence. These sensors detect disturbances to the fence—such as those caused by an intruder attempting to climb the fence or by attempting to cut or lift the fence fabric. Exterior fence-associated sensors include fence-disturbance sensors, taut-wire sensor fences, and electric field or capacitance sensors. Details on each of these sensor types are:

- *Fence-disturbance sensors* detect the motion or vibration of a fence that can be caused by an intruder attempting to climb or cut through. In general, fence-disturbance sensors are used on chain-link fences or on other fence types where a moveable fence fabric is hung between fence posts.

- *Taut-wire sensor fences* are similar to fence-disturbance sensors except that instead of attaching the sensors to a loose fence fabric, the sensors are attached to a wire that is stretched tightly across the fence. These types of systems are designed to detect changes in the tension of the wire rather than vibrations in the fence fabric. Taut-wire sensor fences can be installed over existing fences or as stand-alone fence systems.

- *Electric field or capacitance sensors* detect changes in capacitive coupling between wires that are attached to, but electrically isolated from, the fence. As opposed to other fence-associated intrusion sensors, both electric field and capacitance sensors generate an electric field that radiates out from the fence line, resulting in an expanded zone of protection relative to other fence-associated sensors, and allowing the sensor to detect an intruders' presence before they arrive at the fence line. Note: proper spacing is necessary during installation of the electric field sensor to detect a would-be intruder from slipping between largely spaced wires.

3. *Free-Standing Sensors*—These sensors, which include active infrared, passive infrared, bistatic microwave, monostatic microwave, dual-technology, and video motion detection (VMD) sensors, consist of individual sensor units or components that can be set up in a variety of configurations to meet a user's needs. They are installed above ground, and depending on how they are oriented relative to each other, they can be used to establish a protected perimeter or a protected space. More details on each of these sensor types are:

- *Active infrared sensors* transmit infrared energy into the protected space and monitor for changes in this energy caused by intruders entering that space. In a typical application, an infrared light beam is transmitted from a transmitter unit to a receiver unit. If an intruder crosses the beam, the beam is blocked and the receiver unit detects a change in the amount of light received, triggering an alarm. Different sensors can see single- and multiple-beam arrays. Single-beam infrared sensors transmit a single infrared beam. In contrast, multiple-beam infrared sensors transmit two or more beams parallel to each other. This multiple-beam sensor arrangement creates an infrared "fence."

- *Passive infrared (PIR) sensors* monitor the ambient infrared energy in a protected area and evaluate changes in that ambient energy that may be caused by intruders moving through the protected area. Detection ranges can exceed 100 yards on cold days with size and distance limitations dependent upon the background temperature. PIR sensors generate a non-uniform detection pattern (or "curtain") that has areas (or "zones") of more sensitivity and areas of less sensitivity. The specific shape of the protected area is determined by the detector's lenses. The general shape common to many detection patterns is a series of long "fingers" emanating from the PIR and spreading in various directions. When intruders enter the detection area, the PIR sensor detects differences in temperature due to the intruder's body heat and triggers an alarm. While the PIR leaves unprotected areas between its fingers, an intruder would be detected if he passed from a non-protected area to a protected area.

- *Microwave sensors* detect changes in received energy generated by the motion of an intruder entering into a protected area. Monostatic microwave sensors incorporate transmitter and receiver in one unit, while bistatic sensors separate the transmitter and the receiver into different units. Monostatic sensors are limited to a coverage area of 400 feet, while bistatic sensors can cover an area up to 1,500 feet. For bistatic sensors, a zone of no detection exists in the first few feet in front of the antennas. This distance from the antennas to the point at which the intruder is first detected is known as the offset distance. Due to this offset distance, antennas must be configured so that they overlap one another (as opposed to being adjacent to each other), thereby creating long perimeters with a continuous line of detection.
- *Dual-technology sensors* consist of two different sensor technologies incorporated together into one sensor unit. For example, a dual technology sensor could consist of a passive infrared detector and a monostatic microwave sensor integrated into the same sensor unit.
- *Video motion detection* (VMD) *sensors* monitor video images from a protected area for changes in the images. Video cameras are used to detect unauthorized intrusion into the protected area by comparing the most recent image against a previously established one. Cameras can be installed on towers or other tall structures so that they can monitor a large area.

Fences

A fence is a physical barrier that can be set up around the perimeter of an asset. Fences often consist of individual pieces (such as individual pickets in a wooden fence or individual sections of a wrought iron fence) that are fastened together. Individual sections of the fence are fastened together using posts, which are sunk into the ground to provide stability and strength for the sections of the fence hung between them. Gates are installed between individual sections of the fence to allow access inside the fenced area.

Many fences are used as decorative architectural features to separate physical spaces from each other. They may also be used to physically mark the location of a boundary (such as a fence installed along a properly line). However, a fence can also serve as an effective means for physically delaying intruders from gaining access to a financial service sector asset. For example, many utilities install fences around their primary facilities, around remote pump stations, or around hazardous petrochemical materials storage areas or sensitive areas within a facility. Access to the area can be controlled through security at gates or doors through the fence (e.g., by posting a guard at the gate or by locking it). In order to gain access to the asset, unauthorized persons could either have to go around or through the fence.

Fences are often compared with walls when determining the appropriate system for perimeter security. While both fences and walls can provide adequate perimeter security, fences are often easier and less expensive to install than walls. However, they do not usually provide the same physical strength that walls do. In addition, many types of fences have gaps between the individual pieces that make up the fence (i.e., the spaces between chain links in a chain-link fence or the space between pickets in a picket fence). Thus, many types of fences allow the interior of the fenced area to be seen. This may allow intruders to gather important information about the locations or defenses of vulnerable areas within the facility.

There are numerous types of materials used to construct fences, including chain-link iron, aluminum, wood, or wire. Some types of fences, such as split rails or pickets, may not be appropriate for security purposes because they are traditionally low fences, and they are not physically strong. Potential intruders may be able to easily defeat these fences either by jumping or climbing over them or by breaking through them. For example, the rails in a split fence may be broken easily.

Important security attributes of a fence include the height to which it can be constructed, the strength of the material comprising the fence, the method and strength of attaching the individual sections of the fence together at the posts, and the fence's ability to restrict the view of the assets inside the fence. Additional considerations should include the ease of installing the fence and the ease of removing and reusing sections of the fence. Table 9.10 provides a comparison of the important security and usability features of various fence types.

Some fences can include additional measures to delay, or even detect, potential intruders. Such measures may include the addition of barbed wire, razor wire, or other deterrents at the top of the fence. Barbed wire is sometimes employed at the base of fences as well. This can impede a would-be intruder's progress in even reaching the fence. Fences may also be fitted with security cameras to provide visual surveillance of the perimeter. Finally, some facilities have installed motion sensors along their fences

Table 9.10. Comparison of Different Fence Types

Specifications	Chain Link	Iron	Wire (Wirewall)	Wood
Height limitations	12′	12′	12′	8′
Strength	Medium	High	High	Low
Installation Requirements	Low	High	High	Low
Ability to Remove/Reuse	Low	High	Low	High
Ability to Replace/Repair	Medium	High	Low	High

Source: USEPA, 2005.

to detect movement on the fence. Several manufacturers have combined these multiple perimeter security features into one product and offer alarms and other security features.

The correct implementation of a fence can make it a much more effective security measure. Security experts recommend the following when a facility constructs a fence:

- The fence should be at least 7–9 feet high.
- Any outriggers, such as barbed wire, that are affixed on top of the fence should be angled out and away from the facility and not toward the facility. This will make climbing the fence more difficult and will prevent ladders from being placed against the fence.
- Other types of hardware can increase the security of the fence. This can include installing concertina wire along the fence (this can be done in front of the fence or at the top of the fence) or adding intrusion sensors, cameras, or other hardware to the fence.
- All undergrowth should be cleared for several feet (typically six feet) on both sides of the fence. This will allow for a clearer view of the fence by any patrols in the area.
- Any trees with limbs or branches hanging over the fence should be trimmed so that intruders cannot use them to go over the fence. Also, it should be noted that fallen trees can damage fences, and so management of trees around the fence can be important. This can be especially important in areas where fencing goes through a remote area.
- Fences that do not block the view from outside the fence to inside the fence allow patrols to see inside the fence without having to enter the facility.
- "No Trespassing" signs posted along a fence can be a valuable tool in prosecuting any intruders who claim that the fence was broken and that they did not enter through the fence illegally. Adding signs that highlight the local ordinances against trespassing can further persuade simple troublemakers for illegally jumping/climbing the fence. Electrical substation and other electrical component installations should have clearly visible signage warning of HIGH VOLTAGE and the dangers of electrical shock.

Films for Glass Shatter Protection

Many financial service sector entities have numerous windows on the outside of buildings, in doors, and in interior offices. In addition, many facilities have glass doors or other glass structures, such as glass walls or display cases. These glass objects are potentially vulnerable to shattering when heavy objects are thrown or launched at them, when explosions occur near them, or when there are high winds (for exterior glass). If the glass is shattered, intruders may potentially enter an area. In addition, shattered glass projected into a room from an explosion or from an object being thrown through a door or window can injure and potentially incapacitate personnel in the room. Materials that prevent glass from shattering can help to maintain the integrity of the door, window, or other glass object, and can delay an intruder from gaining access. These materials can also prevent flying glass and thus reduce potential injuries.

Materials designed to prevent glass from shattering include specialized films and coatings. These materials can be applied to existing glass objects to improve their strength and their ability to resist shattering. The films have been tested against many scenarios that could result in glass breakage, including penetration by blunt objects, bullets, high winds, and simulated explosions. Thus, the films are tested against both simulated weather scenarios (which could include both the high winds themselves and the force of objects blown into the glass), as well as more criminal/terrorist scenarios where the glass is subject to explosives or bullets. Many vendors provide information on the results of these types of tests, and thus potential users can compare different product lines to determine which products best suit their needs.

The primary attributes of films for shatter protection are:

- The materials from which the film is made
- The adhesive that bonds the film to the glass surface
- The thickness of the film

Standard glass safety films are designed from high strength polyester. Polyester provides both strength and elasticity, which is important in absorbing the impact of an object, spreading the force of the impact over the entire film, and resisting tearing. The polyester is also designed to be resistant to scratching, which can result when films are cleaned with abrasives or other industrial cleaners.

The bonding adhesive is important in ensuring that the film does not tear away from the glass surface. This can be especially important when the glass is broken so that the film does not peel off the glass and allow it to shatter. In addition, films applied to exterior windows can be subject to high concentrations of UV light, which can break down bonding materials.

Film thickness is measured in gauge or mils. According to test results reported by several manufacturers, film thickness appears to affect resistance to penetration/tearing, with thicker films being more resistant to penetration and tearing. However, the appreciation of a thicker film did not decrease glass fragmentation.

Many manufacturers offer films in different thicknesses. The "standard" film is usually one 4 mil layer; thicker films are typically composed of several layers of the standard 4 mil sheet. However, newer technologies have allowed the polyester to be "microlayered" to produce a stronger film without significantly increasing its thickness. In this microlayering process, each laminate film is composed of multiple micro-thin layers of polyester woven together an alternating angles. This provides increased strength for the film while maintaining the flexibility and thin profile of one film layer.

As described above, many vendors test their products in various scenarios that would lead to glass shattering, including simulated bomb blasts and simulation of the glass being struck by wind-blown debris. Some manufacturers refer to the Government Services Administration standard for bomb blasts, which require resistance to tearing for a 4 PSI blast. Other manufacturers use other measures and tests for resistance to tearing. Many of these tests are not "standard," in that no standard testing or reporting methods have been adopted by any of the accepted standards-setting institutions. However, many of the vendors publish the procedure and the results of these tests on their websites, and this may allow users to evaluate the protectiveness of these films. For example, several vendors evaluate the "protectiveness" of their films and the "hazard" resulting from blasts near windows with and without protective films. Protectiveness is usually evaluated based on the percentage of glass ejected from the window and the height at which that ejected glass travels during the blast (e.g., if the blasted glass tends to project upward in to a room—potentially toward people's faces—it is a higher hazard than if it is blown downward into the room toward people's feet). There are some standard measures of glass breakage. For example, several vendors indicated that their products exceed the American Society for Testing and Materials (ASTM) standard 64Z-95 "Standard Test Method for glazing and Glazing Systems Subject to Air Blast Loadings." Vendors often compare the results of some sort of penetration or force test, ballistic tests, or simulated explosions with unprotected glass versus glass onto which their films have been applied. Results generally show that applying films to the glass surfaces reduces breakage/penetration of the glass and can reduce the amount and direction of glass ejected from the frame. This in turn reduces the hazard from flying glass.

In addition to these types of tests, many vendors conduct standard physical tests on their products, such as tests for tensile strength and peel strength. Tensile strength indicates the strength per area of material, while the peel strength indicates the force it would take to peel the product from the glass surface. Several vendors indicate that their products exceed American National Standards Institute (ANSI) standard Z97.1 for tensile strength and adhesion.

Vendors typically have a warranty against peeling or other forms of deterioration of their products. However, the warranty requires that the films be installed by manufacturer-certified technicians to ensure that they are applied correctly and therefore that the warranty is in effect. Warranties from different manufacturers may vary. Some may cover the cost of replacing the material only, while others include material plus installation. Because installation costs are significantly greater than material costs, different warranties may represent large difference in potential costs.

Fire Hydrant Locks

Fire hydrants are installed at strategic locations throughout a community's water distribution system to supply water for fire fighting. However, because there are many hydrants in a system that are often located in residential neighborhoods, industrial districts, and other areas where they cannot be easily observed and/or guarded, they are potentially vulnerable to unauthorized access. Many municipalities, states, and EPA regions have recognized this potential vulnerability and have instituted programs to lock hydrants. For example, EPA Region 1 has included locking hydrants as number 7 on its "Drinking Water Security and Emergency Preparedness" top ten list for small groundwater suppliers.

A "hydrant lock" is a physical security device designed to prevent unauthorized access to the water supply through a hydrant. It can also ensure water and water pressure availability to fire fighters and prevent water theft and associated lost water revenue. These locks have been successfully used in numerous municipalities and in various climates and weather conditions.

Fire hydrant locks are basically steel covers or caps that are locked in place over the operating nut of a fire hydrant. The lock prevents unauthorized persons from accessing the operating nut and opening the fire hydrant valve. The lock also makes it more difficult to remove the bolts from the hydrant and access the system that way. Finally, hydrant locks shield the valve from being broken off. Should a vandal attempt to breach the hydrant lock by force and succeed in breaking the hydrant lock, the vandal will only succeed in bending the operating valve. If the hydrant's operating valve is bent, the hydrant will not be operational, but the water asset remains protected and inaccessible to vandals. However, the entire hydrant will need to be replaced.

Hydrant locks are designed so that the hydrants can be operated by special "key wrenches" without removing the lock. These specialized wrenches are generally distributed to the fire department, public works department, and other authorized persons so that they can access the hydrants as needed. An inventory of wrenches and their serial numbers is generally kept by a municipality so that the location of all wrenches is known. These operating key wrenches may only be purchased by registered lock owners.

The most important features of hydrants are their strength and the security of their locking systems. The locks must be strong so that they cannot be broken off. Hydrant locks are constructed from stainless or alloyed steel. Stainless steel locks are stronger and are ideal for all climates; however, they are more expensive than alloy locks. The locking mechanisms for each fire hydrant locking system ensures that the hydrant can only be operated by authorized personnel who have the specialized key to work the hydrant.

Hatch Security

A hatch is basically a door that is installed on a horizontal plane (such as in a floor, a paved lot, or a ceiling) instead of on a vertical plane (such as in a building wall). Hatches are usually used to provide access to assets that are either located underground (such as hatches to basements or underground vaults and storage areas) or to assets located above ceilings (such as emergency roof exits). At some IT sector sites, hatches are typically used to provide access to underground vaults containing pumps, meter chambers, valves, or piping, or to the interior of chemical tanks or covered water reservoirs. Securing a hatch by locking it or upgrading materials to give the hatch added strength can help to delay unauthorized access to any asset behind the hatch.

Like all doors, a hatch consists of a frame anchored to the horizontal structure, a door or doors, hinges connecting the door/doors to the frame, and a latching or locking mechanism that keeps the hatch door/doors closed.

It should be noted that improving hatch security is straightforward, and that hatches with upgraded security features can be installed new or retrofit, for existing applications.

Depending on the application, the primary security-related attributes of a hatch are the strength of the door and frame, its resistance to the elements and corrosion, its ability to be sealed against water or gas, and its locking features.

Hatches must be both strong and lightweight so that they can withstand typical static loads (such as people or vehicles walking or driving over them) while still being easy to open.

In addition, because hatches are typically installed at outdoor locations, they are usually designed from corrosion-resistant metal that can withstand the elements. Therefore, hatches are typically constructed from high gauge steel or lightweight aluminum.

Aluminum is typically the material of choice for hatches because it is lightweight and more corrosion resistant relative to steel. Aluminum is not as rigid as steel, so aluminum hatch doors may be reinforced with aluminum stiffeners to provide extra strength and rigidity. The doors are usually constructed from single or double layers (or "leaves") of material. Single-leaf designs are standard for smaller hatches, while double-leaf deigns are required for larger hatches. In addition, aluminum products do not require painting. This is reflected in the warranties available with different products. Product warranties range from ten years to lifetime.

Steel is heavier per square foot than aluminum, and thus steel hatches will be heavier and more difficult to open than aluminum hatches of the same size. However, heavy steel hatch doors may have spring-loaded, hydraulic, or gas openers or other specialized features that help in opening the hatch and in keeping it open.

Many hatches are installed in outdoor areas, often in roadways or pedestrian areas. Therefore, the hatch installed for any given application must be designed to withstand the expected load at that location. Hatches are typically solid to withstand either pedestrian of vehicle loading. Pedestrian loading hatches are typically designed to withstand either 150 or 300 pounds per square feet of loading. The vehicle loading standard is the American Association of State Highway and Transportation Officials (AASHTO) H-20 wheel loading standard of 16,000 pounds over an 8 inch by 20 inch area. It should be noted that these design parameters are for static loads and not dynamic loads; thus, the loading capabilities may not reflect potential resistance to other types of loads that may be more typical of an intentional threat, such as repeated blows from a sledge hammer or pressure generated by bomb blasts or bullets.

The typical design for a watertight hatch includes a channel frame that directs water away from the hatch. This can be especially important in a hatch on a storage tank because it will prevent liquid contaminants from being dumped on the hatch and leaking through into the interior. Hatches can also be constructed with gasket seals that are air-, odor-, and gas-tight.

Typically, hatches for pedestrian loading applications have hinges located on the exterior of the hatch, while hatches designed for H-20 loads have hinges located in the interior of the hatch. Hinges located on the exterior of the hatch may be able to be removed thereby allowing intruders to remove the hatch door and access the asset behind the hatch. Therefore, installing H-20 hatches even for applications that do not require H-20 loading levels may increase security because intruders will not be able to tamper with the hinges and circumvent the hatch this way.

In addition to the location of the hinges, stock hinges can be replaced with heavy-duty or security hinges that are more resistant to tampering.

The hatch locking mechanism is perhaps the most important part of hatch security. There are a number of locks that can be implemented for hatches, including:

- Slam locks (internal locks that are located within the hatch frame)
- Recessed cylinder locks
- Bolt locks
- Padlocks

Ladder Access Control

Financial services sector facilities have a number of assets that are raised above ground level, including electrical substations, transmitting stations, raised conduit systems, and roof access points into buildings. In addition, communications equipment, antennae, or other electronic devices may be located on the top of these raised assets. Typi-cally, these assets are reached by ladders that are permanently anchored to the asset. For example, raised petrochemical/water tanks typically are accessed by ladders that are bolted to one of the legs of the tank. Controlling access to these raised assets by controlling access to the ladder can increase security at an IT sector services facility.

A typical ladder access control system consists of some type of cover that is locked or secured over the ladder. The cover can be a casing that surrounds most of the lad-der, or a door or shield that covers only part of the ladder. In either case, several rungs of the ladder (the number of rungs depends on the size of the cover) are made inac-cessible by the cover, and these rungs can only be accessed by opening or removing the cover. The cover is locked so that only authorized personnel can open or remove it and use the ladder. Ladder access controls are usually installed at several feet above ground level, and they usually extend several feet up the ladder so that they cannot be circumvented by someone accessing the ladder above the control system.

The important features of ladder access control are the size and strength of the cover and its ability to lock or otherwise be secured from unauthorized access.

The covers are constructed from aluminum or some type of steel. This should provide adequate protection from being pierced or cut through. The metals are cor-rosion resistant so that they will not corrode or become fragile from extreme weather conditions in outdoor applications. The bolts used to install each of these systems are galvanized steel. In addition, the bolts for each cover are installed on the inside of the unit so they cannot be removed from the outside.

Locks

A lock is a type of physical security device that can be used to delay or prevent a door, a gate, a window, a manhole, a filing cabinet drawer, or some other physical feature from being opened, moved, or operated. Locks typically operate by connecting two pieces together—such as by connecting a door to a door jamb or a manhole to its casement. Every lock has two modes—engaged (or "locked") and disengaged (or "opened"). When a lock is disengaged, the asset on which the lock is installed can be accessed by anyone, but not when the lock is engaged.

Before discussing locks and their applicability it is important to discuss key control. Based on our experience, many IT service sector facilities (and others) have no idea how many keys for various site/equipment locks have been issued to employees over the years. Many facilities simply issue keys to employees at hiring with no account-ability for the keys upon the employee's departure. Needless to say this is not good security policy. You can have the best made locks available installed throughout your facilities but if you do not have proper key control, you do not have proper security.

Locks are excellent security features because they have been designed to function in many ways and to work on many different types of assets. Locks can also provide different levels of security depending on how they are designed and implemented. The security provided by a lock is dependent on several factors, including its ability to withstand physical damage (i.e., can it be cut off, broken, or otherwise physically disabled) as well as its requirements for supervision or operation (i.e., combinations may need to be changed frequently so that they are not compromised and the locks remain secure). While there is no single definition of the "security" of a lock, locks are often described as minimum, medium, or maximum security. Minimum security locks are those that can be easily disengaged (or "picked") without the correct key or code, or those that can be disabled easily (such as small padlocks that can be cut with bolt cutters). Higher security locks are more complex and thus more difficult to pick, or are sturdier and more resistant to physical damage.

Many locks, such as many door locks, only need to be unlocked from one side. For example, most door locks need a key to be unlocked only from the outside. A person opens such devices, called single-cylinder locks, from the inside by pushing a button or by turning a knob or handle. Double-cylinder locks require a key to be locked or unlocked from both sides.

Manhole Intrusion Sensors

Manholes are found at some IT service sector sites. Manholes are designed to provide access to the underground utilities, meter vaults, petrochemical pumping rooms, etc. and therefore they are potential entry points to a system. Because many utilities run under other infrastructures (roads, buildings), manholes also provide potential access points to critical infrastructure as well as petrochemical process assets. In addition, because the portion of the system to which manholes provide entry is primarily located underground, access to a system through a manhole increases the chance that an intruder will not be seen. Therefore, protecting manholes can be a critical component of guarding an entire plant site and a surrounding community.

There are multiple methods for protecting manholes, including preventing unauthorized personnel from physically accessing the manhole and detecting attempts at unauthorized access to the manhole.

A manhole intrusion sensor is a physical security device designed to detect unauthorized access to the facility through a manhole. Monitoring a manhole that provides access to a chemical plant or processing system can mitigate two distinct types of threats. First, monitoring a manhole may detect access of unauthorized personnel to chemical systems or assets through the manhole. Second, monitoring manholes may also allow the detection of intruders attempting to place explosive or other destructive (WMD) devices into the petrochemical system.

Several different technologies have been used to develop manhole intrusion sensors, including mechanical systems, magnetic systems, and fiber optic and infrared sensors. Some of these intrusion sensors have been specifically designed for manholes, while others consist of standard, off-the-shelf intrusion sensors that have been implemented in a system specifically designed for application in a manhole.

Manhole Locks

A "manhole lock" is a physical security device designed to delay unauthorized access to the financial service sector facility or system through a manhole.

Passive Security Barriers

One of the most basic threats facing any facility is from intruders accessing the facility with the intention of causing damage to its assets. These threats may include intruders actually entering the facility, as well as intruders attacking the facility from outside without actually entering it (i.e., detonating a bomb near enough to the facility to cause damage within its boundaries).

Security barriers are one of the most effective ways to counter the threat of intruders accessing a facility or the facility perimeter. Security barriers are large heavy structures that are used to control access through a perimeter by either vehicles or personnel. They can be used in many different ways depending on how/where they are located at the facility. For example, security barriers can be used on or along driveways or roads to direct traffic to a checkpoint (i.e., a facility may install jersey barriers in a road to direct traffic in a certain direction). Other types of security barriers (crash beams, gates) can be installed at the checkpoint so that guards can regulate which vehicles can access the facility. Finally, other security barriers (i.e., bollards or security planters) can be used along the facility perimeter to establish a protective buffer area between the facility and approaching vehicles. Establishing such a protective buffer can help in mitigating the effects of the type of bomb blast described above, both by potentially absorbing some of the blast and also by increasing the "stand-off" distance between the blast and the facility (the force of an explosion is reduced as the shock wave travels further from the source and thus the further the explosion is from the target, the less effective it will be in damaging the target).

Security barriers can be either "active" or "passive." "Active" barriers, which include gates, retractable bollards, wedge barriers, and crash barriers, are readily movable and thus they are typically used in areas where they must be moved often to allow vehicles to pass—such as in roadways at entrances and exits to a facility. In contrast to active security barriers, "passive" security barriers, which include jersey barriers, bollards, and security planters, are not designed to be moved on a regular basis and thus they are typically used in areas where access is not required or allowed—such as along building perimeters or in traffic control areas. Passive security barriers are typically large heavy structures that are usually several feet high and designed so that even heavy-duty vehicles cannot go over or though them. Therefore, they can be placed in a roadway parallel to the flow of traffic so that they direct traffic in a certain direction (such as to a guardhouse, a gate, or some other sort of checkpoint), or perpendicular to traffic such that they prevent a vehicle from using a road or approaching a building or area.

Security for Doorways-Side Hinged Doors

Doorways are the main access points to a facility or to rooms within a building. They are used on the exterior or in the interior of buildings to provide privacy and security for the areas behind them. Different types of doorway security systems may be installed in different doorways depending on the needs or requirements of the buildings or rooms. For example, exterior doorways tend to have heavier doors to withstand the elements and to provide some security to the entrance of the building. Interior doorways in office areas may have lighter doors that may be primarily designed to provide privacy rather than security. Therefore, these doors may be made of glass or lightweight wood. Doorways in industrial areas may have sturdier doors than do other interior doorways and may be designed to provide protection or security for areas behind the doorway. For example, fireproof doors may be installed in chemical storage areas or in other areas where there is a danger of fire.

Because they are the main entries into a facility or a room, doorways are often prime targets for unauthorized entry into a facility or an asset. Therefore, securing doorways may be a major step in providing security at a facility.

A doorway includes four main components:

- The door, which blocks the entrance. The primary threat to the actual door is breaking or piercing through it. Therefore, the primary security features of doors are their strength and resistance to various physical threats, such as fire or explosions.
- The door frame, which connects the door to the wall. The primary threat to a door frame is that the door can be pried away from the frame. Therefore, the primary security feature of a door frame is its resistance to prying.
- The hinges, which connect the door to the door frame. The primary threat to door hinges is that they can be removed or broken, which will allow intruders to remove the entire door. Therefore, security hinges are designed to be resistant to breaking. They may also be designed to minimize the threat of removal from the door.

- The lock, which connects the door to the door frame. Use of the lock is controlled through various security features, such as keys, combinations, etc. such that only authorized personnel can open the lock and go through the door. Locks may also incorporate other security features, such as software or other systems to track overall use of the door or to track individuals using the door, etc.

Each of these components is integral in providing security for a doorway, and upgrading the security of only one of these components while leaving the other components unprotected may not increase the overall security of the doorway. For example, many facilities upgrade door locks as a basic step in increasing the security of a facility. However, if the facilities do not also focus on increasing security for the door hinges or the door frame, the door may remain vulnerable to being removed from its frame, thereby defeating the increased security of the door lock.

The primary attribute for the security of a door is its strength. Many security doors are 4-20 gauge hollow metal doors consisting of steel plates over a hollow cavity reinforced with steel stiffeners to give the door extra stiffness and rigidity. This increases resistance to blunt force used to try to penetrate through the door. The space between the stiffeners may be filled with specialized materials to provide fire-, blast-, or bullet resistance to the door.

The Windows and Doors Manufacturers Association have developed a series of performance attributes for doors. These include:

- Structural resistance
- Forced entry resistance
- Hinge style screw resistance
- Split resistance
- Hinge resistance
- Security rating
- Fire resistance
- Bullet resistance
- Blast resistance

The first five bullets provide information on a door's resistance to standard physical breaking and prying attacks. These tests are used to evaluate the strength of the door and the resistance of the hinges and the frame in a standardized way. For example, the Rack Load Test simulates a prying attack on a corner of the door. A test panel is restrained at one end and a third corner is supported. Loads are applied and measured at the fourth corner. The Door Impact Test simulates a battering attack on a door and frame using impacts of 200-foot pounds by a steel pendulum. The door must remain fully operable after the test. It should be noted that door glazing is also rated for resistance to shattering, etc. Manufacturers will be able to provide security ratings for these features of a door as well.

Door frames are an integral part of doorway security because they anchor the door to the wall. Door frames are typically constructed from wood or steel, and they are installed such that they extend for several inches over the doorway that has been cut into the wall. For added security, frames can be designed to have varying degrees of overlap with, or wrapping over, the underlying wall. This can make prying the frame from the wall more difficult. A frame formed from a continuous piece of metal (as opposed to a frame constructed from individual metal pieces) will prevent prying between pieces of the frame.

Many security doors can be retrofit into existing frames; however, many security door installations include replacing the door frame as well as the door itself. For example, bullet-resistance per Underwriter's Laboratory (UL) 752 requires resistance of the door and frame assembly, and thus replacing the door only would not meet UL 752 requirements.

Valve Lockout Devices

Valves are utilized as control elements in fuel oil/natural gas and petrochemical process piping networks. They regulate the flow of both liquids and gases by opening, closing, or obstructing a flow passageway. Valves are typically located where flow control is necessary. They can be located in-line or at pipeline and tank entrance and exit points. They can serve multiple purposes in a process pipe network, including:

- Redirecting and throttling flow
- Preventing backflow
- Shutting off flow to a pipeline or tank (for isolation purposes)
- Releasing pressure
- Draining extraneous liquid from pipelines or tanks
- Introducing chemicals into the process network
- As access points for sampling process water

Valves may be located either aboveground or below ground. It is critical to provide protection against valve tampering. For example, tampering with a pressure relief valve could result in a pressure buildup and potential explosion in the piping network. On a larger scale, addition of a contaminant or non-compatible chemical substance to the chemical processing system through an unprotected valve could result in the catastrophic release of that contaminant to the general population.

Different security products are available to protect above ground versus below-ground valves. For example, valve lockout devices can be purchased to protect valves and valve controls located aboveground. Vaults containing underground valves can be locked to prevent access to these valves.

As described above, a lockout device can be used as a security measure to prevent unauthorized access to aboveground valves located within petrochemical processing systems. Valve lockout devices are locks that are specially designed to fit over valves and valve handles to control their ability to be turned or seated. These devices can be used to lock the valve into the desired position. Once the valve is locked, it cannot be turned unless the locking device is unlocked or removed by an authorized individual.

Various valve lockout options are available for industrial use, including:

- Cable lockouts
- Padlocked chains/cables
- Valve-specific lockouts

Many of these lockout devices are not specifically designed for use in the financial service sector industry (i.e., chains, padlocks), but are available from a local hardware store or manufacturer specializing in safety equipment. Other lockout devices (e.g., valve-specific lockouts or valve box-locks) are more specialized and must be purchased from safety or valve-related equipment vendors.

The three most common types of valves for which lockout devices are available are gate, ball, and butterfly valves. Each is described in more detail below.

- Gate Valve Lockouts—Gate valve lockouts are designed to fit over the operating hand wheel of the gate valve to prevent it from being turned. The lockout is secured in place with a padlock. Two types of gate valve lockouts are available: diameter-specific and adjustable. Diameter-specific lockouts are available for handles ranging from 1 inch to 13 inches in diameter. Adjustable gate valve lockouts can be adjusted to fit any handle ranging from 1 inch to 6+ inches in diameter.
- Ball Valve Lockouts—There are several different configurations available to lock-out ball valves, all of which are designed to prevent rotation of the valve handle. The three major configurations available are a wedge shape for 1 inch to 3 inch valves, a lockout that completely covers 3/8 inch to 8 inch ball valve handles, and a universal lockout that can be applied to quarter-turn valves of varying sizes and geometric handle dimensions. All three types of ball valve lockouts can be installed by sliding the lockout device over the ball valve handle and securing it with a padlock.
- Butterfly Valve Lockouts—The butterfly valve lockout functions in a similar manner to the ball valve lockout. The polypropylene lockout device is placed over the valve

handle and secured with a padlock. This type of lockout has been commonly used in the bottling industry.

A major difference between valve-specific lockout devices and the padlocked chain or cable lockouts discussed earlier is that they do not need to be secured to an anchoring device in the floor or the piping system. In addition, valve-specific lockouts eliminate potential tripping or access hazards that may be caused by chains or cable lockouts applied to valves located near walkways or frequently maintained equipment.

Valve-specific lockout devices are available in a variety of colors, which can be useful in distinguishing different valves. For example, different colored lockouts can be used to distinguish the type of liquid passing through the valve (i.e., treated, untreated, potable, petrochemical), or to identify the party responsible for maintaining the lockout. Implementing a system of different-colored locks on operating valves can increase system security by reducing the likelihood of an operator inadvertently opening the wrong valve and causing a problem in the system.

Security For Vents

Vents are installed in some aboveground IT services sector storage areas to allow safe venting of off-gases. The specific vent design for any given application will vary depending on the design of the chemical storage vessel. However, every vent consists of an open air connection between the storage container and the outside environment. Although these air exchange vents are an integral part of covered or underground chemical storage containers, they also represent a potential security threat. Improving vent security by making the vents tamper-resistant or by adding other security features, such as security screens or security covers, can enhance the security of the entire petrochemical processing system.

Many municipalities already have specifications for vent security at their local chemical industrial assets. These specifications typically include the following requirements:

- Vent openings are to be angled down or shielded to minimize the entrance of surface and/or rainwater into the vent through the opening.
- Vent designs are to include features to exclude insects, birds, animals, and dust.
- Corrosion-resistant materials are to be used to construct the vents.

Visual Surveillance Monitoring

Visual surveillance is used to detect threats through continuous observation of important or vulnerable areas of an asset. The observations can also be recorded for later review or use (e.g., in court proceedings). Visual surveillance systems can be used to monitor various parts of production, distribution, or pumping/compressing systems, including the perimeter of a facility, outlying pumping stations, or entry or access points into specific buildings. These systems are also useful in recording individuals who enter or leave a facility, thereby helping to identify unauthorized access. Images can be transmitted live to a monitoring station where they can be monitored in real time, or they can be recorded and reviewed later. Many financial service sector facilities have found that a combination of electronic surveillance and security guards provides an effective means of facility security.

Visual surveillance is provided through a closed circuit television (CCTV) system, in which the capture, transmission, and reception of an image is localized within a closed "circuit." This is different than other broadcast images, such as over-the-air television, which is broadcast over the air to any receiver within range.

At a minimum, a CCTV system consists of:

- One or more cameras
- A monitor for viewing the images
- A system for transmitting the images from the camera to the monitor

Specific attributes and features of camera systems, lenses, and lighting systems are presented in table 9.11.

COMMUNICATION INTEGRATION

In this section, those devices necessary for communication and integration of IT service sector industrial processing operations, such as electronic controllers, two-way radios, and wireless data communications are discussed. In regard to security applications, electronic controllers are used to automatically activate equipment (such as lights, surveillance cameras, audible alarms, or locks) when they are triggered. Triggering could be in response to a variety of scenarios, including tripping of an alarm or a motion sensor; breaking of a window or a glass door; variation in vibration sensor readings; or simply through input from a timer.

Two-way wireless radios allow two or more users that have their radios tuned to the same frequency to communicate instantaneously with each other without the radios being physically lined together with wires or cables.

Wireless data communications devices are used to enable transmission of data between computer systems without individual components being physically linked together via wires or cables. In financial processing systems these devices are often used to link remote monitoring stations or portable computers (i.e., laptops) to computer networks without using physical wiring connections.

Table 9.11. Attributes of Camera, Lenses, and Lighting Systems

	Camera Systems	
Attribute	Discussion
Camera Type	Major factors in choosing the correct camera are the resolution of the image required and lighting of the area to be viewed. • **Solid State** (including charge coupled devices, charge priming device, charge injection device, and metal oxide substrate)— these cameras are becoming predominant in the marketplace because of their high resolution and their elimination of problems inherent in tub cameras. • **Thermal**—These cameras are designed for night vision. They require no light and use differences in temperature between objects in the field of view to produce a video image. Resolution is low compared to other cameras and the technology is currently expensive relative to other technologies. • **Tube**—These cameras can provide high resolution burnout and must be replaced after 1-2 years. In addition, tube performance can degrade over time. Finally, tube cameras are prone to burn images in the tube replacement.
Resolution (the ability to see fine details)	User must determine the amount of resolution required depending on the level of detail required for threat determination. A high definition focus with a wide field of vision will give an optimal viewing area.
Field of vision width	Cameras are designed to cover a defined field of vision, which is usually defined in degrees. The wider the field of vision, the more area a camera will be able to monitor.
Type of image produced (color, black and white, thermal)	Color images may allow the identification of distinctive markings, while black and white images may provide sharper contrast. Thermal imaging allows the identification of heat sources (such as human beings or other living creatures) from low light environments; however, thermal images are not effective in identifying specific individuals (i.e., for subsequent legal processes).
Pan/Tilt/Zoom (PTZ)	Panning (moving the camera in a horizontal plane), tilting (moving the camera in a vertical plane), and zooming (moving the lens to focus on objects that are at different distances from the camera) allow the camera to follow a moving object. Different systems allow these functions to be controlled manually or automatically. Factors to be considered in PTZ cameras are the degree of coverage for pan and tilt function and the power of the zoom lens.

	Lenses	
Format	Lens format determines the maximum image size to be transmitted.
Focal length	This is the distance from the lens to the center of the focus. The greater the focal length, the higher the magnification but the narrower the field of vision.
F number	F number is the ability to gather light. Smaller F numbers may be required for outdoor applications where light cannot be controlled as easily.
Distance and width approximation	Distance and width approximations are used to determine the geometry of the space that can be monitored at the best resolution.

	Lighting Systems	
Intensity	Light intensity must be great enough for the camera type to produce sharp images. Light can be generated from natural or artificial sources. Artificial sources can be controlled to produce the amount and distribution of light required for a given camera and lens.
Evenness	Light must be distributed evenly over the field of view so that there are no dark or shadowy areas. If there are lighter versus darker areas, brighter areas may appear washed out (i.e., details cannot be distinguished) while no specific objects can be viewed from dark areas.
Location	Light sources must be located above the camera so that light does not shine directly into the camera.

Electronic Controllers

An electronic controller is a piece of electronic equipment that receives incoming electric signals an uses preprogrammed logic to generate electronic output signals based on the incoming signals. While electronic controllers can be implemented for any application that involves inputs and outputs (e.g., control of a piece of machinery in a factory), in a security application these controllers essentially act as the system's "brain" and can respond to specific security-related inputs with preprogrammed output response. These systems combine the control of electronic circuitry with a logic function such that circuits are opened and closed (and thus equipment is turned on and off) through some preprogrammed logic. The basic principle behind the operation of an electrical controller is that it receives electronic inputs from sensors or any device generating an electrical signal (e.g., electrical signals from motion sensors), and then uses it's preprogrammed logic to produce electrical outputs (e.g., these outputs could turn on power to a surveillance camera or to an audible alarm). Thus, these systems automatically generate a preprogrammed, logical response to a preprogrammed input scenario.

The three major types of electronic controllers are timers, electromechanical relays, and programmable logic controllers (PLCs), which are often called "digital relays." Each type is discussed in more detail below.

Timers use internal signal/inputs (in contrast to externally—generated inputs) and generate electronic output signals at certain times. More specifically, timers control electric current flow to any application to which they are connected and can turn the current on or off on a schedule pre-specificed by the user. Typical timer range (amount of time that can be programmed to elapse before the timer activates linked equipment) is from 0.2 seconds to 10 hours, although some of the more advanced timers have ranges of up to 60 hours. Timers are useful in fixed applications that don't require frequent schedule changes. For example, a timer can be used to turn on the lights in a room or building at a certain time every day. Timers are usually connected to their own power supply (usually 120–240 V).

In contrast to timers, which have internal triggers based on a regular schedule, electromechanical relays and PLCs have both external inputs and external outputs. However, PLCs are more flexible and more powerful than are electromechanical relays, and thus this section focuses primarily on PLCs as the predominant technology for security-related electronic control applications.

Electromechanical relays are simple devices that use a magnetic field to control a switch. Voltage applied to the relay's input coil creates a magnetic field, which attracts an internal metal switch. This causes the relay's contacts to touch, closing the switch and completing the electrical circuit. This activates any linked equipment. These types of systems are often used for high voltage applications, such as in some automotive and other manufacturing processes.

Two-Way Radios

Two-way radios, as discussed here, are limited to a direct unit-to-unit radio communication, either via single unit-to-unit transmission and reception or via multiple hand-held units to a base station radio contact and distribution system. Radio frequency spectrum limitations apply to all hand-held units and directed by the FCC. This also distinguishes a handheld unit from a base station or base station unit (such as those used by an amateur (ham) radio operator), which operate under different wavelength parameters.

Two-way radios allow a user to contact another user or group of users instantly on the same frequency and to transmit voice or data without the need for wires. They use "half-duplex" communications—or communication that can be only transmitted or received—it cannot transmit and receive simultaneously. In other words, only one person may talk, while other personnel with radio(s) can only listen. To talk, the user depresses the talk button and speaks into the radio. The audio then transmits the voice wirelessly to the receiving radios. When the speaker has finished speaking and the channel has cleared, users on any of the receiving radios can transmit; either to answer the first transmission, or to begin a new conversation. In addition to carrying voice data, many types of wireless radios also allow the transmission of digital data, and these radios may be interfaced with computer networks that can use or track this data. For example, some two-way radios can send information such as global positioning system data, or the ID of the radio. Some two-way radios can also send data through a SCADA system.

Wireless radios broadcast these voice or data communications over the airwaves from the transmitter to the receiver. While this can be an advantage in that the signal emanates in all directions and does not need a direct physical connection to be received at the receiver, it can also make the communications vulnerable to being blocked, intercepted, or otherwise altered. However, security features are available to ensure that the communications are not tampered with.

Wireless Data Communications

A wireless data communication system consists of two components: a "Wireless Access Point" (WAP), and a "Wireless Network Interface Card" (sometimes also referred to as a "Client), which work together to complete the communications link. These wireless systems can link electronic devices, computers, and computer systems together using radio waves, thus eliminating the need for these individual components to be directly connected together through physical wires. While wireless data communications have widespread application in water and wastewater systems, they also have limitations. First, wireless data connections are limited by the distance between components (radio waves scatter over a long distance and cannot be received efficiently unless special directional antenna are used). Second, these devices only function if the individual components are in a direct line of sight with each other, since radio waves are affected by interference from physical obstructions. However, in some cases, re-peater units can be used to amplify and retransmit wireless signals to circumvent these problems. The two components of wireless devices are discussed in more detail below.

(1) WAP: The WAP provides the wireless data communication service. It usually consists of a housing (which is constructed from plastic or metal depending on the environment it will be used in) containing a circuit board; flash memory that holds software; one of two external ports to connect to existing wired networks; a wireless radio transmitter/receiver; and one or more antenna connections. Typically, the WAP requires a one-time user configuration to allow the device to interact with the Local Area Network (LAN). This configuration is usually done via a web-driven software application that is accessed via a computer.

(2) Wireless Network Interface Card/Client: A wireless card is a piece of hardware that is plugged in to a computer and enables that computer to make a wireless network connection. The card consists of a transmitter, functional circuitry, and a receiver for the wireless signal, all of which work together to enable communication between the computer, its wireless transmitter/receiver, and its antenna connection. Wireless cards are installed in a computer through a variety of connections, including USB adapters, or Laptop CardBus (PCMCIA), or Desktop Peripheral (PCI) cards. As with the WAP, software is loaded onto the user's computer allowing configuration of the card so that it may operate over the wireless network

Two of the primary applications for wireless data communications systems are to enable mobile or remote connections to a LAN and to establish wireless communica-tions links between SCADA remote telemetry units (RTUs) and sensors in the field. Wireless car connections are usually used for LAN access from mobile computers. Wireless cards can also be incorporated into RTUs to allow them to communicate with sensing devices that are located remotely.

CYBER PROTECTION DEVICES
Various cyber protection devices are currently available for use in protecting IT ser-vice sector computer systems. These protection devices include antivirus and pest eradication software, firewalls, and network intrusion hardware/software. These prod-ucts are discussed in this section.

Antivirus and Pest Eradication Software
Antivirus programs are designed to detect, delay, and respond to programs or pieces of code that are specifically designed to harm computers. These programs are known as "malware." Malware can include computer viruses, worms, and Trojan horse pro-grams (programs that appear to be benign but which have hidden harmful effects).

Pest eradication tools are designed to detect, delay, and respond to "spyware" (strategies that websites use to track user behavior, such as by sending "cookies" to the user's computer) and hacker tools that track keystrokes (keystroke loggers) or passwords (password crackers).

Viruses and pests can enter a computer system through the Internet or through infected floppy discs or CDs. They can also be placed onto a system by insiders. Some of these programs such as viruses and worms then move within a computer's drives and files or between computers if they are networked to each other. This malware can deliberately damage files, utilize memory and network capacity, crash application programs, and initiate transmissions of sensitive information from a PC. While the specific mechanisms of these programs differ, they can infect files and even the basic operating program of the computer firmware/hardware.

The most important features of an antivirus program are its abilities to identify potential malware and to alert a user before infection occurs, as well as its ability to respond to a virus already resident on a system. Most of these programs provide a log so that the user can see what viruses have been detected and where they were detected. After detecting a virus, the antivirus software may delete the virus automatically or it may prompt the user to delete the virus. Some programs will also fix files or programs damaged by the virus.

Various sources of information are available to inform the general public and computer system operators about new viruses being detected. Since antivirus programs use signatures (or snippets of code or data) to detect the presence of a virus, periodic updates are required to identify new threats. Many antivirus software providers offer free upgrades that are able to detect and respond to the latest viruses.

Firewalls

A firewall is an electronic barrier designed to keep computer hackers, intruders, or insiders from accessing specific data files and information on a financial services sector's computer network or other electronic/computer systems. Firewalls operated by evaluating and then filtering information coming through a public network (such as the Internet) into the utility's computer or other electronic system. This evaluation can include identifying the source or destination addresses and ports and allowing or denying access based on this identification.

There are two methods used by firewalls to limit access to the utility's computers or other electronic systems from the public network:

- The firewall may deny all traffic unless it meets certain criteria.
- The firewall may allow all traffic through unless it meets certain criteria.

A simple example of the first method is to screen requests to ensure that they come from an acceptable (i.e., previously identified) domain name and Internet protocol address. Firewalls may also use more complex rules that analyze the application data to determine if the traffic should be allowed through. For example, the firewall may require user authentication (i.e., use of a password) to access the system. How a firewall determines what traffic to let through depends on which network layer it operates at and how it is configured. Some of the pros and cons of various methods to control traffic flowing in and out of the network are provided in table 9.12.

Firewalls may be a piece of hardware, a software program, or an appliance card that contains both.

Advanced features that can be incorporated into firewalls allow for the tracking of attempts to log on to the local area network system. For example, a report of successful and unsuccessful long-in attempts may be generated for the computer specialist to analyze. For systems with mobile users, firewalls allow remote access in to the private network by the use of secure log-on procedures and authentication certificates. Most firewalls have a graphical user interface for managing the firewall.

In addition, new Ethernet firewall cards that fit in the slot of an individual computer bundle additional layers of defense (like encryption and permit/deny) for individual computer transmissions to the network interface function. These new cards have only a slightly higher cost than traditional network interface cards.

Network Intrusion Hardware/Software

Network intrusion detection and prevention system are software- and hardware-based programs designed to detect unauthorized attacks on a computer network system.

While other applications, such as firewalls and antivirus software, share similar objectives with network intrusion systems, network intrusion systems provide a deeper layer of protection beyond the capabilities of these other systems because they evaluate pattern of computer activity rather than specific files.

It is worth noting that attacks may come from either outside or within the system (i.e., from an insider), and that network intrusion detection systems may be more applicable for detecting patterns of suspicious activity from inside a facility (i.e., accessing sensitive data, etc.) than are other information technology solutions.

Network intrusion detection systems employ a variety of mechanisms to evaluate potential threats. The types of search and detection mechanisms are dependent upon the level of sophistication of the system. Some of the available detection methods include:

- Protocol analysis—Protocol analysis is the process of capturing, decoding, and interpreting electronic traffic. The protocol analysis method of network intrusion

Table 9.12. Pros and Con of Various Firewall Methods for Controlling Network Access

Method	Description	Pros	Cons
Packet Filtering	Incoming and outgoing packets (small chunks of data) are analyzed against a set of filters. Packets that make it through the filters are sent to the requesting system and all others are discarded. There are two type of packet filtering: static (the most common) and dynamic.	Static filtering is relatively inexpensive and little maintenance required. It is well-suited for closed environments where access to or from multiple addresses is not allowed.	Leaves permanent open holes in the network; allows direct connection to internal hosts by external sources; offers no user authentication, method can be unmanageable in large networks.
Proxy Service	Information from the Internet is retrieved by the firewall and then sent to the requesting system and vice versa. In this way, the firewall can limit the information made known to the requesting system, making vulnerabilities less apparent.	Only allows temporary open holes in the network perimeter. Can be used for all types of internal protocol services.	Allows direct connections to internal hosts by external clients; offers no user authentication.
Stateful Pattern Recognition	This method examines and compares the contents of certain key parts of an information packet against a database of acceptable information. Information traveling from inside the firewall to the outside is monitored for specific then incoming information is compared to these characteristics. If the comparison yields a reasonable match, the information is allowed through. If not, the information is discarded.	Provides a limited time window to allow pockets of information to be sent; does not allow any direct connections between internal and external hosts; supports user-level authentication.	Slower than packet filtering; does not support all types of connections.

USEPA, 2005.

detection involves the analysis of data captured during transactions between two or more systems or devices and the evaluation of these data to identify unusual activity and potential problems. Once a problem is isolated and recorded, problems or potential threats can be linked to pieces of hardware or software. Sophisticated protocol analysis will also provide statistics and trend information on the captured traffic.

- Traffic anomaly detection—Traffic anomaly detection identifies potential threatening activity by comparing incoming traffic to "normal" traffic patterns and identifying deviations. It does this by comparing user characteristics against thresholds and triggers defined by the network administrator. This method is designed to detect attacks that span a number of connections rather than a single session.
- Network honeypot—This method establishes non-existent services in order to identify potential hackers. A network honeypot impersonates services that don't exist by sending fake information to people scanning the network. It identifies the attacker when they attempt to connect to the service. There is no reason for legitimate traffic to access these resources because they don't exist; therefore any attempt to access them constitutes an attack.
- Antiintrusion detection system evasion techniques—These methods are designed by attackers who may be trying to evade intrusion detection system scanning. They include methods called IP defragmentation, TCP streams reassembly, and deobfuscation.

While these detection systems are automated, they can only indicate patterns of activity and a computer administer or other experienced individual must interpret activities to determine whether or not they are potentially harmful. Monitoring the logs generated by these systems can be time consuming, and there may be a learning curve to determine a baseline of "normal" traffic patterns from which to distinguish potential suspicious activity.

NOTE

1. It is important to point out that even though the following USEPA security asset and device recommendations were first made for the water/wastewater critical infrastructure; these recommendations are applicable to all other critical infrastructure sectors, including the CS sector where practicable.

REFERENCES AND RECOMMENDED READING

DHS (2009). *National Infrastructure Protection Plan*. Retrieved 05/11/17 @http://www.dhs. gov/ xlibrary/assets/NIPP.Plan.pdf.

DHS (2003). The National Strategy for the Physical Protection of Critical Infrastructures and Key Assets. Accessed @ https://www.dhs.gov/xlibrary/assets/physical_Strat.

DHS (2013). Homeland Security Directive 7: Critical Infrastructure Identification, Prioritization, and Protection accessed @ https://www.dihs.gov/xabout/laws/gc_1214597989952.shtm.

DHS (2016). *Information Technology Sector—An Annex to the National Infrastructure Protection Plan*. Washington, DC: Department of Homeland Security.

Garcia, M. L. (2001). *The Design and Evaluation of Physical Protection Systems*. Oxford, UK: Butterworth-Heinemann.

IBWA (2004). *Bottled Water Safety and Security*. Alexandria, VA: International Bottled Water Association.

NAERC (2002). *Security Guidelines for the Electricity Sector*. Washington, DC: North American Electric Reliability Council.

Schneier, B. (2000). *Secrets & Lies*. New York: Wiley.

USEPA (2005). *Water and Wastewater Security Product Guide*. Accessed 4/14/16 @ http://cfpub.epa.gov.safewater/watersecurity/guide.

10

The Paradigm Shift

It takes disasters to trigger change because dangers that remain hypothetical fail to trigger appropriate sensory response.

—*D. D. P. Johnson and E. M. P Madin*

The 9/11 shift: There is a new world view in the making.

If men would learn from history, what lessens it might teach us!

—*Samuel Coleridge*

The events of 9/11 dramatically changed the United States and focused Americans on combating terrorism. As a result, in 2003 and subsequent years, the Department of Homeland Security (DHS) in conjunction with members from the general public, state and local agencies, and private groups concerned with the safety of critical infrastructures, established a Water Security Working Group (WSWG) to consider and make recommendations on infrastructure security issues. Although initially created to make recommendations for water/wastewater security, WSWG is an excellent template for use with other critical infrastructures, including IT service assets. For example, the WSWG identified active and effective security practices for critical infrastructure and provide an approach for adopting these practices. It also recommended mechanisms to provide incentives that facilitate broad and receptive response among critical infrastructure sectors to implement active and effective security practices. Finally, WSWG recommended mechanisms to measure progress and achievements in implementing active and effective security practices and identify barriers to implementation.

The WSWG recommendations on security are structured to maximize benefits to critical industries by emphasizing actions that have the potential both to improve the quality or reliability of service and to enhance security. These recommendations, based on original recommendations from the 2003 National Drinking Water Advisor

Council (NDWAC), were designed primarily, as the name suggests, for use by water systems of all types and sizes, including systems that serve less than 3,300 people. However, it is the authors' opinion, based on personal experience, that NDWAC's recommendations, when properly adapted to applicable circumstances and locations, can be applied to any and all critical infrastructure sectors, including the financial services sector.

The NDWAC identified fourteen features of active and effective security programs that are important to increasing security and relevant across the broad range of utility circumstances and operating conditions. USEPA (2003) points out that the fourteen features are, in many cases, consistent with the steps needed to maintain technical, managerial, and operational performance capacity related to overall water quality; as pointed out earlier, these steps can be applied to other critical infrastructures as well. Many facilities may be able to adopt some of the features with minimal, if any, capital investment.

FOURTEEN FEATURES OF ACTIVE AND EFFECTIVE SECURITY

It is important to point out that the fourteen features of active and effective programs emphasize that "one size does not fit all" and is not a cookie-cutter approach to effective implementation of security measures. There will be variability in security approaches and tactics among commercial securities sector facilities, based on industry-specific circumstances and operating conditions. The fourteen features:

- Are sufficiently flexible to apply to all IT Services Sector assets, regardless of size
- Incorporate the idea that active and effective security programs should have measurable goals and time lines
- Allow flexibility for IT sector facilities to develop specific security approaches and tactics that are appropriate to industry-specific circumstances

IT sector facilities can differ in many ways including:

- Number of supply sources
- Energy capacity
- Operation risk
- Location risk
- Security budget
- Spending priorities
- Political and public support
- Legal barriers
- Public versus private ownership

IT sector facilities should address security in an informed and systematic way, regardless of these differences. Financial services sector facilities need to fully understand the specific local circumstances and conditions under which they operate and develop a security program tailored to those conditions. The goal in identifying common features of active and effective security programs is to achieve consistency in security program outcomes among IT sector facilities while allowing for and encouraging facilities to develop utility-specific security approaches and tactics. The features are based on a comprehensive "security management layering system" approach that incorporates a combination of public involvement and awareness, partnerships, and physical, chemical, operational, and design controls to increase overall program performance. They address industry security in four functional categories: *organization, operation, infrastructure*, and *external*. These functional categories are discussed in greater detail below.

- **Organizational**—There is always something that can be done to improve security. Even when resources are limited, the simple act of increasing organizational attentiveness to security may reduce vulnerability and increase responsiveness. Preparedness itself can help deter attacks. The first step to achieving preparedness is to make security a part of the organizational culture so that it is in the day-to-day thinking of front-line employees, emergency responders, and management of every IT facility in this country. To successfully incorporate security into "business as usual," there must be a strong commitment to security by organization leadership and by the supervising body, such as the board of stockholders. The following features address how a security culture can be incorporated into an organization.
- **Operational**—In addition to having a strong culture and awareness of security within an organization, an active and effective security program makes security part of operational activities, from daily operations, such as monitoring of physical access controls, to scheduled annual reassessments. IT service sector entities will often find that by implementing security into operations they can also reap cost benefits and improve the quality or reliability of the energy service.
- **Infrastructure**—These recommendations advise utilities to address security in all elements of IT sector infrastructure—from source to distribution and through processing and product delivery.
- **External**—Strong relationships with response partners and the public strengthen security and public confidence. Two of the recommended features of active end effective security programs address this need.

Fourteen Features

Feature 1. Make an explicit and visible commitment of the senior leadership to security.
IT service sector facilities should create an explicit, easily communicated, enterprise-wide commitment to security, which can be done through:

- Incorporating security into a utility-wide mission or vision statement, addressing the full scope of an active and effective security program—that is, protection of worker/public health, worker/public safety, and public confidence, and that is part of core day-to-day operations.
- Developing an enterprise-wide security policy or set of policies.

IT service sector entities should use the process of making a commitment to security as an opportunity to raise awareness of security throughout the organization, making the commitment visible to all employees and customers, and to help every facet of the enterprise to recognize the contribution they can make to enhancing security.

Feature 2. Promote security awareness throughout the organization.
The objective of a security culture should be to make security awareness a normal, accepted, and routine part of day-to-day operations. Examples of tangible efforts include:

- Conducting employee training
- Incorporating security into job descriptions
- Establishing performance standards and evaluations for security
- Creating and maintaining a security tip line and suggestion box for employees
- Making security a routine part of staff meetings and organization planning
- Create a security policy

Feature 3. Assess vulnerabilities and periodically review and update vulnerability assessments to reflect changes in potential threats and vulnerabilities.
Because circumstances change, IT sector facilities should maintain their understanding and assessment of vulnerabilities as a "living document," and continually adjust their security enhancement and maintenance priorities. IT service sector facilities should consider their individual circumstances and establish and implement a schedule for review of their vulnerabilities.

Assessments should take place once every three to five years at a minimum. IT service sector facilities may be well served by performing assessments annually.

The basic elements of sound vulnerability assessments are:

- Characterization of the chemical processing system, including its mission and objectives
- Identification and prioritization of adverse consequences to avoid
- Determination of critical assets that might be subject to malevolent acts that could result in undesired consequences
- Assessment of the likelihood (qualitative probability) of such malevolent acts from adversaries
- Evaluation of existing countermeasures
- Analysis of current risk and development of a prioritized plan for risk reduction

Feature 4. Identify security priorities and, on an annual basis, identify the resources dedicated to security programs and planned security improvements, if any.
Dedicated resources are important to ensure a sustained focus on security. Investment in security should be reasonable considering utilities' specific circumstances. In some circumstances, investment may be as simple as increasing the amount of time and attention that executives managers give to security. Where threat potential or potential consequences are greater, greater investment likely is warranted.

This feature establishes the expectation that IT facilities should, through their annual capital, operations, and maintenance, and staff resources plans, identify and set aside resources consistent with their specific identified security needs. Security priorities should be clearly documented and should be reviewed with utility executives at least once per year as part of the traditional budgeting process.

Feature 5. Identify managers and employees who are responsible for security and establish security expectations for all staff.
- Explicit identification of security responsibilities is important for development of a security culture with accountability.
- At minimum, communication sector facilities should identify a single, designated individual responsible for overall security, even if other security roles and responsibilities will likely be dispersed throughout the organization.
- The number and depth of security-related roles will depend on an asset's specific circumstances.

Feature 6. Establish physical and procedural controls to restrict access to chemical industrial infrastructure to only those conducting authorized, official business and to detect unauthorized physical intrusions.
Examples of physical access controls include fencing critical areas, locking gates and doors, and installing barriers at site access points. Monitoring for physical intrusion can include maintaining well-lighted facility perimeters, installing motion detectors, and utilizing intrusion alarms. The use of neighborhood watches, regular employee

rounds, and arrangements with local police and fire departments can support identifying unusual activity in the vicinity of facilities.

Examples of procedural access controls include inventorying keys, changing access
codes regularly, and requiring security passes to pass gates at access sensitive area. In
addition, utilities should establish the means to readily identify all employees including contractors and temporary workers with unescorted access to facilities.

*Feature 7. Employee protocols for detection of contamination consistent with the
recognized limitations in current contaminant detection, monitoring, and
surveillance technology.*
Until progress can be made in the development of practical and affordable online
contaminant monitoring and surveillance systems, most IT sector facilities must use
other approaches to contaminant monitoring and surveillance.

*Feature 8. Define security-sensitive information; establish physical, electronic,
and procedural controls to restrict access to security-sensitive information; detect
unauthorized access; and ensure information and communications systems will function
during emergency response and recover.*
Protecting IT systems largely involves using physical hardening and procedural steps
to limit the number of individuals with authorized access and to prevent access by unauthorized individuals. Examples of physical steps to harden SCADA and IT networks
include installing and maintaining fire walls and screening the network for viruses.
Examples of procedural steps include restricting remote access to data networks and
safeguarding critical data through backups and storage in safe places. Utilities should
strive for continuous operation of IT and telecommunications systems, even in the
event of an attack, by providing uninterruptible power supply and back-up systems,
such as satellite phones.

In addition to protecting IT systems, security sensitive information should be identified and restricted to the appropriate personnel. Security sensitive information could
be contained within:

- Facility maps and blueprints
- Operations details
- Hazardous material utilization and storage
- Tactical level security program details
- Any other information on utility operations or technical details that could aid in
  planning or execution of an attack

Feature 9. Incorporate security considerations into decisions about acquisition, repair, major maintenance, and replacement of physical infrastructure; include consideration of opportunities to reduce risk through physical hardening and adoption of inherently lower-risk design and technology options.

Prevention is a key aspect of enhancing security. Consequently, consideration of security issues should begin as early as possible in facility construction (i.e., it should be a factor in building plans and designs). However, to incorporate security considerations into design choices, IT facilities need information about the types of security design approaches and equipment that are available and the performance of these designs and equipment in multiple dimensions. For example, IT sector facilities would want to evaluate not just the way that a particular design might contribute to security, but would also look at how that design would affect the efficiency of day-to-day plant operations and worker safety.

Feature 10. Monitor available threat-level information and escalate security procedures in response to relevant threats.

Monitoring threat information should be a regular part of a security program manager's job, and utility-, facility-, and region-specific threat levels and information should be shared with those responsible for security. As part of security planning, financial service sector facilities should develop systems to access threat information, procedures that will be followed in the event of increased industry or facility threat levels, and should be prepared to put these procedures in place immediately so that adjustments are seamless. Involving local law enforcement and the FBI is critical.

IT service sector facilities should investigate what networks and information sources might be available to them locally and at the state and regional level. If a utility cannot gain access to some information networks, attempts should be made to align with those who can and will provide effective information to the financial service sector facility.

Feature 11. Incorporate security considerations into emergency response and recovery plans, test and review plans regularly, and update plans to reflect changes in potential threats, physical infrastructure, chemical processing operations, critical interdependencies, and response protocols in partner organizations.

IT service sector facilities should maintain response and recovery plans as "living documents." In incorporating security considerations into their emergency response and recovery plans, chemical facilities also should be aware of the National Incident Management System (MIMS) guidelines, established by DHS, and of regional and local incident management commands and systems, which tend to flow from the national guidelines.

IT service sector facilities should consider their individual circumstances and establish, develop, and implement a schedule for review of emergency response and recovery plans. IT service sector facility plans should be thoroughly coordinated with emergency response and recovery planning in the larger community. As part of this coordination, a mutual program should be established to arrange in advance for exchanging resources (personnel or physical assets) among agencies within a region in the event of an emergency or disaster that disrupts operation. Typically, the exchange of resource is based on a written formal mutual agreement. For example, Florida's Water-Wastewater Agency Response Network (FlaWARN), deployed after Hurricane Katrina, allowed the new "utilities helping utilities" network to respond to urgent requests from Mississippi for help to bring facilities back on-line after the hurricane.

The emergency response and recovery plans should be reviewed and updated as needed annually. This feature also establishes the expectation that chemical facilities should test or exercise their emergency response and recovery plans regularly.

Feature 12. Develop and implement strategies for regular, ongoing security-related communications with employees, response organizations, rate setting organizations, and customers.

An active and effective security program should address protection of public health, public safety (including infrastructure), and public confidence. IT service sector facilities should create an awareness of security and an understanding of the rationale for their overall security management approach in the communities they reside in and/ or serve.

Effective communication strategies consider key messages; who is best equipped/ trusted to deliver the key messages; the need for message consistency, particularly during an emergency; and the best mechanisms for delivering messages and for receiving information and feedback from key partners. The key audiences for communication strategies are: utility employees, response organizations, and customers.

Feature 13. Forge reliable and collaborative partnerships with the communities served, managers of critical interdependent infrastructure, response organizations, and other local utilities.

Effective partnerships build collaborative working relationships and clearly define roles and responsibilities so that people can work together seamlessly if an emergency should occur. It is important for IT sector facilities within a region and neighboring regions to collaborate and establish a mutual aid program with neighboring utilities, response organizations, and sectors such as the power sector, on which utilities rely or impact. Mutual aid agreements provide for help from other organizations that can be prearranged and accessed quickly and efficiently in the event of a terrorist attack or natural disaster. Developing reliable and collaborative partnerships involves reaching out to managers and key staff and other organizations to build reciprocal understanding and to share information about the facility's security concerns and planning. Such efforts will maximize the efficiency and effectiveness of a mutual aid program during an emergency response effort, as the organizations will be familiar with each others' circumstances and thus will be better able to serve each other.

It is also important for IT sector facilities to develop partnerships with the communities and customers they serve. Partnerships help to build credibility within communities and establish public confidence in utility operations. People who live near financial service sector facility structures can be the eyes and ears of the facility and can be encouraged to notice and report changes in operating procedures or other suspicious behaviors.

IT service sector facilities and public health organizations should establish formal agreements on coordination to ensure regular exchange of information between facilities and public health organizations and outline roles and responsibilities during response to and recovery from an emergency. Coordination is important at all levels of the public health community—national public health, county health agencies, and healthcare providers, such as hospitals.

Feature 14. Develop IT services facility-specific measures of security activities and achievements and self-assess against these measures to understand and document program progress.
Although security approaches and tactics will be different depending on IT-specific circumstances and operating conditions, we recommend that all financial service sector facilities monitor and measure a number of common types of activities and achievements, including existence of program policies and procedures, training, testing, and implementing schedules and plans.

The Fourteen Feature Matrix
In the following, a matrix of recommended measures to assess effectiveness of a IT service sector facility's security program is presented. Each feature is grouped according to its functional category: organization, operation, infrastructure, and external.

Ultimately, the goal of implementing the fourteen security features (and all other security provisions) is to create a significant improvement in IT sector facilities on a national scale by reducing vulnerabilities and therefore risk to public health from terrorist attacks and natural disasters. To create a sustainable effect, the IT sector as a whole must not only adopt and actively practice the features, but also incorporate the features into "business as usual."

Table 10.1. Fourteen Features of Active and Effective Security Matrix

Features	Checklist: Potential Measures of Progress
Organizational Features	
Feature 1—Explicit commitment to security	Does a written, enterprise-wide security policy exist, and is the policy reviewed regularly and updated as needed?
Feature 2—Promote security awareness	Are incidents reported in a timely way and are lessons learned from incident responses reviewed and, as appropriate, incorporated into future utility security efforts?
Feature 5—Defined security roles and employee expectations	Are managers and employees who are responsible for security identified?
Operational Features	
Feature 3—Vulnerability assessment up to date?	Are reassessments of vulnerabilities made after incidents and are lessons learned and other relevant information incorporated into security practices?
Feature 4—Security resources assigned to them?	Are security priorities clearly identified, and to what extent and implementation priorities do security priorities have?
Feature 7—Contamination detection	Is there a protocol/procedure in place to identify and respond to suspected contamination events?
Feature 10—Threat-level based protocols	Is there a protocol/procedure of responses that will be made if threat levels change?
Feature 11—Emergency response plan tested and up to date	Do exercise address the full range of threats—physical, cyber, and contamination—and is there a protocol/procedure to incorporate lessons learned from exercises and actual response into updates to emergency response and recovery plans?
Feature 14—Industry-specific measures and self assessment	Does the utility perform self-assessment at least annually?
Infrastructure Features	
Feature 6—Intrusion detection and access control	To what extent are methods to control access to sensitive assets in place?
Feature 8—Information protection and continuity	Is there a procedure to identify and control security-sensitive information, is information correctly categorized, and how to control measures performed under testing?
Feature 9—Design and construction standards	Are security considerations incorporated into internal utility design and construction standards for new facilities/ infrastructure and major maintenance projects?
External Features	
Feature 12—Communications	Is there a mechanism for utility employees, partners, and the community to notify the utility of suspicious occurrences and other security concerns?
Feature 13—Partnerships	Have reliable and collaborative partnerships with customers, managers of independent interrelated infrastructure, and response organizations been established?

Source: USEPA, 2003.

REFERENCES AND RECOMMENDED READING

Coleridge, Samuel (1800). *The Lessons of Living.* London

DHS (2009). *National Infrastructure Protection Plan.* Retrieved 05/11/17 @http://www.dhs.gov/ xlibrary/assets/NIPP.Plan.pdf.

DHS (2003). The National Strategy for the Physical Protection of Critical Infrastructures and Key Assets. Accessed @ https://www.dhs.gov/xlibrary/assets/physical_Strat.

DHS (2007). *Banking and Finance.* Washington, DC: U.S. Department of Homeland Security.

DHS (2013). Homeland Security Directive 7: Critical Infrastructure Identification, Prioritization, and Protection accessed @ https://www.dihs.gov/xabout/laws/ gc_1214597989952.shtm.

DHS (2016). *Information Technology Sector—An Annex to the National Infrastructure Protection Plan.* Washington, DC: Department of Homeland Security.

Johnson, D. D. P., and E. M. P. Madin (2014) *Why Does It Take Disasters to Trigger Change?* Oxford, UK: University of Oxford Press.

USEPA (2003). *Active and Effective Water Security Programs.* Accessed 6/2006 @ http://cfpub .epa.gov/safewater/watersecurity/14 features.cfm.

11

Preparation

When is Enough, Enough?

Question: When preparing to respond to terrorist acts against people, malls, schools, sports stadiums, libraries, communications systems, government facilities and financial services assets when is enough, enough?
Answer: Until we can read the terrorists' minds, enough preparation is never enough. Simply, preparation is ongoing and never-ending.

—Frank R. Spellman

The possibility of terrorism—attacks on U.S. information technology services sector infrastructure—doesn't generate the same attention as potential nuclear, biological, or chemical terrorism. Why? Simply, when you ask a citizen about U.S. information technology service sector assets, he or she just looks at you like you are some kind of wacko. I know, I have asked. Anyway, because of the seriousness of the threat of terrorism to the nation's IT service sector and the enormous economic and security implications of such attacks, US FCC, USDOE, USEPA, USDHS, and other agencies have worked nonstop since 9/11 in gathering and providing as much advice and guidance as possible to aid IT service securities sector personnel in protecting IT service sector assets and associated critical support infrastructure. In this chapter we provide an overview of important tools that can be used in protecting IT service sector to guard against the threat of terrorism. In the discussion, keep in mind that even though this is an IT service sector issue, the guidance provided could be used to protect other critical infrastructure sectors.

THREATS AND INCIDENTS

Based on evidence of potential losses from past accidents, indication of the potential human and environmental losses and economic costs from an attack on a IT service sector facility or producer comes from major incidents that have occurred both abroad and in the United States. Those events indicate that the human and environmental losses could be significant (CBO, 2004).

IT service sector threats and incidents may be of particular concern due to the range of potential consequences:

- Creating an adverse impact on public health within a population
- Disrupting system operations and interrupting the supply of critical military components
- Causing physical damage to system infrastructure
- Reducing public confidence in the financial services system
- Long-term denial of basic security and protection and the cost of replacement

Keep in mind that some of these consequences would only be realized in the event of a successful terrorist incident; however, the mere threat of terrorism can also have an adverse impact on industries that depend on a safe, steady supply of commercial and financial services. In addition, the economic implications of such attacks are potentially enormous. For example, many believe that the reason we are looking at oil at more than $60 a barrel is the fact that we have a "terror premium" factored into the price of a barrel of oil.

While it is important to consider the range of possibilities associated with a particular threat, assessments are typically based on the probability of a particular occurrence. Determining probability is somewhat subjective and is often based on intelligence and previous incidents. As mentioned, there are historical accounts of accidental incidents that have caused tremendous death and destruction.

Threat Warning Signs

A threat warning is an occurrence or discovery that indicates a potential threat that triggers an evaluation of the threat. It is important to note that these warnings must be evaluated in the context of typical industry activity and previous experience in order to avoid false alarms. Following is a brief description of potential warnings.

- *Security Breach.* Physical security breaches, such as unsecured doors, open hatches, and unlocked/forced gates, are probably the most common threat warnings. In most cases, the security breach is likely related to lax operations or typical criminal activity such as trespassing, vandalism, and theft. However, it may be prudent to assess any security breach with respect to the possibility of attack.

- *Witness Account.* Awareness of an incident may be triggered by a witness account of tampering. IT service sector sites/facilities should be aware that individuals observing suspicious behavior near IT service sector facilities will likely call 911. In this case, the incident warning technically might come from law enforcement, as described below. *Note*: the witness may be a commercial service employee engaged in their normal duties.
- *Direct Notification by Perpetrator.* A threat may be made directly to the IT service sector site, plant, or facility, either verbally or in writing. Historical incidents would indicate that verbal threats made over the phone are more likely than written threats. While the notification may be a hoax, threatening a IT service sector unit is a crime and should be taken seriously.
- *Notification by Law Enforcement.* An IT service sector site/facility may receive notification about a threat directly from law enforcement, including local, country, state, or federal agencies. As discussed previously, such a threat could be a result of suspicious activity reported to law enforcement, either by a perpetrator, a witness, or the news media. Other information, gathered through intelligence or informants, could also lead law enforcement to conclude that there may be a threat to the IT service sector site/facility. While law enforcement will have to be lead in the criminal investigation, the IT service sector site/facility has primary responsibility for the safety of its equipment and processes. Thus, the plant's role will likely be to help law enforcement to appreciate the public health implications of a particular threat as well as the technical feasibility of carrying out a particular threat.
- *Notification by News Media.* A threat to destroy an IT service site/facility might be delivered to the news media, or the media may discover a threat. A conscientious reporter would immediately report such a threat to the police and either the reporter or the police would immediately contact the IT service sector site/facility. This level of professionalism would provide an opportunity for the asset to work with the media and law enforcement to assess the credibility of the threat before any broader notification is made.

RESPONSE TO THREATS

Note: This section is not designed to discuss what specific steps to take in responding to a terrorist threat. Rather, the questions addressed in this section are "Why is it necessary to plan to respond to IT service sector threats at all?" and "When have I done enough?"

Federal, state, and local programs already exist that—with varying degrees of effectiveness—encourage or require the operators of IT service sector sites/facilities to boost their efforts to promote safety and security and to share information that can help local governments plan for emergencies.

Proper planning is a delicate process because public health measures are rarely noticed or appreciated (such as buried utility pipes, they are often hidden functions except when they fail)—then they are very visible. The result to too little action, including no response at all, can have disastrous consequences potentially resulting in public injuries or fatalities. One overriding question is "When has an IT service producer done enough?" This question may be particularly difficult to address when considering the wide range of agencies that may be involved in a threat situation. Other organizations such as US FCC, USEPA, USDHA, USDOE, CDC, USDOT, law enforcement agencies, public health departments, etc. will each have unique obligations or interests in responding to a severe release or explosion threat.

When is Enough, Enough?

The guiding principle for responding to severe release or explosion threats is one of "due diligence" or "What is a suitable and sensible response to a threat?" As discussed above, some response to IT service sector failures is warranted due to the public health implications of an actual dangerous incident.

Ultimately, the answer to the question of "due diligence" must be decided at the local level and will depend on a number of considerations. Among other factors, local authorities must decide what level of risk is reasonable in the context of a perceived threat. Careful planning is essential to developing an appropriate response to terrorist threats, and in fact, one primary objective of USEPA's *Response Protocol Tool Boxes* (RPTBs) is to aid users in the development of their own site-specific plans that are consistent with the needs and responsibilities of the user. Beyond planning, the RPTB considers a careful evaluation of any terrorist threat, and an appropriate response based on the evaluation, to be the most important element of due diligence.

In the RPTB, the threat management process is considered in three successive stages: "possible," "credible," and "confirmed." Thus, as the threat escalates through these three states, the actions that might be considered due diligence expand accordingly. The following paragraphs describe, in general terms, actions that might be considered as due diligence at these various stages.

- Stage 1: "Is the threat possible?" If an IT service facility is faced with a terrorism threat, it should evaluate the available information to determine whether or not the threat is "possible" (i.e., could something have actually happened). If the threat is "possible," immediate operational response actions might be implemented and activities such as site characterization would be initiated to collect additional information to support the next stage of the threat evaluation.
- Stage 2: "Is the threat credible?" Once a threat is considered "possible," additional information will be necessary to determine if the threat is "credible." The threshold

at the credible stage is higher than that at the possible stage, and in general there must be information to corroborate the threat in order for it to be considered "credible."

- Stage 3: "Has the incident been confirmed?" Confirmation implies that definitive evidence and information have been collected to establish the presence of a threat to the IT service sector. Obviously, at this stage the concept of due diligence takes on a whole new meaning since authorities are now faced with death and destruction and a potential public health crisis. Response actions at this point include all steps necessary to protect public health, property and the environment.

PREPARATION

IT service sector facility managers and employees must know their facilities. For these persons, there is no excuse for not knowing every square inch of the facility site. In particular, workers should know about any and all construction activities underway on the site; the actual construction parameters of the facility; and especially operation of all transactional unit processes. In addition, management must not only know their operating staff but also their customers.

Construction and Operation

Each IT service sector facility is unique with respect to age, operation, and complexity. This is important, particularly in evaluating the potential of a commercial service failure or malicious action causing an IT service failure.

Personnel

IT service sector employees are generally its most valuable asset in preparing for and responding to threats and incidents. They have knowledge of the system and potential problem areas. The importance of knowledgeable and experienced personnel is highlighted by the complexity of most commercial financial service systems. This complexity makes a specific terrorist target contingent upon detailed knowledge of the system configuration and usage patterns. If perpetrators have somehow gained a sophisticated understanding of an IT service communications network system, the day-to-day experience of network production will prove an invaluable tool to countering any attacks. For instance, personnel may continually look for unusual aspects of daily operation that might be interpreted as a potential threat warning, and may also be aware of specific characteristics of the system that make it vulnerable to malware attacks or worse.

Customers

A customer's knowledge of IT service availability, functionality, and delivery is an important component of preventing and managing system intrusion incidents.

Prevention is based largely on understanding potential types of malware attacks and the type of target facility. Steps taken to protect the customer's financial services tie-ins and in addition its employees and property, such as enhancements to the physical security of the sender's and receiver's financial services system may deter the attack itself.

IT service customers vary significantly with regard to their expectations of what constitutes acceptable service, so it is necessary to consider the manner in which IT service sector services are used in a particular system. Planning, preparation, and allo-cation of IT service resources should be directed toward protecting the public at large, beyond specific demographic groups or individual users.

Perform Training and Desk/Field Exercises

In addition to a lack of planning, another reason that emergency response plans fail is lack of training and practice. Training provides the necessary means for everyone involved to acquire the skills to fulfill their role during an emergency. It may also provide important "buy-in" to the response process from both management and staff, which is essential to the success of any response plan. Desk exercise (also known as "tabletops," or "sand lot," or "dry runs") along with field exercises allow participants to practice their skills. Also, these exercises will provide a test of the IT service security plan itself, revealing strengths and weakness that may be used to improve the overall plan.

Enhance Physical Security

Where possible, deny physical access to non-pedestrian sites; within the IT service sec-tor system this may act as a deterrent to a perpetrator. When we consider that many of the IT service sector backup support units such as power generating and tower trans-mission systems are often in remote, wide-open spaces, this can be a huge challenge. Terrorists often seek the easiest route of attack, just like a burglar prefers a house with an open window or an open automobile with keys in the ignition. Aside from deterring actual attacks, enhancing physical security has other benefits. For example, security cameras can be used to review security breaches and determine if the incident was simply due to trespassing or is a potential contamination threat. The costs of enhancing physical security may be justified by comparison to the cost of respond-ing to just one "credible" munitions explosion or contamination threat involving site characterization and lab analysis for potential contaminants.

THE BOTTOM LINE

This chapter has emphasized the importance of ensuring the physical security of IT service sector facilities and equipment. But it is important to point out that true IT service sector security goes beyond the physical plant; the sector requires security of a different kind. This is the case of course because IT service facilities are wide-open, soft targets that can be accessed by just about anyone. Placing a fence, barricades, and locking systems around a Wal-Mart or a sports stadium to prevent entry makes little sense when the purpose of these facilities, and other like facilities, is to provide convenient access for customers. However, cybersecurity is a different matter; much of the IT service infrastructure, including control architecture, is vulnerable to cyberattack from either inside or outside of the network. The fact is that perhaps the largest vulnerability and dependency of the IT service infrastructure as well as the infrastructure for other sectors is on cybersecurity. The control of IT service networks and all of its functional components are vulnerable to various degrees of cyberattacks on the software operating systems by either the idle hacker or the more malicious intruder participating in information warfare. This is also true of all the networks within other sectors. The bottom line, the networks must be protected and guarded from attack.

REFERENCES AND RECOMMENDED READING

CBO (2004) *Homeland Security and the Private Sector.* Washington, DC: Congressional Budget Office.

DHS (2009). *National Infrastructure Protection Plan.* Retrieved 05/11/17 @http://www.dhs. gov/ xlibrary/assets/NIPP.Plan.pdf.

DHS (2003). The National Strategy for the Physical Protection of Critical Infrastructures and Key Assets. Accessed @ https://www.dhs.gov/xlibrary/assets/physical_Strat.

DHS (2013). Homeland Security Directive 7: Critical Infrastructure Identification, Prioritization, and Protection accessed @ https://www.dihs.gov/xabout/laws/ gc_1214597989952.shtm.

DHS (2016). *Information Technology Sector—An Annex to the National Infrastructure Protection Plan.* Washington, DC: Department of Homeland Security.

Henry, K. (2002). New face of security. *Gov. Security*, pp. 30–37.

Spellman, F. R. (1999). *Process Safety Management.* Lancaster, PA: Technomic Publishing Co.

USEPA (2004). *Response Protocol Toolbox: Planning for and Responding to Drinking Water Contamination Threats and Incidents.* Washington, DC: United States Environmental Protection Agency.

USEPA (2011). *Response Protocol Toolbox: Planning for and Responding to Wastewater Contamination Threats and Incidents.* Washington, DC: United States Environmental Protection Agency.

Glossary

Cybersecurity and Terrorism

Acid bomb—A crude bomb made by combining muriatic acid with aluminum strips in a 2-liter soda bottle.

Adware—Any software application that displays advertising banners while the program is running. Adware often includes code that tracks a user's personal information and passes it on to third parties without the user's authorization or knowledge. And if your gather enough to if, adware slows down your computer significantly. Over time, performance may be so degraded that you may have trouble working productivity.

Aerosol—A fine mist or spray that contains minute particles.

Aflatoxin—A toxin created by bacteria that grow on stored foods, especially on rice, peanuts, and cotton seeds.

All-Hazards—A grouping classification encompassing all conditions, environmental or manmade, that have the potential to cause injury, illness, or death; damage to or loss of equipment, infrastructure services, property, or alternatively causing functional degradation to social, economic, or environmental aspects.

Afghanistan—At the time of 9/11, Afghanistan was governed by the Taliban and Osama bin Laden called it home. Amid U.S. air strikes, which began on October 7, 2001, the United States sent in more than $300 million in humanitarian aid. In December 2001, Afghanistan reopened their embassy for the first time in more than 20 years.

Agency—A division of government with a specific function, or a non-governmental organization (e.g., private contractor, business, etc.) that offers a particular kind of assistance. In the incident command system, agencies are defined as jurisdictional (having statutory responsibility for incident mitigation) or assisting and/or cooperating (providing resources and/or assistance).

Air marshal—A federal marshal whose purpose is to ride commercial flights dressed in plain clothes and armed to prevent hijackings. Israel's use of air marshals on El Al is credited as the reason Israel has had a single hijacking in 31 years. The United States started using air marshals after September 11. Despite President Bush's urging there are not enough air marshals to go around, many flights do not have them.

Airborne—Carried by or through the air.

Al Jazeera—Satellite television station based in Qatar and broadcast throughout the Middle East, al Jazeera has often been called the "CNN" of the Arab world.

Al Qaeda—Meaning "the Base"; an international terrorist group founded in approximately 1989 and dedicated to opposing non-Islamic governments with force and violence. One of the principal goals of al Qaeda was to drive the U.S. armed forces out of the Saudi Arabian peninsula and Somalia by violence. Currently wanted for several terrorist attacks, including those on the U.S. embassy in Kenya and Tanzania as well as the first and second World Trade Center bombings, and the attack on the Pentagon.

Al Tahwid—A Palestinian group based in London that professes a desire to destroy both Israel and the Jewish people throughout Europe. Eleven al Tahwid were arrested in Germany allegedly as they were about to begin attacking that country.

Alpha radiation—The least penetrating type of nuclear radiation. Not considered dangerous unless particles enter the body.

American Airlines Flight 11—The Boeing 767 carrying 81 passengers, 9 flight attendants, and 2 pilots, which was high jacked and crashed into the north tower of the World Trade Center at 8:45 a.m. Eastern Time on September 11, 2001. Flight 11 was en route to Los Angeles from Boston.

American Airlines Flight 77—The Boeing 757 carrying 58 passengers, 4 flight attendants, and 2 pilots, which was high jacked and crashed into the Pentagon at 9:40 a.m. Eastern Time on September 11, 2001. Flight was en route to Los Angeles from Dulles International Airport in Virginia.

Ammonium nitrate-fuel oil (ANFO)—A powerful explosive made by mixing fertilizer and fuel oil. The type of bomb used in the first World Trade Center attack as well as the Oklahoma City bombing.

Analyte—The name assigned to a substance or feature that describes it in terms of its molecular composition, taxonomic nomenclature, or other characteristic.

Anthrax—An often fatal infectious disease contracted from animals. Anthrax spores have a long survival period; the incubation period is short; disability is severe, making anthrax a bioweapon of choice by several nations.

Antidote—A remedy to counteract the effects of poison.

Antigen—A substance that stimulates an immune response by the body; the immune system recognizes such substances as foreign and produces antibodies to fight them.

Antitoxin—An antibody that neutralizes a biological toxin.

Antivirus software—Software designed to detect and potentially eliminate viruses before they have had a chance to wreak havoc within the system. Antivirus software can also repair or quarantine files that have already been infected by virus activity.

Application—Software that performs automated functions for a user, such as word processing, spreadsheets, graphics, presentations, and databases—as opposed to operating system (OS) software.

Armed Islamic Group (GIA)—An Algerian Islamic extremist group that aims to overthrow the secular regime in Algeria and replace it with an Islamic state. The GIA began its violent activities in early 1992 after Algiers voided the victory of the largest Islamic party, Islamic Salvation Front (FIS), in the December 1991 elections.

Asset—A person, structure, facility, information, material, or process that has value. In the context of the National Infrastructure Protection Plan (NIPP), people are not considered assets.

Asymmetric threat—The use of crude or low-tech methods to attack a superior or more high-tech enemy.

Axis of Evil—Iran, Iraq, and North Korea as mentioned by President G.W. Bush during his State of the Union speech in 2002 as nations that were a threat to U.S. security due to harboring terrorism.

Attachment—A file that has been added to an e-mail—often an image or document. It could be something useful to you or something harmful to your computer.

Authentication—Confirming the correctness of the claimed identity of an individual user, machine, software component, or any other entity.

Authorization—The approval, permission, or employment for someone for something to do something.

Baath Party—The official political party in Iraq until the United States debaathified Iraq in May 2003 after a war that lasted a little over a month. Saddam Hussein, the former ruler of the Baath Party, was targeted by American-led coalition forces and fled. Baath Party members have been officially banned from participating in any new government in Iraq.

Backdoor—Hidden software or hardware mechanism used to circumvent security controls.

Backup—File copies that are saved as protection against loss, damage, or unavailability of the primary data. Saving methods include high-capacity type, separate disk subsystems or on the Internet. Off-site backup storage is ideal, sufficiently far away to reduce the risks of environmental damage such as floods, which might destroy both the primary and the backup if kept nearby.

Bandwidth—The capacity of a communication channel to pass data such as text, images, video, or sound through the channel in a given amount of time. Usually express in bits per second.

Beltway Sniper—For nearly a month in October 2002, the Washington, D.C., Maryland, and Virginia area was the hunting grounds for 41-year-old John Allen Muhammad and 17-year-old Lee Boyd Malvo. Dubbed "the Beltway Sniper" by the media, they shot people at seemingly random places such as schools, restaurants, and gas stations.

Bioaccumulative—Substances that concentrate in living organisms as the organism breathes in contaminated air or drinks contaminated water or eats contaminated food; the contaminants are not eliminated through natural processes.

Biosafety Level 1—Suitable for work involving well-characterized biological agents not known to consistently cause disease in healthy adult humans, and of minimal potential hazard to lab personnel and the environment. Work is generally conducted on open bench tops using standard microbiological practices.

Biosafety Level 2—Suitable for work involving biological agents of moderate potential hazard to personnel and the environment. Lab personnel should have specific training in handling pathogenic agents and be directed by competent scientists. Access to the lab should be limited when work is being conducted, extreme precautions should be taken with contaminated sharp items, and certain procedures should be conducted in biological safety cabinets or other physical containment equipment if there is a risk of creating infectious aerosols or splashes.

Biosafety Level 3—Suitable for work done with indigenous or exotic biological agents that may cause serious or potentially lethal disease as a result of exposure by inhalation. Lab personnel must have specific training in handling pathogenic and potentially lethal agents and be supervised by competent scientists who are experienced in working with these agents. All procedures involving the manipulation of infectious material are conducted within biological safety cabinets or other physical containment devices, or by personnel wearing appropriate personal protective clothing and equipment. The lab must have special engineering and design features.

Biosafety Level 4—Suitable for work with the most infectious biological agents. Access to the two Biosafety Level 4 labs in the United States is highly restricted.

Bioterrorism Act—The Public Health Security and Bioterrorism Preparedness and Response Act of 2002.

Biochemical warfare—Collective term for use of both chemical warfare and biological warfare weapons.

Biochemterroism—Terrorism using as weapons biological or chemical agents.

Biological ammunition—Ammunition designed specifically to release a biological agent used as the warhead for biological weapons. Biological ammunition may take many forms, such as a missile warhead or bomb.

Biological attacks—The deliberate release of germs or other biological substances that cause illness.

Bioterrorism—The use of biological agents in a terrorist operation. Biological toxin would include anthrax, Ricin, botulism, the plague, smallpox, and tularemia.

Biowarfare—The use of biological agents to cause harm to targeted people either directly, by bringing the people into contact with the agents or indirectly, by infecting other animals and plants, which would in turn cause harm to the people.

Blacklisting Software—A form of filtering that blocks only websites specified as harmful. Parents and employers sometimes use such software to prevent children and employees from visiting certain websites. You can add and remove sites from the "not permitted" list. This method of filtering allows for more full use of the Internet, but is less efficient at preventing access to any harmful material that is not on the list.

Blister agents—Agents that cause pain and incapacitation instead of death and might be used to injure many people at once, thereby overloading medical facilities and causing fear in the population. Mustard gas is the best known blister agent.

Blood agents—Agents based on cyanide compounds. More likely to be used for assassination than for terrorism.

Blended Threat—A computer network attack that seeks to maximize the severity of damage and speed of contagion by combining methods—for example, using characteristics of both viruses and worms.

Blog—Short for "Web log," a blog is usually defined as an online diary or journal. It is usually updated frequently and offered in a dated log format with the most recent entry at the top of the page. It often contains links to other websites along with commentary about those sites or specific subjects, such as politics, news, pop culture, or computers.

Botulism—An illness caused by the botulinum toxin, which is exceedingly lethal and quite simple to produce. It takes just a small amount of the toxin to destroy the central nervous system. Botulism may be contracted by the ingestion of contaminated food or through breaks or cuts in the skin. Food supply contamination or aerosol dissemination of the botulinum toxin are the two ways most likely to be used by terrorists.

Broadband—General term used to refer to high-speed network connections such as cable modem and Digital Subscriber Line (DSL). These types of "always on" Internet connections are actually more susceptible to some security threats than computers that access the web via dial–up service.

Browser—A client software program that can retrieve and display information from servers on the World Wide Web. Often known as a "Web Browser" or "Internet Browser," examples include Microsoft's Internet Explorer, Google's Chrome, Apple's Safari, and Mozilla's Firefox.

Brute Force Attack—An exhaustive password-cracking procedure that tries all possibilities, one by one.

Bush Doctrine—The policy that holds responsible nations that harbor or support terrorist organizations and says that such countries are considered hostile to the United States From President Bush's speech: "A country that harbors terrorists will either deliver the terrorist or share in their fate. . . . People have to choose sides. They are either with the terrorists, or they're with us."

Business Continuity—The ability of an organization to continue to function before, during, and after a disaster.

BWC—Officially known as the "Convention on the Prohibition of Development, Production, and Stockpiling of Bacteriological (Biological) and Toxin Weapons and Destruction." The BWC works toward general and complete disarmament, including the prohibition and elimination of all types of weapons of mass destruction.

Camp X-Ray—The Guantanamo Bay, Cuba, which houses al-Qaeda and Taliban prisoners.

Carrier—A person or animal that is potentially a source of infection by carrying an infectious agent without visible symptoms of the disease.

Cascading event—The occurrence of one event that causes another event.

Causative agent—The pathogen, chemical, or other substance that is the cause of disease or death in an individual.

Cell—The smallest unit within a guerrilla or terrorist group. A cell generally consists of two to five people dedicated to a terrorist cause. The formation of cells is born of the concept that an apparent "leaderless resistance" makes it hard for counterterrorists to penetrate.

Chain of custody—The tracking and documentation of physical control of evidence.

Chemical agent—A toxic substance intended to be used for operations to debilitate, immobilize, or kill military or civilian personnel.

Chemical ammunition—A munition, commonly a missile, bomb, rocket, or artillery shell, designed to deliver chemical agents.

Chemical attack—The intentional release of toxic liquid, gas, or solid in order to poison the environment or people.

Chemical warfare—The use of toxic chemicals as weapons, not including herbicide used to defoliate battlegrounds or riot control agents such as gas or mace.

Chemical weapons—Weapons that produce effects on living targets via toxic chemical properties. Examples would be sarin, VX nerve gas, or mustard gas.

Chemterrorism—The use of chemical agents in a terrorist operation. Well-known chemical agents include sarin and VX nerve gas.

Choking agent—Compounds that injure primarily in the respiratory tract (i.e., nose, throat, and lungs). In extreme cases membranes swell up, lungs become filled with liquid, and death results from lack of oxygen.

Cipro—A Bayer antibiotic that combats inhalation anthrax.

Communications architecture elements—Assets, systems, and networks that make up the communications architecture. The following are sample categories of architecture elements:

- *Core network/Internet backbone*—The portion of the communications network that consists of high-capacity network elements servicing nationwide, regional, and international connectivity.
- *Signaling and control systems*—Systems that exchange information regarding the establishment of a connection and control the management of the network.
- *Shared assets and systems*—Assets and systems owned and operated by multiple companies, including facilities where equipment is collocated and systems are shared by network operators.
- *Access*—Primarily the local portion of the network connecting end users to the backbone that enables users to send or receive communications. Access includes equipment and system such as Public Switched Telephone Network (PSTN) switches, asynchronous transfer mode (ATM) switches, video servers for video on demand, and Internet Protocol (IP) routers for Internet Service Providers (ISPs).
- *Customer equipment*—Equipment owned and operated by the end user or located at the end user's facility. Customers include individuals, organizations, businesses, and government.

Clear Desk Policy—A policy that directs all personnel to clear their desks at the end of each working day and file everything appropriately. Desks should be cleared of all documents and papers, including the contents of the "in" and "out" trays—not simply for cleanliness, but also to ensure that sensitive papers and documents are not exposure to unauthorized persons outside of working hours.

Clear Screen Policy—A policy that directs all computer users to ensure that the contents of the screen are protected from prying eyes and opportunistic breaches of confidentially. Typically, the easiest means of compliance is to use a screensaver that engages either on request or after a specified short period of time.

Communications sector—Public and private sector entities that have equities in the provisioning, use, protection, or regulation of communications networks and services. The communications sector is made up of five industry sectors:

- *Wireline.* Consists primarily of the PSTN, but also includes enterprise networks. The PSTN is a domestic communications network accessed by telephones, key telephone systems, private branch exchange (PBX) trunks, and data arrangements. Despite industry's transition to packet-based networks, the traditional PSTN remains the backbone of the communications infrastructure includes landline telephone, the Internet, and submarine cable infrastructure.
- *Wireless.* Refers to telecommunication in which electromagnetic waves (rather than some form of wire) carry the signal over part of or the entire communication path.

Consists of cellular phone, paging, personal communication services, high-frequency radio, unlicensed wireless, and other commercial and private radio services.

- *Satellite.* This is a space vehicle launched into orbit to relay audio, data, or video signals as part of a telecommunications network. Signals are transmitted to the satellite from earth station antennas, amplified, and sent back to Earth for reception by other earth station antennas. Satellites are capable of linking two points, one point with many others, or multiple locations with other multiple locations. Uses a combination of terrestrial and space components to deliver various communications, Internet data, and video services.

- *Cable.* This wireline network offers television, Internet, and voice services that interconnect with the PSTN through end offices. Primary cable television (CATV) network components include headends and fiber-optic and/or HFC. Because the CATV network was designed primarily for downstream transmission of television signals, most of the existing network is being refitted to support two-way data transmissions.

- *Broadcasting.* Broadcasting systems consist of free, over-the-air radio and television stations that offer analog and digital audio and video programming services and data services. Broadcasting has been the principal means of providing emergency alerting services to the public for six decades. Broadcasting systems operate in three frequency bands: medium frequency (MF (AM radio)), very high frequency (VHF (FM radio and television)), and ultra-high frequency (VHF (FM radio and television)), and ultra-high frequency (UHF (television)). The recent transition to digital television (DTV) and ongoing transition to digital radio provide broadcast stations with enhanced capabilities, include the ability to multicast multiple programs on a single channel.

"Confirmed"—In the context of the threat evaluation process, a water contamination incident is definitive evidence that the water has been contaminated.

Consequence—The effect of an event, incident, or occurrence. For the purposes of the NIPP, consequences are divided into four main categories: public health and safety, economic, psychological, and governance impacts.

Control center—A sophisticated monitoring and control system responsible for balancing power generation and demand; monitoring flows over transmission lines to avoid overloading; planning and configuring the system to operate reliably; maintaining system stability; preparing for emergencies; and placing equipment in and out of service for maintenance and emergencies.

Control systems—Computer-based systems used within many infrastructures and industries to monitor and control sensitive processes and physical functions. These systems typically collect measurement and operation data from the field, process and display the information, and relay control commands to local or remote equipment or human-machine interfaces (operators). Examples of types of control systems include SCADA system, Process Control Systems, and Distributed Control Systems.

Cookie—A small file that is downloaded by some websites to store a packer to information on your browser. Companies and organizations use cookies to remember your login or registration identification, site prefers, pages view, and online "shopping-cart" so that the next you visit a site, your stored information can automatically be pulled up for you. A cookie is obviously convenient but also presents potential security issues. You can configure your browser to alert you whenever a cookie is being sent. You can refuse to accept all cookies or ease all cookies saved on your browser.

Counterterrorism—Measures used to prevent, preempt, or retaliate against terrorist attacks.

"Credible"—In the context of the threat evaluation process, a water contamination threat is characterized as "credible" if information collected during the threat evaluation process corroborates information from the threat warning.

Credit Card—A card indicating the holder has been granted a line of credit. Often sought after by criminals looking for an easy way to purchase things without having to pay for them. For this reason and others, a credit card preferable to a debit card for only shopping since it provides a buffer between buyer and seller, affording more protections to the buyer in case there is a problem with the order or the car number is compromised.

Critical Infrastructure—Systems and assets, whether physical or virtual, so vital that the incapacity or destruction of such may have a debilitating impact on the security, economy, public health or safety, environment, or any combination of these matters, across any federal, state, regional, territorial, or local jurisdiction.

Cutaneous—Related to or entering through the skin.

Cutaneous anthrax—Anthrax that is contracted via broken skin. The infection spreads through the bloodstream causing cyanosis, shock, sweating, and finally death.

Cyberbullying—Sending or posting harmful, cruel, rude, or threatening messages or slanderous information, text, or images using the Internet or other digital communication devices.

Cybersecurity—The prevention of damage to, unauthorized use of, or exploitation of, and, if needed, the restoration of electronic information and communications systems and the information contained therein to ensure confidentially, integrity, and availability. Cybersecurity includes protection and restoration, when needed, or information networks and wireline, wireless, satellite, public safety answering points, and 911 communications systems and control systems.

Cyber System—Any combination of facilities, equipment, personnel, procedures, and communications integrated to provide cyber services. Examples include business systems, control systems, and access control systems.

Cyberterrorism—Attacks on computer networks or systems, generally by hackers working with or for terrorist groups. Some forms of cyberterrorism include denial of service attacks, inserting viruses, or stealing data.

Debit Card—A card linked directly to the holder's bank account, withdrawing money from the account. Not as safe as credit cards for online shopping since if problems arise, the buyer's money has already been spent and is harder to get back.

Defensive critical asset—An asset of such extraordinary important to operations in peace crisis and war that its incapacitation or destruction would have a very serious, debilitating effect on the ability of the Department of Defense to fulfill its missions.

Denial of Service Attack—The prevention of authorized access to a system resource or the delaying of system operations and functions. Often this involves a cyber criminal generating a large volume of data requests.

Dependency—The one-directional reliance of an asset, system network, or collection thereof, within or across sectors, in input, interaction, or other requirement from other sources in order to function properly.

Dictionary Attack—A password-cracking attack that tries all of the phrases or words in a dictionary.

Digital Certificate—The electronic equivalent of an ID card that establishes your credentials when doing business or other transactions on the web. It contains your name, a serial number, expiration dates, a copy of the certificate holder's public key (used for encrypting messages and digital signatures), and the digital signature of the certificate-issuing authority so that a recipient can verify that the certificate is real.

Dirty Bomb—A makeshift nuclear device that is created from radioactive nuclear waste material. While not a nuclear blast, an explosion of a dirty bomb causes localized radioactive contamination as the nuclear waste material is carried into the atmosphere where it is dispersed by the wind.

Domain Hijacking—An attack in which an attacker takes over a domain by first blocking access to the domain's DNS server and them putting his own server up in its place.

Domain Name System (DNS)—The DNS is the way that Internet domain names are located. A website's domain name is easier to remember than its IP (Internet Protocol) address.

Dumpster Diving—Recovering files, letters, memos, photographs, IDs, passwords, checks, account statements, credit card offers, and more from garbage cans and recycling bins. This information can then be used to commit identity theft.

eBomb (for e-bomb)—Electromagnetic bomb that produces a brief pulse of energy that affects electronic circuitry. At low levels, the pulse temporarily disables electronic systems, including computers, radios, and transportation systems. High levels completely destroy circuitry, causing mass disruption of infrastructure while sparing life and property.

Ecotage—Is the portmanteau of the "eco-" prefix and "sabotage." It is used to describe illegal acts of vandalism and violence committed in the name of environmental protection.

Ecoterrorism—A neologism for terrorism that includes sabotage intended to hinder activities that are considered damaging to the environment.

Electromagnetic Pulse (EMP)—A burst of electromagnetic radiation by deliberate means, such as nuclear attack, or through natural means, such as a large-scale geomagnetic storm. Magnetic and electric fields resulting from EMP have the potential to disrupt electrical and electronic systems by causing destructive current and voltage surges.

Electronic Infections—Often called "viruses," these malicious program send codes harmful your computer and compromise your privacy. In addition to the traditional viruses, other common types include worms and Trojan horses. They sometimes work in tandem to do maximum damage.

Encryption—A data security technique used to protect information from unauthorized inspection or alteration. Information is encoded so that it appears as a meaningless string of letters and symbols during delivery or transmission. Upon receipt, the information is decoded using an encryption key.

End User License Agreement (EULA)—A contract between you and your software's vendor of development. Many times the EULA is presented as a dialog box that appears the first time you open the software and forces you to check "I accept" before you can proceed. Before accepting, though, read through it and make sure you understand and are comfortable with the terms of the agreement. If the software EULA is hard to understand or you can't fine it, beware!

Energy Asset and System Parameters—Six general asset or system characteristics that are important parameters for evaluating the vulnerabilities of energy infrastructure and developing risk management programs. They include physical and location attributes, cyber attributes, volumetric or throughput attributes, temporal/load profile attributes, human attributes, and the important of an asset of system to the energy network.

Euroterrorism—Associated with left wing terrorism of the 1960s, 1970s and 1980s involving the Red Brigade, Red Army Faction, and November 17th Group, among other groups that targeted U.S. interests in Europe and NATO. Other groups include Orange Volunteers, Red Hand Defenders, Continuity IRA, Loyalist Volunteer Force, Ulster Defense Association, and First of October Anti-Fascist Resistance Group.

Evil Twins—A fake wireless Internet hot spot that looks like a legitimate service. When victims connect to the wireless network, a hacker can launch a spying attack on their transactions on the Internet, or just ask for credit card information in the standard pay-for-access deal.

fallout—The descent to the earth's surface of particles contaminated with radioactive material from a radioactive cloud. The term can also be applied to the contaminated particulate matter itself.

Fatah—Meaning "conquest by means of jihad"; a political organization created in the 1960s and led by Yasser Arafat. With both a military and intelligence wing, it has carried out terrorist attacks on Israel since 1965. It joined the PLO in 1968. Since 9/11, the Fatah was blamed for attempting to smuggle 50 tons of weapons into Israel.

Fatwa—A legal ruling regarding Islamic Law.

Fedayeen Saddam—Iraq's paramilitary organization said to be an equivalent to the Nazi's "SS." The militia is loyal to Saddam Hussein and is responsible for using brutality on civilians who are not loyal to the policies of Saddam. They do not dress in uniform.

File-Sharing Programs—Sometimes called peer-to-peer (P2P) programs, these allow many different users to access the same file at the same time. These programs are often used to illegally upload and download music and other software. Examples include Napster, Grokster, Kazaa, iMesh, Ares, and Limewire.

Firewall—A hardware or software link in a network that inspects all data packets coming and going from a computer, permitting only those that are authorized to reach the other side.

Flooding—An attack that attempts to cause a failure in the security of a computer by providing more input, such as a large volume of data requests, than it can properly process.

Frustration-Aggression Hypothesis—A hypothesis that every frustration leads to some form of aggression and every aggressive act results from some prior frustration. As defined by Gurr: "The Necessary precondition for violent civil conflict is relative deprivation, defined as actors' perception of discrepancy between their value expectations and their environment's apparent value capabilities. This deprivation may be individual or collective."

Function—A service, process, capability, or operation performed by an asset, system, network, or organization.

Fundamentalism—Conservative religious authoritarianism. Fundamentalism is not specific to Islam; it exists in all faiths. Characteristics include literal interpretation of scriptures and a strict adherence to traditional doctrines and practices.

Geneva Protocol 1925—The first treaty to prohibit the use of biological weapons. The 1925 Geneva Protocol for the Prohibition of the Use In War of Asphyxiating, Poisonous or Other Gases and Bacteriological Methods of Warfare.

Germ Warfare—The use of biological agents to cause harm to targeted people either directly, by bringing the people into contact with the agents or indirectly, by infecting other animals and plants, which would in turn cause harm to the people.

Glanders—An infectious bacterial disease known to cause inflammation in horses, donkeys, mules, goats, dogs, and cats. Human infection has not been seen since 1945, but because so few organisms are required to cause disease, it is considered a potential agent for biological warfare.

Government Coordinating Council (GCC)—The government counterpart to the SCC of each sector established to enable interagency coordination. The GCC comprises representatives across various levels of government (federal, state, local, tribal, and territorial) as appropriate to the security and operations landscape of each individual sector.

Grab Sample—A single sample collected at a particular time and place that represents the composition of the water, air, or soil only at that time and location.

Grooming—Using the Internet to manipulate and gain trust of a minor as a first step toward the future sexual abuse, production, or exposure of that minor. Sometimes involves developing the child's sexual awareness and may take days, weeks, months or in some cases years to manipulate the minor.

Ground Zero—From 1946 until 9/11, ground zero was the point directly above, below, or at which a nuclear explosion occurs or the center or origin of rapid, intense, or violent activity or change. After 9/11, the term, when used with initial capital letters, refers to the ground at the epicenter of the World Trade Center attacks.

Hacker—An individual who attempts to break into a computer without authorization.

Hamas—A radical Islamic organization that operates primarily in the West Bank and Gaza Strip whose goal is to establish an Islamic Palestinian state in place of Israel. On the one hand, Hamas operates overtly in their capacity as social services deliverers, but its activists have also conducted many attacks, including suicide bombings, against Israeli civilians and military targets.

Hazard—An inherent physical or chemical characteristic that has the potential for causing harm to people, the environment, or property.

Hazard assessment—The process of evaluating available information about the site to identify potential hazards that might pose a risk to the site characterization team. The hazard assessment results in assigning one of four levels to risk: lower hazard, radiological hazard, high chemical hazard, or high biological hazard.

Hemorrhagic Fevers—In general, the term viral hemorrhagic fever is used to describe severe multisystem syndrome wherein the overall vascular system is damaged, and the body becomes unable to regulate itself. These symptoms are often accompanied by hemorrhage; however, the bleeding itself is not usually life-threatening. While some types of hemorrhagic fever viruses can cause relatively mild illnesses.

High-Impact, Low-Frequency (HILF)—HILF events are occurrences that are relatively unusual but have the potential to cause catastrophic disruption. Examples include pandemic disease, terrorist attack, and electromagnet pulse.

Hizbollah (Hezbollah)—Meaning the "Party of God." One of many terrorist organizations that seek the destruction of Israel and the United States. They have taken credit for numerous bombings against civilians and have declared that civilian targets are warranted. Hezbollah claims it sees no legitimacy for the existence of Israel and that their conflict becomes one of legitimacy that is based on religious ideals.

Homeland Security Office—An agency organized after 9/11 with former Pennsylvania governor Tom Ridge heading it up. The Office of Homeland Security is at the top of approximately forty federal agencies charged with protecting the United States against terrorism.

HTTPS—When used in the first part of a URL (e.g., http://), this term specifics the use of hypertext transfer protocol (HTTP) enhanced by a security mechanism such as Secure Socket Layer (SSL). Always look for the HTTPS on the checkout or order form page when shopping online or when logging into a site and providing your username and password.

Hybrid Attack—Builds on other password-cracking attacks by adding numerals and symbols to dictionary words.

Incident—A confirmed occurrence that requires response actions to prevent or minimize loss of life or damage to property and/or natural resources. A drinking water contamination incident occurs when the presence of a harmful contaminant has been confirmed.

Infrastructure—The framework of interdependent networks and systems comprising identifiable industries, (including people and procedures), and distribution capabilities that provide a reliable flow of products and services essential to the defense of economic security of the United States, the smooth functioning of government at all levels, and society as a whole. Consistent with the definition in the Homeland Security Act, infrastructure includes physical, cyber, and/or human elements.

Inhalation anthrax—A form of anthrax that is contracted by inhaling anthrax spores. This results in pneumonia, sometimes meningitis, and finally death.

ISIS (ISIL) Islamic State of Iraq and the Levant—Islamic extremist rebel group that presently controls territory and brutalizes and/or murders various groups in various countries, including Syria, Iraq, Libya, Nigeria, and others.

Instant Messaging (IM)—A service that allows people to send and get messages almost instantly. To send messages using instant messaging you need to download an instant messaging program and know the instant messaging address of another person who uses the same IM program.

Interdependency—Mutually reliant relationship between entities (objects, individuals, or groups). The degree of interdependency does not need to be equal in both directions.

Intifada (intifadah) (alternatively Intifadah, from Arabic "shaking off")—The two intifadas are similar in that both were originally characterized by civil disobedience by the Palestinians, which escalated into the use of terror. In 1987, following the killing of several Arabs in the Gaza Strip, the first intifada began and went on until 1993. The second intifada began in September 2000, following Ariel Sharon's visit to the Temple Mount.

IP (Internet Protocol) Address—A computer's inter-network address, written as a series of four 8-bit numbers separated by periods, such as 123.45.678.990. Every website has an IP address, although finding a website is considerably easier to do when using its domain name instead.

Internet Service Provider (ISP)—A company that provides Internet access to customers.

Islam—Meaning "submit." The faith practiced by followers of Muhammad. Islam claims more than a billion believers worldwide.

Jihad—Meaning "struggle." The definition is a subject of vast debate. There are two definitions generally accepted. The first is a struggle against oppression, whether political or religious. The second is the struggle within oneself, or a spiritual struggle.

Key Resources—As defined in the Homeland Security Act, key resources are publicly or privately controlled resources essential to the minimal operations of the economy and government.

Keystroke Logger—A specific type of electronic infection that records victims' keystrokes and sends them to an attacker. This can be done with either hardware or software.

Koran—The holy book of Islam, considered by Muslims to contain the revelations of God to Mohammed. Also called the Qu'ran.

Laboratory Response Network (LRN)—A network of labs developed by the CDC, APHL, and FBI for the express purpose of dealing with bioterrorism threats, including pathogens and some biotoxins.

Links—The means (road, rail, barge, or pipeline) by which a chemical is transported from one node to another.

Malware—A generic term for a number of different types of malicious code.

Man-In-the-Middle Attack—Posing as an online bank or merchant, a cyber criminal allows a victim to sign in over a Secure Sockets Layer (SSL) connection. The attacker then logs onto the real server using the client's information and steals credit card numbers.

Mindset—According to *American Heritage Dictionary*: "1. A fixed mental attitude or disposition that predetermines a person's response to an interpretation of situations; 2. and inclination or a habit." *Merriam Webster's Collegiate Dictionary* (10th ed.) defines it as "1. A mental attitude or inclination; 2. a fixed state of mind." The term dates from 1926 but apparently is not included in dictionaries of psychology.

Mitigation—Ongoing and sustained action to reduce the probability of or lessen the impact of an adverse incident.

Molotov cocktail—A crude incendiary bomb made of a bottle filled with flammable liquid and fitted with a rag wick.

Monitoring Software—Software products that allow parents to monitor or track the websites or e-mail messages that child visits or reads.

Mullah—A Muslim, usually holding an official post, who is trained in traditional religious doctrine and law.

Muslim (also Moslem)—Followers of the teachings of Mohammed, or Islam.

Narcoterrorism—The view of many counterterrorist experts that there exists an alliance between drug traffickers and political terrorists.

National Pharmaceutical Stockpile—A stock of vaccines and antidotes that are stored at Centers for Disease Control in Atlanta to be used against biological warfare.

Network—A group of components that share information or interact with each other in order to perform a function; two or more computer systems that are grouped together to share information, software, and hardware.

Nodes—A facility at which a chemical is produced, store, or consumed.

Operating System (OS)—Programs that manage all the basic functions and programs on a computer, such as allocating system resources, providing access and security controls, maintaining file systems, and managing communications between end users and hardware devices. Examples include Microsoft's Windows, Apple's Macintosh, and Red Hat's Linux.

Opportunity Contaminant—A contaminant that might be readily available in a particular area even though they may not be highly toxic or infectious or easily dispersed and stable in treated drinking water.

Osama bin Laden (also spelled "Usama")—A native of Saudi Arabia, was born the seventeenth of twenty-four sons of Saudi Arabian builder Mohammed bin Oud bin Laden, a Yemeni immigrant. Early in his career, he helped the mujahedeen fight the Soviet Union by recruiting Arabs and building facilities. He hated the United States and apparently this was because he viewed the United States as having desecrated holy ground in Saudi Arabia with their presence during the first Gulf War. Expelled from Saudi Arabia in 1991 and from Sudan in 1996, he operated terrorist training camps in Afghanistan. His global network al Qaeda is credited with the attacks on the United States on September 11, 2001, the attack on the USS *Cole* in 2000, and other terrorist attacks.

Owners/operators—Those entities responsible for day-to-day operation and investment in a particular asset or system.

Password—A secret sequence of characters that is used as a means of authentication to confirm you identity in a computer program or online.

Password Cracking—Password cracking is the process of attempting to guess passwords, given the password file information.

Password Sniffing—Passive wiretapping, usually on a local area network, to gain knowledge of passwords.

Patch—A patch is a small security update released by a software manufacturer to fix bugs in existing programs. Your computer's software programs and/or operating system may be configured to check automatically for patches, or you may need to periodically visit the manufacturers' websites to see if there have been any updates.

Pathogen—Any agent that can cause disease.

Pathways—The sequence of nodes and links by which a chemical is produced, transported, and transformed from its initial source to its ultimate consumer.

Physical Security—The use of barriers and surveillance to protect resources, personnel, and facilities against crime, damage, or unauthorized access.

Political terrorism—Terrorist acts directed at governments and their agents and motivated by political goals (i.e., national liberation).

"possible"—In the context of the threat evaluation process, a water contamination threat is characterized as "possible" if the circumstances of the threat warning appear to have provided an opportunity for contamination.

Pharming—Redirecting visitors from a real website to a bogus one. A user enters what is believed to be a valid web address and is unknowingly redirected to an illegitimate site that steals the user's personal information. On the spoofed site, criminals may mimic real transactions and harvest private information unknowingly shared by users. With this, the attacker can then access the real website and conduct transactions using the credentials of a valid user.

Phishing—Soliciting private information from customers or members of a business, bank, or other organization in an attempt to fool them into divulging confidential personal and financial information. People are lured into sharing user names, passwords, account information, or credit cared numbers, usually by an official-looking message in an e-mail or pop-up advertisement that urges them to act immediately, usually by clicking on a link provided.

Preparedness—The activities necessary to build, sustain, and improve readiness capabilities to prevent, protect against, respond to, and recover from natural or manmade incidents. Preparedness is a continuous process involving efforts at all levels of government and between government and the private sector and nongovernmental organizations to identify threats, determine vulnerabilities, and identify required resources to prevent, respond to, and recover from major incidents.

Presumptive results—Results of chemical and/or biological field testing that need to be confirmed by further lab analysis. Typically used in reference to the analysis of pathogens.

Prevention—Actions taken and measures put in place for the continual assessment and readiness of necessary actions to reduce the risk of threats and vulnerabilities, to intervention and stop an occurrence, or to mitigate effects.

Prioritization—In the context of the NIPP, prioritization is the process of using risk assessment results to identify where risk reduction or mitigation efforts are most needed and to subsequently determine which protective actions should be instituted in order to have the greatest effect.

Protection—Actions or measures taken to cover or shield from exposure, injury, or destruction. In the context of the NIPP, protection includes actions to deter the threat, mitigate the vulnerabilities, or minimize the consequences associated with a terrorist attack or other incident. Protection can include a wide range of activities, such as hardening facilities, building resilience and redundancy, incorporating hazard resistance into initial facility design, initiating active or passive countermeasures, installing security systems and redundancy, incorporating hazard resistant into initial facility design, initiating active or passive countermeasures, installing security systems, promoting workforce surety, training, and exercises, and implementing cybersecurity measures, among various others.

Psychopath—A mentally ill or unstable person, especially one having a psychopathic personality (*q.v.*), according to *Webster's*.

Psychopathy—A mental disorder, especially an extreme mental disorder marked usually by egocentric and antisocial activity, according to *Webster's*.

Psychopathology—The study of psychological and behavioral dysfunction occurring in mental disorder or in social disorganization, according to *Webster's*.

Psychotic—Of, relating to, or affected with psychosis, which is a fundamental mental derangement (as schizophrenia) characterized by defective or lost contact with reality, according to *Webster's*.

Rapid Field Testing—Analysis of water during site characterization uses rapid field water testing technology in an attempt to tentatively identify contaminants or unusual water quality.

Recovery—The development, coordination, and execution of service- and site-restoration plans for affected communities and the reconstitution of government operations and services through individual, private sector, nongovernmental, and public assistance programs that identify needs and define resources; provide housing and promote restoration; address long-term care and treatment of affected persons; implement additional measures for community restoration; incorporate mitigation measures and techniques as flexible; evaluate the incident to identify lessons learned and develop initiatives to mitigate the effects of future incidents.

Red Teaming—As used in this text, a group exercise to imagine all possible terrorist attack scenarios against the chemical infrastructure and their consequences.

Redundancy—An energy reliability strategy based on the notion that multiple systems provide needed backup if one system fails or cannot meet demand.

Resilience/resiliency—The ability to resist, absorb, recover from, or successfully adapt to adversity or a change in conditions. In the context of energy security, resilience is measured into terms of robustness, resourcefulness, and rapid recovery.

Response—Activities that address the short-term, direct effects of an incident, including immediate actions to save lives, protect property, and meet basic humans needs. Response also includes the execution of emergency operations plans and incident mitigation activities designed to limit the loss of life, personal injury, property damage, and other unfavorable outcomes. As indicated by the situation, response activities include applying intelligence and other information to lessen the effects or consequences of an incident; increasing security operations; continuing investigations into the nature and source of the threat; ongoing surveillance and testing processes; immunizations, isolation, or quarantine; and specific law enforcement operations aimed at preempting, interdicting, or disrupting illegal activity, and apprehending actual perpetrators and bringing them to justice.

Retentate—In ultrafiltration, the retentate is the solution that contains the particles that do not pass through the membrane filter. The retentate is also called the concentrate.

Risk—The potential for an unwanted outcome resulting from an incident, event, or occurrence, as determined by its likelihood and the associated consequences.

Router—A hardware device that connects two or more networks and routes incoming data packets to the appropriate network. Many internet service providers (ISPs) provide these devices to their customers, and they often contain firewall protections.

Script—A file containing active content—for example, commands or instructions to be executed by the computer.

Sector—A logical collection of assets, systems, or networks that provide a common function to the economy, government, or society. The NIPP addresses eighteen critical infrastructure sectors indentified by the criteria set forth in HSPD-7.

Sentinel Laboratory—An LRN lab that reports unusual results that might indicate a possible outbreak and refers specimens that may contain select biological agents in reference labs within the LRN.

Shoulder Surfing—Looking over a person's shoulder to get confidential information. It is an effective way to get information in crowded places because it's relatively easy to stand next to someone and watch as they fill out a form, enter a PIN number at an ATM machine, or type a password. Can also be done long-distance with the aid of binoculars or other vision-enhancing devices. To combat it, experts recommend that you shield paperwork or your keypad from view by using your body or cupping your hand. Also, be sure you password-protect your computer screen when you must leave it unattended, and clear your desk at the end of the day.

Site Characterization—The process of collecting information from an investigation site in order to support the evaluation of a drinking water contamination threat. Site characterization activities include the site investigation, field safety screening, rapid field testing of the water, and sample collection.

Situational Awareness—An understanding of the current environment and the ability to accurately anticipate future problems in order to respond effectively.

Skimming—A high-tech method by which thieves capture your personal or account information from your credit card, driver's license, or even passport using an electronic device called a "skimmer." Such devices can be purchased online for under fifty dollars. Your card is swiped through the skimmer and the information contained in the magnetic strip on the card is then read into and stored on the device or an attached computer. Skimming is predominantly a tactic used to perpetuate credit care fraud, but is also gaining in popularity among identity thieves.

Smart Grid—The electric delivery network, from electrical generation to end-use customer, integrated with the latest advances in digital and information technology to improve electric-system reliability, security, and efficiency.

Social Engineering—A euphemism for non-technical or low-technology means—such as lies, impersonation, tricks, bribes, blackmail, and threats—used to attack information systems. Sometimes telemarketers or unethical employees employ such tactics.

Social Networking Websites—Sites specifically focused on the building and verifying of social networks for whatever purpose. Many social networking services are also blog hosting services. There are more than three hundred known social networking websites, including Facebook, Myspace, Friendster, Xanga, and Blogspot. Such sites enable users to create online profiles and post pictures and share personal data such as their contact information, hobbies, activities, and interests. The sites facilitate connecting with other users with similar interests, activities, and locations. Sites vary in who may view a user's profile—some have settings that may be changed so that profiles can be viewed only by "friends."

Sociopath—Basically synonymous with psychopath (q.v.). Sociopathic symptoms in the adult sociopath include an inability to tolerate delay or frustration, a lack of guild feelings, a relative lack of anxiety, a lack of compassion for others, a hypersensitivity to personal ills, and a lack of responsibility. Many authors prefer the term sociopath because this type of person had defective socialization and a deficient childhood.

Spam—Unwanted, unsolicited e-mail from someone you don't know. Often sent in an attempt to sell you something or get you to reveal personal information.

Spim—Unwanted, unsolicited instant messages from someone you don't know. Often sent in an attempt to sell you something or get you to reveal personal information.

Spoofing—Masquerading so that a trusted IP address is used instead of the true IP address. A technique used by hackers as a means of gaining access to a computer system.

Spyware—Software that uses your Internet connection to send personally identifiable information about you to a collecting device on the Internet. It is often packaged with software that you download voluntarily, so that even if you remove the downloaded program later, the spyware may remain.

SSL (Secure Socket Layer)—An encryption system that protects the privacy of data exchanged by a website and the individual user. Used by websites whose URLs begin with https instead of http.

System—Any combination of facilities, equipment, personnel, procedures, and communications integrated for a specific purpose.

Terrorism—Premeditated threat or act of violence against non-combatant persons, property, and environmental or economic targets to induce fear, intimate, coerce, or affect a government, the civilian population, or any segment thereof, in furtherance of political, social, ideological, or religious objectives.

Terrorist Group—A group that practices or has significant elements that are involved in terrorism.

Threat—An indication that a harmful incident, such as contamination of the drinking water supply, may have occurred. The threat may be direct, such as a verbal or written threat, or circumstantial, such as a security breach or unusual water quality.

Toxin—A poisonous substance produced by living organisms capable of causing disease when introduced into the body tissues.

Transportation Security Administration (TSA)—A new agency created by the Patriot Act of 2001 for the purpose of overseeing technology and security in U.S. airports.

Trojan horse—A computer program that appears to be beneficial or innocuous but also has a hidden potentially malicious function that evades security mechanisms. A "keystroke logger," which records victims' keystrokes and sends them to an attacker or remote-controlled "zombie computers" are examples of the damage that can be done by Trojan horses.

URL—Abbreviation for "Uniform (or Universal) Resource Locator." A way of specifying the location of publicly available information on the Internet. Also known as a web address.

URL Obfuscation—Taking advantage of human error, some scammers use phishing e-mails to guide recipients to fraudulent sites with names very similar to established sites They use a slight misspelling or other subtle different in the URL, such as "monneybank.com" instead of "moneybank.com" to redirect users to share their personal information unknowingly.

Value Proposition—A statement that outlines the national and homeland security interest in protecting the nation's critical infrastructure and articulates the benefits gained by all critical infrastructure partners through the risk management framework and public-private partnership described in the NIPP.

Vector—An organism that carries germs from one host to another.

Virus—A hidden, self-replicating section of computer software, usually malicious logic, that propagates by infection—that is, inserting a copy of itself into and become part of—another program. A virus cannot run by itself; it requires that its host program be run to make the virus active. Often sent through e-mail attachments.

Vishing—Soliciting private information from customers or members of a business, bank, or other organization in an attempt to fool them into divulging confidential personal and financial information. People are lured into sharing user names, passwords, account information, or credit card numbers, usually by an official-looking message in an e-mail or a pop-up advertisement that urges them to act immediately—but in a vishing scam they are urged to call the phone number provided rather than clicking on a link.

Vulnerability—A physical feature or operational attribute that renders an entity open to exploitations or susceptible to a given hazard.

Weapons of Mass Destruction (WMD)—According to the National Defense Authorization Act, any weapon or device that is intended, or has the capability, to cause death or serious bodily injury to a significant number of people through the release, dissemination, or impact of

- toxic or poisonous chemicals or their precursors
- a disease organism
- radiation or radioactivity

Webinar—A live online educational presentation during which participating viewers can submit questions and comments.

Whitelisting Software—A form of filtering that only allows connections to a pre-approved list of sites that are considered useful and appropriate for children. Parents sometimes use such software to prevent children from visiting all but certain websites. You can add and remove sites from the "permitted" list. This method is extremely safe, but allows for only extremely limited use of the Internet.

Worm (acronym for: Write Once, Read Many Times)—A type of electronic infection that can run independently and propagate a complete working version of itself onto other host on a network. Many consume computer resources destructively. Once this malicious software is on a computer, it scans the network for another machine with a specific security vulnerability. When it finds one, it exploits the weakness to copy itself to the new machine and then the worm starts replicating form there as well.

Xenophobia—Irrational fear of strangers or those who are different from oneself.

Zombie Computer—A remote-access Trojan horse installs hidden code that allows your computer to be controlled remotely. Digital thieves then use robot networks of thousands of zombie computers to carry out attacks on other people and cover up their tracks. Authorities have a harder time tracing criminals when they go through zombie computers.

Zyklon b—A form of hydrogen cyanide. Symptoms of inhalation include increased respiratory rate, restlessness, headache, and giddiness followed later by convulsions, vomiting, respiratory failure, and unconsciousness. Used in the Nazi gas chambers in World War II.

Index

AASHTO. *See* American Association of State Highway and Transportation Officials

aboveground equipment, 144–45, 147

access cards, 163

access control: applications, 161; for employees, 57; physical access controls, 199; procedural, 200; systems, 153

accessibility, 141

active security barriers, 147, 153, 179

Address Verification Service, 63

adverse consequences, *109*

adware, 101

alarm systems, 153; exterior intrusion sensors and, 165; fire, 155, 156, *158*; hardwired systems, 156; intrusion sensors, 155–56, *157*; local alarms, 155; sensors in, 154, 156; "supervised" systems, 154; wireless systems, 156

aluminum, 175

American Association of State Highway and Transportation Officials (AASHTO), 176

American National Standards Institute (ANSI), 173

American Society for Testing and Materials (ASTM), 173

American Society of Sanitary Engineers (ASSE), 145

annunciator, 155

ANSI. *See* American National Standards Institute

anti-fraud measures, 63

anti-intrusion detection system evasion techniques, 193

antivirus: programs, 51, 189–90; signature protection, 42

architecture vulnerabilities, 23

Argonne National Laboratory, 66, 68, 75

armed guards, 143

arming station, 154

ASSE. *See* American Society of Sanitary Engineers

asset loss, 112

ASTM. *See* American Society for Testing and Materials

attendance tracking, 161

authentication, 25, 26; access authorization, 113; appropriate level of, 50; mutual, 92; "spot," 92; strong authentication policies, 39; two-factor authentication methods, 44; user, 48, 49, 50

authorization, 25

automated building systems, 71

automatic updating, 45

awareness, 101–2; building, 107

Awareness Training, 101

239

National Drinking Water Advisor Council
  (NDWAC), 195–96
National Electrical Codes (NEC), 145
National Fire Alarm Code, 155
National Fire Protection Association
  (NFPA), 145, 155
National Incident Management System
  (MIMS), 201
National Infrastructure Council (NIAC), 74
National Infrastructure Protection Center
  (NIPC), 26
national interests, 6
national security, 138
National Security Directive PPD-8, 68
national security espionage, 104
natural disaster, *10*, 126, 203; potential
  impact of, 127
Natural Hazards, 78
NC. *See* normally closed
NCSD. *See* National Cybersecurity Division
NDWAC. *See* National Drinking Water
  Advisor Council
NEC. *See* National Electrical Codes
network access, *192*
network architecture, 113
network-based attacks, 54
network demons, 29
network design, 51
network honeypot, 193
network intrusion detection, 191
networks, 23
network security, 33, 42
network security breaches, 71
New Mitigation Measures, 78
NFPA. *See* National Fire Protection
  Association
NIAC. *See* National Infrastructure Council
9/11, 1, 65; DHS and, 99; post 9/11-related
  questions, 126; rescuers at site of, 139;
  uncharted territory of, 125
NIPC. *See* National Infrastructure Protection
  Center

NO. *See* normally open
non-adversarial threats, 11
non-essential perimeter portals, 142
normally closed (NC), 154
normally open (NO), 154
North American Grid, 142
Northeast Blackout, 65
North Korea, 70
"No Trespassing" signs, 171

Occupational Safety and Health
  Administration (OSHA), 145
Offsite Capabilities, 79
online fraud, 40–41
open redirect, *12*
operating system command injection, *12*
operating systems, 48
operational security (OPSEC), 59–60, 117,
  197; OPSEC managers, 61
operational vulnerabilities, 100
OPSEC. *See* operational security
organizational security, 197
organized crime, *10*
OSHA. *See* Occupational Safety and Health
  Administration

packet filtering, *192*
padlocked chain lockouts, 183, 184
Pareto analysis, 119
passive infrared (PIR) sensors, 168–69
passive security barriers, 179–80
passwords, 58; complex, 25; default, 48;
  employees tricked into handing over, 41;
  on mobile devices, 55; policies on, 44;
  strong, 39
patching, 89
path traversal, *12*
payment cards, 61
payments industry, 62
payment systems, 62
PCI. *See* Desktop Peripheral
PCMCIA. *See* Laptop CardBus

About the Author

Frank R. Spellman, PhD, is a retired assistant professor of environmental health at Old Dominion University, Norfolk, Virginia, and the author of more than 109 books covering topics ranging from concentrated animal feeding operations (CAFOs) to all areas of environmental science and occupational health. Many of his texts are readily available online, and several have been adopted for classroom use at major universities throughout the United States, Canada, Europe, and Russia; two have been translated into Spanish for South American markets. Dr. Spellman has been cited in more than 750 publications. He serves as a professional expert witness for three law groups and as an incident/accident investigator for the U.S. Department of Justice and a northern Virginia law firm. In addition, he consults on homeland security vulnerability assessments for critical infrastructures including water/wastewater facilities nationwide and conducts pre-Occupational Safety and Health Administration (OSHA)/Environmental Protection Agency EPA audits throughout the country. Dr. Spellman receives frequent requests to co-author with well-recognized experts in several scientific fields; for example, he is a contributing author of the prestigious text *The Engineering Handbook,* 2nd ed. (CRC Press). Dr. Spellman lectures on sewage treatment, water treatment, biosolids and homeland security and lectures and safety topics throughout the country and teaches water/wastewater operator short courses at Virginia Tech (Blacksburg, Virginia). He has traveled extensively throughout the world and studied water supplies and environmental pollution in the upper Amazon region and Galapagos Islands where he studied various water supplies and Darwin's finches and pollution events in Ecuador. He also spent several days tracing and recording the ancient water supply system at Machu Picchu. He holds a BA, in public administration, a BS in business management, an MBA, and an MS and PhD in environmental engineering.